ROCK

PAPER

FIRE

edited by

MARNI JACKSON
TONY WHITTOME

rock
paper
fire

THE BEST OF MOUNTAIN
AND WILDERNESS WRITING

 The Banff Centre
inspiring **creativity**

To all the writers in The Banff Centre
Mountain and Wilderness Writing program

Rock, paper, fire : the best of mountain and wilderness writing / edited by Marni Jackson, Tony Whittome ; introduction by Charlotte Gill.

Includes bibliographical references.
Issued in print and electronic formats.
ISBN 978-1-894773-67-6 (pbk.)
ISBN 978-1-894773-69-0 (epub)
ISBN 978-1-894773-70-6 (mobi)

1. Outdoor life—Literary collections. 2. Mountains—Literary collections. 3. Wilderness areas—Literary collections. 4. Canadian literature (English)—21st century. I. Jackson, Marni, editor of compilation II. Whittome, Tony, editor of compilation

PS8237.O8R63 2013   C810.8'036   C2013-904879-0   C2013-904880-4

Designed by Jessica Sullivan

Banff Centre Press
Box 1020, 107 Tunnel Mountain Drive
Banff, Alberta, Canada T1L 1H5
www.banffcentrepress.ca

The Banff Centre
inspiring **creativity**

The Banff Centre is pleased to acknowledge the generous donors who have given financial support to the Mountain and Wilderness Writing Program.

Balancing two small trees
between his ears

he mooches through the forest,
slow as a teenager,

head lifted so as not to drop
the twin gemstones

he carries in his skull,
whose amber

stores the customs
of new snow,

habits of grass, a list
of spring's imperatives

and when he turns his stare
towards the house,

it's we who are exhibits,
crowded behind glass.

He stands stock-still,
examines us:

re-homed and happy, strangers
to ourselves at last.

HELEN MORT, "Elk"

(Written during the 2012 Mountain
and Wilderness Writing program)

CONTENTS

FOREWORD

SITUATED IN a national park in the heart of the Rocky Mountains, Banff offers some of the world's finest ice-climbing. This was part of the attraction for the six writers and climbers who came to The Banff Centre in 2005 to participate in the first year of the Mountain Writing program. They would write, and they would climb. What we weren't prepared for, as faculty editors of the program, was the group's insistence that we join them on a frozen waterfall.

They drove us to the edge of town and the base of Cascade, the queenly, symmetrical peak celebrated in local postcards. It was November, and the narrow waterfall that tumbles down one flank had become a bluish-white column of ice. Like children on a daycare outing, we were harnessed, helmeted, secured to ropes, and outfitted with crampons and the murder weapons known as ice axes. Kicking all available points into the curtain of ice, the two of us began to climb.

It is a strangely secure sensation (though a misleading one) to attach oneself like Velcro to the frozen surface of a mountain. The spectre of the route above and below vanishes, replaced by a self-obliterating, laser focus on the moment at hand, and the next move. Like the task of writing—on a good day, at least.

Although climbing a mountain should be the polar opposite of sitting in a room typing, they share many challenges. Both demand unusual focus, patience, and precision. Both require constant decision-making, while offering the ever-present opportunity to fail. In writing as in climbing, the story can seem obscure at the outset, and the route toward it beyond our grasp. Like climbers on a pillar of ice, writers must learn how to anchor themselves in something intrinsically fragile— a string of words that can bear the weight of the story—and carry us forward.

All of the stories in *Rock, Paper, Fire*, with one exception, are by writers who have taken part in The Banff Centre's Mountain and Wilderness Writing program (as it's now called) in the past eight years. Created by Bernadette McDonald during the time she was director of the hugely successful Banff Mountain Film and Book Festival, the MWW program has expanded from an early emphasis on alpine narratives to include projects with other wilderness or environmental themes. Through our writers we have climbed Himalayan giants and the big walls of Yosemite, sailed, kayaked, and surfed the world's oceans, cycled the Silk Road, and explored the precarious survival of our most threatened creatures and ecosystems. We have welcomed participants from all over the world, working in every genre: fiction, biography, memoir, journalism, graphic novels, and poetry.

What the stories in this anthology share is a focus on the physical world and our relationship to it. They are all deeply rooted in a particular landscape—and they owe something to the peace and beauty of Banff as well.

The Mountain and Wilderness Writing program is, we believe, unique in the world. A number of prize-winning books have come out of projects that were developed in Banff, as we sat around the dining room of the Painter House discussing Nanga Parbat, talking crows, nylon ropes, and W.G. Sebald. We're very proud of this enterprise, which combines high literary standards with the increasingly urgent theme of how we interact with the natural world.

For a brilliant example of this in these pages, read Don Gillmor's darkly comic story, "The Descent of Man," in which he compares the accelerating disappearance of the world's glaciers with his own aging process. Or turn to the alert, assured poems of British poet Helen Mort, in which she imagines the lives of several early women climbers. Jon Turk, a National Geographic Adventurer of the Year in 2012, writes about circumnavigating Ellesmere Island in a sea kayak, which represents a polar first. In "The Magic Bus," twenty-five-year-old writer and Yukon guide Niall Fink describes an Alaskan rafting adventure that uncomfortably echoes Jon Krakauer's classic *Into The Wild*. Our other Niall, the Irish-born Niall Grimes, offers a beautifully evocative piece about grief and "grand rocks" on a trip back to County Donegal. Erin Soros explores different kinds of childhood courage in a wartime logging community. And Wayne Sawchuk, formerly a logger and trapper and now a conservationist in the deep wilderness of B.C.'s Muskwa-Kechika region, explores a chilling mystery of death in a Canadian winter.

MOUNTAIN NARRATIVES play an important part in *Rock, Paper, Fire*. Bernadette McDonald's portrait of the great Slovenian alpinist Tomaž Humar shows just what it takes to excel as a mountaineer at the highest level—and what it can cost. Steve Swenson and Barry Blanchard, both at the cutting edge of contemporary Alpinism, provide graphic accounts of fulfilling but dangerous climbs, as does Freddie Wilkinson in his story of a Himalayan ascent with Ueli Steck, the man who has soloed the North Face of the Eiger in two hours forty-seven minutes and thirty-three seconds. Breaking with convention as usual, U.K. climber Andy Kirkpatrick, twice winner of the Boardman-Tasker Prize for mountain literature, shares his live blog—written from a portaledge anchored on the face of the 600-metre Norwegian wall known as the Troll. Katie Ives, the editor of *Alpinist*, digs deep into personal and literary experience to explore the morality of risk in climbing. And *Globe and Mail* writer Ian Brown (not a MWW grad but current chair of the Literary Journalism program at The Banff Centre) unforgettably delivers the experience of backcountry skiing in his eloquent essay, "What the Mountains Mean to Us."

As faculty of the Mountain and Wilderness Writing program, we have been privileged to work with a variety of talented people, firstly of course all the writers who have graced the program, and then everyone at The Banff Centre who has made our work not only possible but immense fun, from Bernadette McDonald and Shannon O'Donoghue in the early days to the present Director of Literary Arts, Steven Ross Smith (whose idea this anthology is), his deputy, Naomi Johnston, and the whole dedicated Literary Arts team. We are also grateful to our Managing Editors, Robyn Read and Leanne Johnson, and to our copyeditor, Melanie Little. In the traditional disclaimer, any faults remaining in *Rock, Paper, Fire* are our own.

We haven't included any maps, by the way. These stories are wild. Let them take you out there.

MARNI JACKSON AND TONY WHITTOME
Faculty Editors
Mountain and Wilderness Writing
The Banff Centre

Charlotte Gill

═══════════

INTRODUCTION

THESE DAYS, it's possible to dwell in a high-rise, sleep hundreds of feet off the ground, and never experience mud or a spider in one's house. Skyscrapers themselves generate their own weather, buffering us from the true bite of the cold. If you live in the heart of a modern city, it is possible to exist almost totally isolated from what we've come to think of as nature.

But, as the American poet Gary Snyder reminded us decades ago, "nature" is a human conceit. When we say wilderness, we mean the terrain beyond the familiar. It's a word we now associate with landscapes severe and extreme—because mostly that's what's left of the wilderness, the marginal outlands. In just a few centuries we have tamed Earth's more benign latitudes with asphalt, electricity, and agricultural fields. But what we call the "environment" is a kind of invention, too. We are a part of our planetary living space, and it is a part of us, written into our DNA.

This evolutionary connection to the wild must be one of the reasons people feel compelled to venture out to the edge of our habitable realm in crampons and Gore-Tex, on skis and in kayaks or on foot. When we go climbing, paddling, on walkabout, we crave an unmitigated, free-range connection with the outdoors. We want to be reminded of what it feels like to be human, as we've been human for almost two million years. This urge is so compelling, apparently, that many of us will risk frostbite, drowning, and altitude sickness—often at great personal expense—with no promise of glory or reward beyond the trip itself.

Why do we do it?

First, there is the mountain, the glacier, the desert, the long trek across the steppe. A landscape passes beneath our feet. In the thick of it, we have no choice but to engage, to breathe the air, feel its jagged surfaces in our hands, to hear it crackle underneath our feet. We are present and immersed. Perhaps we explore merely to break records, to be the first to reach the summit. Or, we want to dip into some hidden well in ourselves that is never accessed indoors. Maybe, when some of us return home, we'll put our fingers to the keyboard.

For thousands of years, people have been doing just this, going on expeditions and then coming home to tell the tale. I imagine the first campfire stories originated this way. Tribal scouts travelled out, explored the beyond, and returned to report on what they'd found. These would not have been mere yarns—the clan would have depended utterly on this knowledge for food and safety. Perhaps storytelling has its roots in this imperative—to create a narrative map of our environment. Even now, wilderness and mountain writing—what we sometimes call adventure stories—seems made for narrative. The act of departing and coming home, climbing up and coming down, coincides perfectly with the shape of a story.

In the twenty-first century, wherever we go on the planet, chances are someone will have gotten there before us. Sometimes our destinations aren't wild places at all. They're wild only to us: unknown. But we can turn this into an advantage. We can take advantage of our unique point of view to create the story. Mount Everest is a fact of geography, buckled up from the earth's crust millions of years ago. That tale isn't new. The mountain has been climbed thousands of times since Edmund Hillary and Tenzing Norgay's first ascent. And yet this isn't the heart of the story, either. Everest is only the raw material. Until a man and a woman see the sun collapse along the ridge, until the place comes alive in their gaze, until then, the mountain is just a hunk of rock. Until they warm their frigid hands with tired breath as spindrift whirls all around, the tale doesn't exist.

It is this potential alchemy—human being plus natural world—that gives the stories in this collection their dramatic, suspenseful magic. Jan Redford writes about the difference between climbing El Capitan and making the wrong moves in love; Karsten Heuer paddles across Canada with his family, revisiting the rivers and paths author Farley Mowat wrote about; Masa Takei explores, as part of his experiment in sustainable living, the complicated emotions of hunting. These essays recapture wild journeys in all their sensory vividness, so that when the writer's heart races, our pulse quickens, too. This intermingling of the printed word and life itself is the hallmark of creative non-fiction, and it has the power to transfix and move us. It's not just the snow on the trail or the sand blowing across the desert, but the experience of it, which is as singular as every one of us who slings on a backpack and steps across the threshold into the wind.

Even then, the adventure alone is probably not enough. An explorer who chooses to tell her story now must be deeply aware of the context. Wherever we go, chances are we'll find humans who already live in these locales. This kind of writing is also an exercise in sensitivity. We must examine the footprints we leave behind, environmental, economic, and cultural. And any story in which a human protagonist struggles valiantly against nature is inevitably flecked with the irony that this wilderness is losing its tug-of-war with us and shrinking every day. In response to these complexities, the genres of mountain and wilderness writing are becoming more hybridized and fascinating by the day. When we pick up an expedition book or essay, chances are it will be part travelogue, part history or ecological saga—and part memoir.

A writer may even come to question her very motives for wanting to venture out in the first place. As readers of nonfiction, we have come to expect that the author will speak to us directly, guilelessly. She must be as brave on the page as she is on the slope. Why hit the trail? Why climb the mountain? Everyone has his own reasons. We must explore those, too. When we tell a true story, often enough it's because we were changed by the experience. And it is that change that readers want most to discover. An expedition is often matched by a corresponding inner journey. A man crosses the trail of another young adventurer who disappeared in the Alaskan backcountry. A woman embarks on a journey of self-exploration as she climbs El Capitan, whose sheer granite face was once considered unassailable. The stories in this collection will take you to the high and far places we long to explore—and, sometimes, to the unmapped places within us as well. The explorers may also find more than they bargained for. En route to a goal that may never be reached, they discover something better, emerging from their voyages enriched and deeply affected by their experience.

All the better for the reader, who comes along for the exhilarating ride.

Barry Blanchard

FIRST ASCENT

A GLOWING STRIP of ice draped down over dark rock bands, linking patches of snow like a silver braid of pearls laid onto black velvet. I immediately thought of the Peruvian Andes or the Himalayas. I grabbed the eight-by-ten glossy from the piles of mountain photos and route descriptions sheaved atop David Cheesmond's desk.

"Where the hell is this?" I said.

"Oh shit, man," he said. His pale auburn eyes slashed left, then right, acute as a fox's. Vulpine eyes. He made a futile grab for the picture. "You weren't supposed to see that!"

"It looks so cool. Where is it? The Himalayas?"

"No, it's... ah..."

"C'mon, man, you have to tell me. Please."

"Oh hell, okay. It's one of Urs Kallen's photos."

"You're telling me that this is in the Rockies?" The ice looked so linear, so perfect, a staircase into the sky. It looked *Great*, as in Greater Ranges "Great." Could it actually be in our backyard?

"Yes. It's on the east face of Mount Fay."

"Mount Fay at Moraine Lake?" The scale wasn't adding up for me.

"Ya, man," David said, in his cultivated South African English. He'd immigrated to Canada just two years ago. "But not the Moraine Lake side, the east face, above Constellation Lakes. That face is much bigger."

"Holy shit! When do we go?"

The first snows of winter had just, that evening, sifted small arcs of white onto the windowsill. We cracked a couple of beers and got down to planning an attempt that coming winter. In my mind's eye, I saw David and me cleanly inserted into Urs's picture. Perfectly present there, the two of us doing what we believed we were meant to do: going up.

Later that night, Dave dropped me off at my mother's house on the far side of Calgary, farther from the mountains. In the morning, I'd board the bus back to Canmore. It was October, 1983.

MY MOTHER had five half-breed kids by three different men in seven years. None of the white fathers made it; all of them left, and it was as if the fabric of our family had changed from a white wedding dress to a faded and patched pair of jeans by the time Stephen came around. At seventeen, Stephen was flunking out of school and already in trouble with the law. He'd been drinking at a party when he got talked into a robbery attempt by an older man who had previously done time.

Just fifteen months earlier, I'd moved to the mountains to take the first steps up the career path of mountain guiding. One of the good men I'd taught to rock climb was a gifted criminal lawyer.

"It will make a strong impression on the judge if as many of your family as possible can be in court to support Stephen," he said.

When the judge asked if there were any family members in court, my mother, brother, sister, and I all stood up. The judge gave Stephen a term of probation conditional on his staying in school.

It was late by the time I finally said goodbye to David and opened the door of my mother's house. Stephen was still out.

"I don't know what to do with him," my mother said. Her forehead sank into her fingers and her elbows trembled against the hard sheen of her kitchen table. A deep sob shook her shoulders. I put my arm around her. I'd seen my mother cry before, but that was usually over Stephen's dad. She'd always been a pillar for us, a tigress.

"Maybe he can come and stay with me," I said. The only way I knew how to help was to take him climbing.

Two days later I found a cheap blue house to rent. It was a single-level, built in the 1950s, and it had seen some hard use with no recent maintenance. It sat on the westmost corner of "Teepee Town"—a collection of valley-bottom flats in old Canmore where Stoney Indians used to camp: perfect. The next week I moved away from my two housemates and into the empty blue house. My mother drove Stephen up on the last day of October and he enrolled in the local high school. We sat on borrowed chairs at a borrowed table and ate a lot of pasta with red sauce. My girlfriend took to calling our house "Sparta."

It felt good to see my little brother go out the door, walk to school, and start to make some friends. I knew he was trying to step up, to be good enough, and I had hope. And although that hope would waver over the next twenty-two years, I realize now that I never really lost it, no matter what my brother did.

MID-DECEMBER, blue ice was laminated in strips onto the grey walls above our valley. Stephen and I had been living together for six weeks and we were doing okay, but I wanted to help him more.

"We should go ice climbing, bro. I think you'd like it." His huge brown eyes widened; interest and imagination glinted.

The Canmore Junkyards are so named because early in the town's history, people started dumping junk there, including several cars, all for the redneck shits and giggles of it. Since I didn't have a car, Stephen and I walked for two hours instead of driving for ten minutes and hiking for five. We were doing the best that we could.

My brother stood six feet—three inches taller than me—and at 200 pounds, he had thirty on me. He took pride in his physique. We'd been hitting the gym together, and while I trained to be a better climber, getting leaner and harder, Stephen just got bigger. He looked more native than I did and I'd joke with him, call him an "FBI" (Fucking Big Indian).

He did fine with the ice climbing, and I hoped it would capture him as it had captured me. "How do you like it, bro?"

"It's pretty cool, Bear," he said. "But it's scary."

"Fear can be your friend," I said. "It can make you stronger."

"I don't know, man."

The muffled crackling of water emanated through the blue ice and from higher up, above where Stephen stood secure on his crampons, came the roar of open water; mist birthing from spray and slowly rising against the stark, black wall of Ha Ling Peak, high above.

IN FEBRUARY, four months after he moved in, Stephen said, "Canmore isn't working for me, brother." We'd been living in our hollow house cooking meals, going to the gym together, getting by. I made sure he went to school. I even tried to get him to run up the road above the Junkyards with me. "Running isn't my thing, Bear," he said. "It's too hard."

Stephen told me that Calgary just had more going on, and he'd decided to move back to my mother's house. We walked to the bus station together. An Arctic airmass had cracked Alberta with a deep frost. Rigid snow squeaked under our boots, like the sound of a ship's timbers flexing.

"Thanks for all your help, Bear," he said.

"It's okay, bro. I hope Calgary is better for you now."

Our hug was a little clumsy, as always: it felt awkward for me to wrap my arms around my brother's floundering. But then I got him close, and I felt my love for him, and I said, "Be good, bro." A glassy sheen of tears shimmered over my eyes.

"I will, Bear," he said. His voice quavered. "I will."

We'd tried. I walked back to Sparta, wishing I could help him more, but not knowing how.

AT 11 P.M., five hours after Stephen stepped onto the bus, David Cheesmond and Carl Tobin pulled up to the front door of the blue house and we hit the road for Lake Louise. David sang along to a Juluka cassette about the scatterlings of Africa. Strong guttural male voices issued the chorus: "YUN! BO! HA!" and I saw lines of Zulu warriors pounding the earth with bare feet, cowhide shields, thrusting spears, preparation for battle. David's Econoline van barrelled down the dark and deserted highway and inside that sanctum Carl and I joined David in chanting out the chorus. Our pact of ascent was a given.

"BUGGER!" THE TOE BAIL on my binding had snapped clean and cold as a frozen twig. I stabbed the broken skis into the snow and wrestled my second pair out from the load in my blue plastic sled.

Our plan was to ski, by headlamp, eight miles up the closed Moraine Lake Road and bed down in a cook shelter for four hours. We'd cache one pair of skis there to facilitate our return down the north side of the mountain, and at 8 A.M., we'd ski on the second set up a branching valley that led to the east face. We had just two days for the climb, Saturday and Sunday, and Monday for the ski out. David had to be at work on Tuesday morning. Carl, who was on vacation from Alaska, intended to ski back in later that week to pick up the set we'd leave below the east face. Now, down to one pair of skis, I'd have to walk out behind them from the cook shelter.

The grey strip of road rolled through dark timber. I skied through clouds of exhaled breath, my ski skins creaking over the coarse, frozen track. A halo of frost grew on my chest. I thought of Stephen back at our mother's house and hoped that he was at home. It felt good to move through the cold, skiing toward what I'd imagined Urs's photo to be: a beautiful alpine dream.

"I'M GOING TO JUMP!" Carl yelled down to David and me the next day. He was halfway up an aquamarine pillar of ice that dropped plumb from the apex of an outward-leaning, 100-foot-high black wall of limestone.

"What do you mean?" I shouted back. I didn't believe ice existed that Carl couldn't climb; to me, he always looked like Tarzan. I'd seen him shirtless in the gym and his pectoral muscles were like plates of metal—broad, flat, and efficient, none of the bloated bulk of the bodybuilder. A grid of abdominal muscles armoured his gut like cut white marble. "You can't fucking jump!"

"I can't hang on anymore! I'm going to jump. Fuck!"

David's eyes flashed wide at mine, then we both looked at our meagre anchor of shallowly driven pitons and picketed ice tools. We were 1,000 feet off the deck. And then Carl let go of his ice tools and jumped. I stopped breathing. David and I lunged into the wall as Carl sailed through the frame of our vision and nailed a perfect gymnast's dismount on top of a snow ledge. Flexing his knees and thrusting his arms out, he stayed in balance and didn't even weight the rope. *Pure action superhero shit*, I thought.

Minutes of deep breathing passed. Carl made his way back to us, and then David turned to me. "Right then, now it's your turn."

To this day, that pillar remains one of the hardest trials I've had on ice. I only got up it by clipping Carl's in-situ axes for protection, then weighting one of my tools, twenty feet higher, to place a screw. I pulled over the top with my lungs coming through my nostrils and my heart hammering. It took the remainder of the day to get us, and our packs, up that blue column of ice.

Cold to the bone, I woke up shivering. The top of my home-made bivvy sack had slipped down and my shoulder had melted a hollow into the chrome-coloured water ice that formed the back wall of our cramped snow cave. Water had sat-urated my sleeping bag. I rearranged my pit and struggled to find some warmth. I shivered. I pumped my legs up and down, punched my arms down the plane of my body again and again. The shivering would come again and I'd clench my body into a fist and hold, forcing exhalations. I had to sleep, I had to stay warm enough, I prayed for the dawn.

FINALLY, THE SUN. Heat radiated into my dark clothing, and I felt warm. One hundred and thirty feet overhead, Carl was tacked onto a silver strip of ice. A rock pillar rose from the top of the ice above him like the handle of a sword affixed to a gleaming silver blade. The stone glowed in an aura of oblique light, and we envisioned a direct finish that way to the summit. Then—*Crack!* The air vibrated with the whir of a large object accelerating. I glanced up: the belly of a cornice was bearing down on Carl.

"Avalanche!" I wailed, and the sky exploded. I dove forward, weighting my tools as the chunks thumped into the snow all around me. Something like a sledgehammer smacked into the back of my right shoulder. Pinpricks of hot, white light scatter-shot through black. I slid six inches before my body snapped to and flexed harder into the slope. I stopped. The roar drew off down the mountain, and then hushed into a hiss.

In the silence, I looked for Carl. He was still on the ice—white from helmet to frontpoint, but still attached. We bellowed frantically at each other:

"Should we go down?"

"Do you think it could happen again?"

David and Carl were both okay, and we decided to keep going up.

My shoulder blade was bruised, stiff, and throbbing. I was out of the leading. I hung back and followed, riding the jumars on the steep sections. It was marvellous to watch how well David and Carl worked as a team. At one anchor David handed Carl a carabiner full of pitons indexed by size, then he silently clipped an etrier onto a vacant gear loop on Carl's harness. Ready, Carl locked his eyes onto David's and crinkled into a grin. David's fox eyes twinkled and he said, "Climb like a beast, man." They hadn't mastered the mountain. Instead they'd come to know and accept their place on its side.

That afternoon the storm began, and that night I passed long hours inside our snow cave pumping my limbs, willing myself to stop shivering, trying to keep my teeth from clattering. The dark and the cold isolated me, cornered me. Through my sodden sleeping bag I felt the bottomless cold of the mountain; the wall was pressed against my back. I shivered and I fought and again I prayed for the sun.

HEAVY SNOWFALL obscured Monday's dawn. Our dream of climbing the rock pillar straight to the summit was out. We simply needed to survive. Late in the day, we traversed through the twenty-ninth hour of continuous storm, striving for an escape to the ridgeline of Mount Fay. Waves of spindrift rushed down the wall and I could feel the cold of those ice crystals like metal against my neck and the insides of my wrists. Wind slapped snow across my face and my eyelashes kept freezing together. I'd squeeze my eyes shut for seconds to melt the bind. Snow, fine as ground glass, was pushed into all the openings in my clothing. I turned out from the mountain and began screaming obscenities into the driving snow, challenging the storm. *I wanted perfection in my alpinism, and I was given this. This is what you dream; this is what you get.*

I spent what was left in my lungs and turned back into the snow slope breathless and crumpled. Carl caught up with me, waited for ten heartbeats and then said, "Hey man, it don't gotta be fun to be fun."

Perfect. I had to laugh.

At dusk we dug one last snow cave. The fuel was gone. Dinner was a box of candies split three ways. Sealed within our white vault, we talked about life, and I told them about Stephen. They empathized with me, and listened, graciously prompting me to continue, but a brother in trouble was too big a problem inside our snow cave and the best they could do was to be beside me and reassure me that everything would be okay. David went through each of the empty food wrappers to retrieve the scraps. He licked the powder from peeled-open soup packages. They put me between them, but I still suffered. The cold tried to get my core.

We hit the ridgeline early the next morning and spent all of Tuesday retreating. I staggered out on foot behind David and

Carl. The only food we could get in Lake Louise at one A.M. on a Wednesday was potato chips from the bar.

"Don't worry, man," David said. He leaned against the open door of the van. "It will all be okay. I don't understand my brother either."

I swayed as I climbed the steps to Sparta. My girlfriend was there, and she drew me a hot bath and gently helped me into it. The hallucinations were magnificent. Four hours of sleep, and then I had to get up and move that day from the house where Stephen and I had lived for four months. All that time we'd spent there seemed written into the walls, a form of physical remembrance like the faint patinas of evaporation that ring a Mason jar.

THREE YEARS LATER, I tried to help Stephen again. This time, I took him climbing in Peru. He wasn't a kid anymore, and he'd gotten bigger. All of my hand-me-down climbing clothing looked tight on him, yet when we stood on top of the white summit of Ishinca and I asked him if he was having fun, he cracked a big, goofy grin and said, "It's fun to be on top, Bear, but it is so much work!"

As we walked out of the Quebrada Santa Cruz, we learned that David had died on Mount Logan. Stephen had never seen death. I had. His brown eyes opened wide. "Oh man," he said. My eyes clenched tight in tears. "Fuck! fuck! fuck!" I cursed, my head in my hands, and sank to my haunches. And then my brother walked over to me and put his arm around my trembling shoulders.

I was teaching ice climbing in New Hampshire in 2005 when my mother called and told me about Stephen's overdose. We both wept.

I realize now that I knew David better than I ever knew my brother. I think that Stephen never felt good enough.

When I look at his grade-school pictures in the album at my mother's house, I cry. Yet I hold fast to another mental image: my brother's laughter when he realized we'd just walked two hours to go ice climbing in a junkyard on that winter's day in 1983. "This is crazy, Bear!"

Norman Maclean's words have helped me immensely over time, and I return to them: "It is those we live with and love and should know who elude us."

I love and I lose, I lose and I love.

We do the best that we can.

Niall Grimes

INTO THE MOUNTAINS

WHEN ALL that can be said is said, and all that can be done is done, when the words have lost their insides, condolences so empty that they seem obscene, I get in the car, and drive, drive toward the county.

ONCE I HEARD the news I would fly home as often as I could, gulping down time together. We would sit silently together in front of the TV, talk nonsense, never mentioning it. When they put her in hospital we laughed about the hair loss, and with the red headscarf tied in a big knot at the back, she called herself Casey Jones.

The last time back, a late flight got me in near the end of the day. I crept into the hospice after hours and found the bed, her body a shadow under the cream sheets. I knelt down beside the bed, took the little hand and kissed it.

"Your baby's here, Ma," I whispered.

I was torn between not wanting to wake her and wanting to grab every second. She lay unconscious, but I needed to talk, needed to make the most of this time together.

"Not been seeing any bright lights lately, have you?" I said again to her stillness.

Two weeks earlier she had reported to our old neighbour Sheena MacMenamin that she had twice seen a bright light outside the window of the hospice, shining on her.

"What do you mean a light, Pauline?" Sheena asked. "What was it like?"

"Lovely."

I held her and, lost for words big enough for the occasion, whispered the words of a song, "The Big Rock Candy Mountain."

Then, in the low night lights of the ward, I saw her eyes open. The sharp humorous glint was now an opaque struggle, trying to see through. It took me by surprise, and I felt nervous.

"It's me, Ma, what about you?"

Her mouth tried to move. I came close to her. With my ear to her lips I heard the barest breath forcing out the words:

"I'm far gone, son."

"Sssshhhhh," I said. "You look fine to me. Now get some rest."

They were the last words she said. Only later did it occur to me that she might have wanted to talk awhile in that lonely darkness with her last-born, that rest was coming for her soon enough. Some days later the family stood round and I watched as she stopped breathing, the tiny rising and falling of the chest finally disappearing. I thought it would be a relief. Instead, it plunged me into a new grief. Swimming breathless and desperate toward the surface, only to find that it's a mirror.

Grown-up talk about "arrangements" filled the days that followed, as duty kept us busy. At the graveyard where we had buried her own mother while she held my arm in the rain, we buried her, and then were left with our own feelings.

I got in the hire car and fled.

AT FIRST I thought I was just getting away, putting distance behind me, but when I passed the abandoned armoured buildings that were once the military checkpoints that separated Northern Ireland from the Republic, I realized where I was going.

Donegal lay ahead, Ireland's northernmost county, a sparsely populated expanse of green hills, orange bogs, and grey mountains. For a little boy in a car-less family it had been just another faraway place, even though it started seven miles from our front door. In my teens, an older boy took me there to go rock climbing one day and from that day on climbing became everything to me.

So too did Donegal. I made a new friend through climbing and together we became obsessed with exploring the county for new outcrops and unexplored cliffs, travelling there any weekend that he could borrow his parents' car. We would examine hillsides with binoculars for rock clean enough, tall enough, and steep enough for climbing. Always looking for something new. We looked in the blanker areas between old routes for harder lines. We would spend hours crossing wet uplands in hope, often finding nothing. But often we found treasure. We climbed the rock and created new ways up the mountains. Our ways. We named them and my connection to them was immense. Later I wrote a guidebook to the area including all of our first ascents and that was it, I was part of history.

But that was nearly twenty years ago: things had changed since then.

The roads in the Republic were as potholed and puddled as I remembered them. I drove the hire car on through small villages and sprawled townlands that I remembered from that easy past. The road led soon to Letterkenny, the county town—"The Fastest Growing Town in Europe," it claimed—and once through its ugly modernity, I took an old road which began to incline gently upward. The rain started, a thick wind-driven drizzle, and I turned on the wipers.

Hedgerows. Holly, blackthorn, and brambles. Barbwire fences and rusted gates. The odd dwelling. As I went higher, the land got worse: damp fields, cows standing in mud. On I went, into the rain, into the mountains. Featureless land lay ahead, anonymous. I recognized this place, not by any physical references, but by the mood of it.

The road I was following had long since left anything as self-conscious as a town; soon, only the orange bog yawned away into the far lonely distance. Featureless, untameable, and forever. A low sky clung to hilltops, each seeming to seek comfort in the other. Grey scours of rain swept here or there in the distance. A single tree might survive in some sheltered spot, leafless, like black lightning cracking back to the heavens, branches scrawning about in senile rants. A small river ran beside the road in a drunken meander, black from the peat that carpeted this inhumane land.

It was a land you yearned for, even in its presence.

The car radio drifted in and out of stations. Pop songs would lose their signal to current affairs, serious men talking of the big issues of our day. I couldn't tune in to their importance. Then static, as the mountaintops cut the signal again, followed by traditional music. The old thin songs of lament, joyous reels, a love poem set to music, interspersed with the Irish language. Nothing stayed tuned for long.

But it was important to keep driving.

I was in the granite highland, enormous and ancient. Rock flows, molten, then cools; an ice age gouges by. Woods and forests grow up and again die. Their trunks rot and melt into the soil, becoming the acidic peat that will line the bog. Famously, into this bog fall the bodies of ancient peoples, and their yawning deathmasks along with bellies full of berries are preserved, mummified by the acid.

In lonely valleys I passed some ruins of houses, huddled in hopeless clusters. Grass and weeds grew inside their small, windowless walls, now mostly tumbled. Amazing to think that anyone could ever have managed to live off this wet, bare, rocky land.

"Them's the houses of the peasants Captain Hill evicted in 1887," Aiden MacKinney had told me one time while drunk. "Sent the whole lot of them out off the land. Two thirds of them died, and the rest went to America."

"Murderous English fucker," he concluded.

It was really just another case of Enclosure, the taking of common land to maximize profit through scale, which would have been happening in England at the same time. But the Irish always managed to see misfortune as some kind of personal insult.

Still, I thought of the dead—compassionate, fond thoughts—and once again my eyes moistened with tears. Even a ruined house could set me off. I drove on, allowing the tears to empty me. The window wipers slouched away and I followed the black line ahead.

Out of habit my eyes constantly scanned the hillsides for rock features. Every now and again, some silvery granite showed itself through the vegetation. Near the bottom of one hill I saw there was a reasonable amount of exposed rock. I stopped my car on the road below and stepped out for some air. After the hire-car clamminess the outside air felt beautifully fresh and damp. I got an orange from the back seat and as I peeled it my eyes turned to the exposed outcrops above and examined them half-consciously. Then something dropped into place.

I suddenly realized that I knew what I was looking at—knew it by heart, in fact. The bare features above were all a part of my past and magically threw themselves into focus. That wasn't just a rocky corner I was staring at, that was Tarquin's Groove, climbed on one of my first days out in the mountains. That wasn't a bare slab over on the right, that was West Buttress, one of my first leads. That wasn't a way down, that was Triversion, which we climbed in the snow. The wall far above, which looked unclimbable, was Deltoid Face, one of my finest first ascents.

There below the cliff was the flat stone where we would change our shoes and drink tea from a tartan flask; the groove where I once fell; the place where I sat and took pictures of Alan. I knew I could now turn round and see a curving lake-shore, where a river, dark from the peat, would flow into the lake at a white sand beach. There would be rows of bags of turf, and beyond, a rocky hillside. I turned round. There was the shore, the beach, the river, the rows of bags, and a wet rocky hillside.

God, I wasn't ready for that. It had taken me back a bit too quickly.

This was Lough Barra Crag. The ancient granite cliff where I had begun climbing, over twenty years ago, on wet Sundays between aimless teenage weeks. The dark river I had driven along was the Owen Barra, where we would fill our bottles to drink the lovely brown water. I was in one of my special places.

Tens of memories came at me in that windy lay-by. I looked down at the sand at my feet and remembered seeing the footprints of my first walking boots among its grains. This was the spot where we would peel off sodden waterproofs and clammy cotton T-shirts and shiver into dry track-suit bottoms at the dead end of a lightless winter afternoon. Dry shoes and socks over brown, waterlogged feet.

Lough Barra, where it all began. After a short day on a small local cliff, Gerard and Raymond had taken me and Paul here. A Sunday in October. An orange Ford Escort and a U2 cassette. On the way in the car, Bono had sung "Sunday Bloody Sunday" and we all called him a wanker. Rain. My terror and my excitement and my ignorance and my obedience.

I stared again at Tarquin's Groove, the route we had all four done that day, and my imagination wove deep into its recesses. Still now it looked beautiful. Subtle, steep, and clean, weaving up for four ropelengths directly to the summit. I remember, my God how clearly, sitting tethered to a nut half-way up, the rough branches of a raven's nest digging into my back, and, with the utmost responsibility, paying the rope out as Raymond led from the stance. I remembered how seriously I took my role, and how I used it to take my mind off the fear I felt. How early such habits form. And how easily such habits form the person. As I stood below, I could reach out and touch those emotions, how that sixteen-year-old felt about the height, the landscape, the newness of this thing he was doing. And I remember the rain on the last section, the whips of water that would fling from the rope as Raymond took it tight, the rivers running down my upstretched hands, into my cuffs, and along my cold arms. The elements, raw, felt like never before.

Deep and dark within the gully was the steep crackline I had tried as my first new route, the first attempt to write my name in the never-read history book of Donegal climbing. And the long fall I had taken onto a runner, and the pride, the respect I had felt from my companions at daring to take a fall. I never did the route, but I would never forget the fall.

The small outcrop we investigated one February. We climbed a crack, then from the height saw that the surface of

Lough Barra had frozen into huge, circular patterns. These were ancient circles of Celtic legend, and we ran and danced across their magic and, when we pushed the magic too far, we went crashing through the ice into the water below. Our screams of terror slowly melted into embarrassed chuckles as we realized we were in water no deeper than our basketball boots.

Comical, almost, to behold it all with fresh eyes. To see that these climbs, so huge in my own self-myth, now look like small scraps of rock poking out from swathes of vegetation. Has nature reclaimed them over the years? Perhaps no one ever climbs here now and they are untravelled. Or maybe they always looked like this and it was only the eyes of youthful self-delusion that saw them as anything more than a wash of wasted Sundays.

In the end I had to tear myself away from the spot. There were too many memories here. Things were different then. I got in the car, started the engine, and pulled back out into the road. I was crying again.

As I drove, the open mountains began closing in to a narrower valley, the mountains funnelling down between its narrowing sides. I passed a farmhouse. A collection of tumble-down ruins and a dirty white bungalow with faded lace curtains in the dusty windows. Rusting farm machinery littered the mucky yard. Opposite the house were threadbare fields that held a handful of sheep, their wool ragged and dirty. Brown smoke smudged from a chimney pot, and the air carried the unmistakable smell of peat being burned—sweet, yet acrid. In forgotten poverty, someone was still working the land here, somehow surviving. I couldn't help but dwell on the farmer giving his life to this valley, his soul disappearing into the soil like the ancient landscape that disappeared to make the peat he now burned to stay warm. I wondered if the smoke and the smell were old spirits escaping from the brown combustible earth, the way someday the farmer's soul might also flee this place.

I TOOK MORE turns in the road. The rain had stopped, and now and again sun strained pale through the low clouds. I still didn't know where I was going. When I saw a curious sign by the road, a big yellow footprint on top of a yellow metal pole, another memory punched to the surface:

—Where are we, son?

—I don't know, Ma, I just wanted to stop beside this sign.

—Does it say where we are?

—No, it's just a yellow foot.

—Well then we must be at Yellow Foot. All we have to do now is find Yellow Leg and we'll be halfway there.

In the time before she became sick I had taken to spending long weekends back home once or twice a year. We really treasured each other's company then and at the time it didn't occur to us that it might not always be there. I'd often hire a car and we'd go on runs in the country. Pointless drives, seldom looking at a map. Perhaps a cup of tea and a bun in a shop if we found one. We'd drive for hours, sometimes talking about nothing, sometimes reminding me of something I did in the past—"Do you remember you once washed a knife with a tea bag?"—mostly in easy silence. Sometimes she'd say things out of the blue—"How are things in Glocca Morra?"—to which I would reply, "The price of hoggets has doubled in this last month alone," and in the rearview mirror I'd see her quietly laughing to herself. We would cruise past breathtaking scenery in silence, until we'd pass a collection of household gnomes or a brightly painted fence and she'd finally exclaim, "Oh, isn't that lovely."

I had spotted the yellow foot on one of those drives. It looked odd, so I pulled the car over and stopped below it. It was a beautiful autumn day. The orange bracken shone golden in late-afternoon sun, and miles beyond it the Atlantic was a dark blue. A gentle wind was blowing, and I watched the long shadow of the car stretch out on the tarmac. I let my eyes rest on an abandoned glove in the roadside ditch, allowing moments to pass. She asked where we were and I had told her.

—There's the grand rock for you, son.

—What's that, Ma?

—Over yonder, I say, there's the grand rock for you.

She had wound down the window and was pointing a slender finger past a barbwire fence into the rough mountain ground. I looked.

There, not thirty metres away, was a huge granite boulder. Its golden bulk shone in the sunshine. Somehow I hadn't noticed it myself. I got out and mounted the wobbling top strand of the fence's wire, jumped down on the other side, and strolled to the boulder. The surface was clean, perfect granite. It was two bodyheights tall, and about the size of a trailer. The sides were steep, with rounded features, all of which fit the hand perfectly. I touched them, felt the granite crystals, imagined holding them, pulling on them, the way a climber does. Across the front face, glowing in the light and warm to the touch, ran a rounded ramp, a perfect line for a traverse. It was a beautiful boulder, a perfect boulder, the kind that we used to spend entire weekends searching for. I looked over toward the car, and just as I did, my mother looked up. I waved, and she back. I ran back to the car.

—That is the grand rock, Ma.

I was surprised. I remember once explaining to her the idea of bouldering, of climbing on little roadside rocks, and had once shown her a picture of someone bouldering in France. It appeared she had remembered, had understood, and, even so many years later, had recognized the qualities of this remote rock for that activity. Quietly, in the back seat of the car, she sat and turned over the pages of a TV magazine.

—Hmmm?

—I say, that is the grand rock. Will we go and climb it?

—No. The prime minister and the parish priest are coming for tea tonight at half six. We better be getting on, son.

Parked once more under the yellow foot, the memory played back, word for word. The sun was low and golden now, as before. It shone on my face. I laughed again at her quirky jokes and collapsed once again into tears.

I let the tearful quaking subside, got out of the car, and looked over the fence. There, inch-perfect, was the boulder still. That's the grand rock for me, I thought to myself.

"A climber keeps his boots and a chalk bag with him at all times."

This had been one of our early mottos, and one I still clung to, more as a badge of identity these days than for any practical purpose. But still, I always tossed a small plastic bag with these items, the most basic climbing equipment, into my baggage on flights home, and usually it would stay in the rental car. I popped open the boot now, took the bag, jumped the fence, and felt again the perfection of the boulder. Even the warmth of the ramp was perfect to my memory.

I had thought about this boulder from time to time since first seeing it that day and had wanted to come back to climb on it. It was the pioneering spirit in me, still wanting to write my name in the book of the place.

It would be nice to do something new again, I thought. So I spent an hour unravelling the problems on the boulder, then began working on the traverse. This took a lot of effort, but I was grateful for something as mindless as having to move leftward across a feature on a rock in the middle of a bog, with my feet just above the ground in a light breeze and the October sunshine. I pulled the sleeve of my grey woollen jumper down over the soft fleshy bottom of my loose fist, using it to scrub away any loose crystals of rock from the surface of the holds. The process took all my spare thought, and for a while I forgot to be sad. Then I would catch myself looking the short distance to my parked car, the yellow foot, and the absence, and fall again to tears.

I could always muscle my mind back to the problem in hand, and persisted. After some time, I managed to complete the traverse. I swung myself from the final holds onto the top of the boulder. I couldn't help but feel pleased with myself: a first ascent, after all these years. And one of this quality. I rationalized with myself over the grade of the problem and then, to fully possess the experience, to make it a *thing,* I gave it a name: Pauline.

The land was before me. Donegal, the first land I had learned to love. The first land I had given myself to; my years and my hopes poured into my days on the cliffs. To my right, gentle wet hills sighed off over rolling summits and rounded valleys. The dying grass and bobbing bog cottons and the breeze-blown heather of the foreground gave way in the middle distance to a more general sense of growth. Beyond that, the surface of the hills was a flat carpet, absorbing all, no sign of houses or trees or people or anything that looked like life had ever lived. Just the forever bog that covered mountains, still with grey clouds haunting their flanks and summits.

I had thought of the idea of claiming the problem like we used to do, of sending it to those who record such things, who publish such things, to make the climb mine. To have a tiny piece of this place named after my achievement, like a memorial to myself. Saying to the world, Remember me!

Will you remember me, and what I have done?

Ghosts. In this land they believe in ghosts. The same happens in any place where the dead are remembered through their spirits rather than through their achievements. Through who they were, not what they did. Monuments crumble, fall to ruin. A climb will become overgrown and forgotten. The land will once again take over.

These quiet mountains. I know what I did today can sink into their soft, absorbent surface, join the ancient forests and the centuries of people who have lived their lives here, have sunk into the bogs and become the bogs, unquestioned, unquestioning. These quiet mountains that allow me the space to feel.

I looked up and waved to the car, empty this time around. I changed into my shoes, walked back, and crossed the fence.

Experience and feeling cannot be owned, just as they can never disappear. Love lives forever. The spirit is a quiet mountain and the heart is a bog. Some weak sunlight was reflecting off a road which led upward to the dark mass of mountains. I started the car, swung it round, and headed for the silver ribbon of the road. I noticed that the fuel was getting low and that sometime soon I would have to turn toward home. But not just yet. I needed to stay lost a little longer.

Jon Turk

A WORLD OF ICE
Circumnavigating Ellesmere

AN ICE FLOE the size of a football field drifted slowly toward the cliff, rotated, and buckled. The air filled with a human-like groan, followed by a sharp crack that echoed off the nearby mountain. Ice crystals exploded and danced rainbows in the sunshine, while ten-foot-thick chunks rose thirty feet out of the sea and smeared against solid rock.

Boomer and I were trapped.

An ocean current was driving the North Pole ice pack into the Robeson Channel, a constriction twelve miles wide between Ellesmere Island and the northern coast of Greenland. Behind this floe, a seemingly infinite reservoir of polar ice was moving southward under compression of tectonic magnitude. Now our path was blocked.

We were an odd couple to contemplate spending eternity together. Erik Boomer is forty years younger than me, closer in age to my grandchildren than to my children. He is a world-class whitewater paddler who before this expedition had never sat in a sea kayak. I was sixty-five years old, and though I hadn't paddled a Class V river in a number of years, I'd rounded Cape Horn and crossed the North Pacific in a sea kayak. The goal on this trip was to circumnavigate Ellesmere Island, on ski and by kayak.

Despite, or perhaps because of our differences, we had already travelled 750 miles across the Arctic icepack, dragging our loaded kayaks over the snow and tortured ice, wading through meltwater pools, and occasionally crawling in heavy slush and ice. We had learned to work together and rely on one another. Boomer and I were a team, and we both felt it deep down, where it counts. We might disagree on which shortcut to take, but the fact was, neither of us knew the answers to the most pressing questions on this venture. *How far can we push our bodies today and still travel every day for three-and-a-half months? How many miles can we maintain on willpower alone, and when do we tickle the dragon of basic metabolic limitations?* We had no idea, at the start, how perilously close we would come to answering that last question.

Between our two little selves and the first output of civilization lay more than 750 miles of hard travel. We had food for about fifty days, depending on how much starvation we could tolerate and still function, but for the past seventeen days we had gone nowhere. We were utterly trapped. If we ventured into dangerous ice, we could be crushed. But if we waited for optimal conditions, we could sit there until our food was gone and winter descended. That option hadn't worked out so well for Sir John Franklin, among other early Arctic explorers.

In order to survive, we needed to find that razor-thin edge between boldness and caution.

BILL BRADT is an old river-running buddy of mine. When his son Tyler was six or seven years old, we sat him in a kayak and launched down the West Fork of the Bitterroot near our homes in Western Montana. He looked so tiny in that cockpit, elbows raised so he could dip his paddle in the water. Over the years, I watched Tyler grow into that kayak. Then, suddenly, it seemed, as Bill and I became progressively older and slower, Tyler was testing his extraordinary talent on the most difficult whitewater on the planet, including making a record-setting plunge over 186-foot Palouse Falls in 2009.

Then, one day, an email popped up. "Hey, maybe we should do an expedition together?"

Age was creeping up. Sixty-five feels significantly older than sixty. Yet I had one big expedition dream left to fulfill: a 1,500-mile circumnavigation of Ellesmere Island by ski and sea kayak. I'd thought about it since 1988, when Chris Seashore and I had paddled from Ellesmere to Greenland. The towering glaciers, moving ice, and stark exposure of that vast and uninhabited seascape had captured my imagination. Incredibly, no one had attempted the circumnavigation, one of the last great prizes in the Arctic. Tyler and I agreed to attempt it together.

We would use two food drops and carry provisions for 100 days, which meant that we'd need to average fifteen miles—half a marathon—every day for more than three months. Experienced polar explorers warned us that rough ice on the north coast would slow our passage to a mile a day, or a few hundred yards, or nothing at all. And once the ice broke up in late summer, we would be paddling overloaded boats through open water exposed to Arctic storms.

Over coffee in Duluth, Minnesota, I talked with polar explorer Lonnie Dupre, who had circumnavigated Greenland in 2001. He advised me that our bodies would simply not withstand the torture of 100 continuous days. We'd need to rest along the way, he said. Well, we knew we wouldn't have enough food or time to rest; yet, for no rational reason, the circumnavigation still seemed possible to us.

The advice did convince us to add more muscle to our team. Tyler suggested Erik Boomer, a whitewater charger revered for his physical strength and clear-headed optimism. When we described the trip's many challenges and the experts' warnings, Boomer smiled casually as if we were discussing a backyard run of a local river. "Sure," he said. "I'm in."

We rounded up a few sponsors. Someone offered to provide boats, another outfit donated paddles, some money flowed our way. Then, on March 21, less than six weeks before our planned departure, another email popped up. It was from Tyler, and the subject line read "Bad News."

"Hi guys, I really fucked up. My boat flattened out halfway down a big falls and I broke my back. I'll know a lot more in the morning when I talk to the neurosurgeon."

Tyler would eventually make a full recovery, but if Boomer and I were to attempt the Ellesmere circumnavigation, we'd have to do it without him. He'd been the force holding us together, the apex of our human triangle. Now Boomer and I were these two strangers, forty years apart, preparing to travel together, in total isolation, for more than three months, with the assurance that we would face life-and-death decisions.

Many people have insisted that I must have had reservations about travelling so far and so long with someone I didn't know, a generation younger than me. We had no music, no books, no playing cards—just eight rumpled pages torn out of the *Tao Te Ching*. What would we talk about? How would we resolve differences in the face of tense situations? We had plenty to worry about in the days before flying north, but I already trusted Boomer. Previously, I had kayaked 2,000 miles across the North Pacific Rim with Misha Petrov, a Russian who had never been in a kayak before. That worked out fine. I think you can trust a person by recognizing the madness that propels them, and in Boomer's madness I saw my own.

In 1971, I had stuffed my Ph.D. diploma in the glove box of a ratty old Ford Fairlane, lashed a canoe on top, and headed into the Arctic. Boomer had also experimented with possessions and jobs. He'd put them aside to go north and run the Stikine, and the Susitna, and Turnback Canyon on the Alsek River. We'd miss Tyler's magnetic personality and contagious laugh, but something even stronger would hold Boomer and me together—the mischievous grin of the Arctic wilderness.

Boomer and I set off on May 7, 2011, from Grise Fiord, the northernmost hamlet in Canada and the only civilian settlement on Ellesmere. This trip would be my retirement party— one last journey into a world that had shaped my life since I dropped out of research chemistry forty years ago. Boomer, for his part, was seeking a new vision of adventure, expanded from his already formidable accomplishments as a world-class whitewater boater.

The temperature was in the mid-teens Fahrenheit when we skied out of town, pulling our kayaks as sleds across a frozen ocean. We were carrying twenty-five days of food, and our total loads, including the boats, weighed 225 pounds each. Everything we'd packed was a compromise because every piece of gear, from kayaks to underwear, had to function in three radically different environments—winter on dry snow; breakup and slush; and open-water Arctic paddling. The Wilderness Systems Tsunami 135 kayak, advertised on the company website as "ideal for female and small-framed paddlers," was clearly smaller than we would have liked, but it was the largest boat that fit into the airplane that flies to Grise.

The first leg of the journey was 400 miles to the Canadian weather station at Eureka, on the west coast of the island. In the frenzy of preparation I'd glued and screwed the skins on my skis backward, so now I hobbled along like a skateboarder with square wheels. Boomer's boots didn't fit well and after a few days he constructed a new mode of footwear out of silver tape and scraps of shoe-like material he scavenged from an outlying hunting cabin.

The temperature dropped to below zero, and the north wind blew the snow into rock-hard drifts. We pulled our hoods tight against our frozen faces and trudged past polar bear tracks and herds of muskoxen. One day we disagreed on whether to take a shortcut overland, and on another day we argued about whether we should take a shortcut across the sea ice. But, very quickly, we learned to trust each other. It wasn't a verbalized emotion; like the eight water-stained pages of the *Tao*, it just was.

We resupplied at the Eureka weather station, which is distinguished for having the lowest average annual temperature of any weather station in Canada. It squatted on a hillside like a spaceship out of time: gleaming stainless steel kitchens, hot water, internet, and television. We rested for a day and a half and packed for the next leg of our expedition, which would take us to a food cache on the north coast, 350 miles away.

We'd been travelling on the west coast of Ellesmere, in the lee of nearby Axel Heiberg Island. Protected from the currents and waves of the open ocean, the sea ice here forms a relatively smooth surface, making travel easy. In contrast, the north coast is exposed to the continuously churning, moving, colliding North Polar ice pack. We'd heard reports of nearly impenetrable pressure ridges, formed from colliding multi-year-old ice.

So, did we need food for twenty days, or fifty? Or was the passage impossible? Should we turn back and abort the mission at the first encounter with rough ice? Or push on into the mayhem, risking the unpleasant possibility of starving to death in the middle of it—unable to move forward, but too far along to retreat?

The line between courage and foolishness is drawn only after the fat lady sings. If you make it, you were courageous. If you die, all the Monday-morning quarterbacks can puff up their chests and call you a fool. In the end we set off with fifty days of food, which was as much as we could carry, mandating that we average seven miles a day.

All along the northwest coast, Boomer and I found magic passages through potentially jagged ice. On many headlands, mini-glaciers flowed into the sea, providing smooth snow and seamless travel over land. We continued onward into the summer solstice, feeling lucky and clever, yet always apprehensive that tomorrow would be the day that our path turned into a dead-end.

The miles passed underfoot, but they didn't come easy. Our feet became blistered and swollen, and our bodies ached. Every day, by late afternoon, my brain was too tired to process the input from my eyes, so I saw double and blurry. I relied on Boomer's younger vision and incredible strength to find routes through the ice.

Yet the game here was to dissociate mental wellness from physical. Yes, of course, our bodies were beat up. What did we expect? But I was exactly where I wanted to be, crossing this frozen void in the spirit of our ancestors, who walked out of Africa, across the desert, during the ice ages, who hunted mammoths on the steppe with pieces of stone tied to the ends of long sticks, who wandered into the high Arctic to raise babies and tend grandparents in the harshest environment on Earth.

By mid-June, the summer sun had melted the previous season's snow cover, revealing sharp chunks of pressure-ridge ice. Boomer's skis broke. He moved his bindings and pushed ahead on the stubs. In this way we crossed the 350 miles in twenty-two days, found our cache, and celebrated with Pringles and rum. Now loaded to 300 pounds, we set out again, still dragging our boats. Near Cape Hecla, we finally encountered the feared maze of pressure ridges. Rock cliffs lined the shore and the sea had metamorphosed into a kaleidoscope of jagged ice, deep slush, and frigid freshwater lakes that pooled on the surface. We walked, paddled, or pushed along with ski poles through the meltwater pools, helped each other over the steepest ice, and crawled across the slush on hands and knees because we couldn't get enough traction using just our feet.

When you're soaking wet and crawling across supersaturated snow, it doesn't do any good to remind yourself that you still have 800 miles to go.

On the afternoon of July 4, we rounded the northeast corner of Ellesmere into the Robeson Channel. Here, the sun and current had fractured the ice into independently moving floes. Some were many acres in size, while others were as large as a house, or a tent, or a baseball. A current was driving ice from the North Polar Sea southward, into the narrow constriction between Ellesmere and Greenland. As a result, all the floes were compressed together, churning, spinning, and threatening to crush anything in their path.

We climbed to a rocky headland and watched the ice parade along the coast, imagining the despair that turn-of-the-century explorers must have felt as their stout wooden ships were crushed in the mayhem. We discussed the unpleasant option of walking to Grise Fiord, overland and half-starved, after the ocean froze again in the fall. But when we tried to imagine a route over the mountains, with no climbing gear and not even adequate backpacks, we realized that it was impossible. There was only one option left. We had to get through the ice.

The days ticked by. Occasionally, we made a mile, or two, or three. For nine days we sat in our tent, going nowhere. We slept, sat silently against sun-warmed rocks to feel our bodies heal molecule by molecule, cell by cell, and read those eight pages of the *Tao* until the ancient Chinese wisdom mixed like spindrift with the Arctic winds. Every day the sun settled lower in the sky, reminding us that although we still enjoyed 24-hour daylight, winter would soon descend upon us with polar speed and ferocity. Our food supply dwindled. Boldness or caution? Caution or boldness? Too much of either would kill us.

We sat on the shore and watched the procession of ice.

Okay, time to think outside of the box. There must be a way. Finally, we convinced ourselves to risk a treacherous passage across moving ice to reach one of the large floes. Our theory was that if we chose a floe strong enough to withstand collisions with the rest of the ice, we could ride it southward with the current.

·On July 13, a large floe, about five to ten acres in size and consisting of thick, multi-year ice, floated to within 400 yards of shore. We reasoned that this floe would survive the ravages of continuous collisions and provide a safe "ship" to carry us south. The current slowed at slack tide, giving us a narrow window of time to cross from shore to the floe.

The intervening distance was choked with small pieces of ice floating in a watery matrix. Some of this ice was large and stable enough to stand on, but other floes were small and tippy. We attached a long line to the boats and jumped from one unstable fragment of ice to another until we reached the safety of the first large chunk. Then we pulled the boats across to join us. But now our continued passage was blocked by a small, open channel wider than we dared jump across. So

Boomer bridged the gap with his kayak and crawled across the deck in a gymnastic tightrope act. I followed. Next, we seal-launched into an even wider passage, paddled a few boat-lengths, and climbed out of the boats and back onto the ice. Moving in this eclectic manner, we travelled a quarter of a mile in three hours.

Once we reached the large floe, we high-fived and set up our tent in the warm sunshine. We were determined to stay aboard this enormous ice shard for a week or more, if necessary, through all changes in tide and weather, as it carried us effortlessly toward Grise Fiord. Initially our GPS told us that we were heading south at 0.3 to 0.4 knots. That wasn't much; but, if sustained, it would multiply to four to five miles a day, which is significantly faster than not going anywhere. Boomer stood on a pressure ridge and held an imaginary steering wheel in his hand, grinning with joy, the captain of a massive, diesel-munching ice breaker.

At the next slack tide, the floe stopped moving and then, in the middle of the night, began drifting north with the ebb at one knot. We found ourselves travelling the wrong way at more than twice the speed of our earlier southward passage. The ice compression relaxed and open water stretched all around us. Then the ice started squeezing together again. I couldn't tell whether we were drifting north and the ice to the north of us was stationary, or if we were stationary and the ice to the north was crashing into us. In any case, in the semi-twilight of the Arctic night, the surrounding water became smaller and smaller, as if it were being sucked into a black hole.

The collision occurred with a slushy, whooshy sound, not a metallic clang. The edges of our floe crumpled and fractured, shooting ice splinters into the air, while the centre, where we were huddled together in fear and awe, rippled, as if it were in the throes of an earthquake. There is no metaphor to describe what was happening. This wasn't *like* anything. It was the Arctic icepack compressing and fracturing into rubble.

At the next slack water, we repeated our tenuous and terrifying passage across small floes in reverse and returned to terra firma, having travelled a net distance of one mile *away* from our goal.

For the next week, we inched southward, averaging about 1,200 yards a day. In places where the shoreline was still covered with winter snowdrifts, we dragged overland. Occasionally we paddled short distances between giant pressure ridges, and once we were forced to portage over talus and rock. Several days we waited, going nowhere. Finally we reached a zone where steep cliffs dropped sharply into the sea. We could no longer travel a mile or two and return safely to land. If we were caught in the strait when the ice closed in on us, we would be crushed between unimaginable forces.

A good friend, Paul Attalla, had advised us, "Be patient. Don't do anything stupid." We broke our bags apart, counted our food, and then grimly packed everything up again. Don't do anything stupid? Fine. It would be stupid to paddle into the ice and get crushed, and equally stupid to wait and starve.

We needed a south wind to push the ice out of the way and hold it clear for the five hours it would take us to race past the cliffs and reach the next safe landing. On the morning of July 21, the compression seemed to be easing up, and we had a weather report of favourable wind. We paddled into narrow channels between the floes. A twenty-foot iceberg collapsed moments after I paddled past it. *Ok, no worries,* I told myself. *Nothing bad actually happened.* But I couldn't stop worrying any more than I could stop breathing.

In whitewater, the current is flowing, but at least the rocks stay still. Here, everything was moving, so there was no stable reality. Our open-water channel slammed shut, so we dragged our boats onto a large floe and started hiking toward the south edge, where a remnant of open water remained. Boomer was ahead and urged me to move faster, but I was going all out. There was no "faster" left inside me. No, this wasn't right. We couldn't continue if our survival constantly depended on split-second timing.

We travelled another mile until, just offshore of Cape Union, fear overpowered desperation. Reluctantly, we retraced our tenuous steps to our old camp, elated to be unscathed.

We slept to let the adrenaline drain away. When we woke, even more open water presented itself, so we paddled out for a second time that day. But after about half a mile, we got scared again and retreated. Discouraged, we pitched the tent and ate dinner. It seemed as if we would never leave this place. After all, when Adolphus Greely set up camp to the south of us in 1881, he was isolated for three years before a resupply ship could break through. Nineteen of his original twenty-five men died of starvation, drowning, hypothermia, and, in one case, firing squad. Greely ordered a man shot for stealing food, after which his comrades may have eaten him (no one knows for sure). I wanted to close my eyes and stop thinking about our predicament, but Boomer took one last scouting mission to watch the ice. He returned breathlessly.

"Looks good out there. I think we can go for it."

For the third time on that long day, we paddled southward toward the rockbound coastline. The summer sun had swung into the northern sky to cast a subdued greyness across the seascape, offset by the soft, white glow of the ice. We were already exhausted from our previous two ordeals, but this is the moment you live for as an adventurer. It is comparable to pulling out of an eddy into a big rapid or turning skis into the fall line and dropping into a steep, snaking couloir. It is the moment when you must trust yourself and your partner absolutely and completely. A trust earned by travelling across the Arctic, alone, together. It is the glorious moment when fear vaporizes because you have decided to commit, and fear is now a needless distraction.

A major league baseball player reaches the Hall of Fame if he connects once out of every three times at bat. An NBA basketball player draws a multimillion-dollar salary if he hits fifty percent. An adventurer must have a lifetime batting average of 1,000. Nothing less. I had a gut feeling that we would make it that night, but don't remind me how much we were depending on blind luck.

It was July 21. For us it was the first day of summer because, after seventy-six days, it was the first time we paddled our kayaks as if we were on a sea kayak expedition. And, in true Arctic fashion, it was the first day of winter as well, because in the wee hours of the morning, as we were battling the fatigue of an all-night ordeal, a thin film of ice formed on the sea. It made a tinkling sound as we dipped our paddles and moved southward, toward home.

As July slowly morphed into August, the sea ice was fractured, moving, and sometimes thick, but not impenetrable. Most days, we paddled in narrow channels through an infinite maze of glistening floes. Occasionally the floes converged and blocked our passage, but after the Robeson Channel, these compressions were short-lived. When we could go no farther, we hauled out on land, or onto a large floe, and waited for a change in tide or wind. Sometimes we dragged on the closely packed ice, jumping across small, tippy floes.

One day, on the water, Boomer was attacked by a walrus— a ton and a half of awkwardly graceful skin, blubber, and muscle, its gleaming ivory tusks rearing above Boomer's head. Or maybe he wasn't attacked after all; maybe the walrus was just curious, getting a better look. In any case, *whack, whack,*

Boomer smacked the monster in the face and paddled away ferociously. On another day when we were camped, a polar bear slobbered over the vestibule and gently bit a small hole in our tent. Was he attacking, or, like the walrus, just visiting in his polar bear way? We'll never know, but we do know that the Arctic and its creatures revealed their power to us and then showed us their gentle side to grant us safe passage.

Boomer and I paddled into Grise Fiord on August 19, after 104 days and 1,500 miles. We celebrated by sautéing up some potatoes, cabbage, and onions, and binging on chips and salsa. We'd done it, together, and hadn't died in the process.

Then, thirty-nine hours after arriving in town, I woke in the night and discovered that I couldn't pee. It's a body function that you normally take for granted, like heartbeat or digestion. But when it failed, my blood pressure and potassium levels shot sky high. The nurse at the local clinic listed my condition as "life threatening." Pilots from Global Rescue flew their jet through a fast-closing weather window to carry me south. They saved my life.

Now I am back home in the mountains of western Montana. My urologist tells me that it was merely a coincidence that my system shut down immediately after the expedition was complete. But endurance athletes, trainers, and naturopathic doctors tell me that in that wonderland of sea and ice, my body was on the brink of collapse and the brain said, "Not yet, old friend. We're in this together, you and me, brain and urinary tract. Hang on. You can shut down after we get to town."

There's no way to know. But I can tell you that out there, surrounded by walruses, storms, polar bears, and ice, I felt a cathartic oneness of all things, animate and inanimate. If it were somehow possible to absorb the essence of a landscape into one's being, I think I would become the Ellesmere coastline.

Niall Fink

═══════════

THE MAGIC BUS

"LEE, CHECK this out."

Lee finished tying our raft to an aspen trunk and scrambled up the grassy bank to join me. When he saw it, surrounded by knee-high fireweed, he too stopped, stunned.

"No way."

I nodded, grinning.

"It's the, you know, the bus, the f-ing—"

"The Magic Bus."

"Jesus. It's not—I mean, is it?"

"It can't be. It's supposed to be close to Denali, which is like four hundred miles away."

Still, though much of the paint had chipped away and the back half was partly crushed, the shape and colour were unmistakable. Dropping our packs, we moved in close to touch the rusted metal. It felt very real.

I tried to laugh, but the sound came out strange. Lee shook his head. "This is bloody creepy, man. Bloody creepy."

It was 2009. *Into the Wild* had been on screens for two years, and Chris McCandless and his magic bus were everywhere. They appeared on posters, album covers, book jackets, and Facebook profiles. I would hear the soundtrack on the radio sometimes, driving out to the mountains for a weekend campout where some engineering student, loosened by fire-light and seven-dollar six packs, would confide that he was secretly dreaming of, you know, taking a year and just *living* out there. Out there in the Wild.

I was sick of it.

But if you were not twenty-something that year, or single, male, middle-class, and desperate to escape the impending yoke of a white collar, then you might not be as familiar with the story, or the bus. So here's the short version.

In September, 1992, a moose hunter found an emaciated body rotting in the back of a converted bus, twenty miles into the backcountry north of Denali State Park. The young man inside it had evidently starved to death that summer. On a sheet of plywood covering one window, he had carved his story:

TWO YEARS HE WALKS THE EARTH. NO PHONE, NO POOL, NO PETS, NO CIGARETTES. ULTIMATE FREE-DOM. AN EXTREMIST: AN AESTHETIC VOYAGER WHOSE HOME IS THE ROAD... TEN DAYS AND NIGHTS OF FREIGHT TRAINS AND HITCHHIKING BRING HIM TO THE GREAT WHITE NORTH. NO LONGER TO BE POI-SONED BY CIVILIZATION HE FLEES, AND WALKS ALONE UPON THE LAND TO BECOME LOST IN THE WILD.

ALEXANDER SUPERTRAMP
MAY 1992

Supertramp was an alias. He was born Christopher John-son McCandless, and came from a well-to-do family in Wash-ington, D.C. He was, by all accounts, a bright academic and an excellent athlete. In 1996, Jon Krakauer published *Into the Wild*, unravelling the full story of the young idealist's odyssey through the American Southwest, Midwest, and finally, fatally, the "great white North." The first edition spent 119 straight weeks on the *New York Times* bestseller list. Eleven years later, in 2007, Sean Penn's film adaptation would gross $56 million in theatres worldwide.

That same year I was on a number of my own "aesthetic voyages." While I was still somewhere in Montana or Arizona, my grey-haired dad bought the *Into the Wild* Collector's Edition DVD, thinking it would make a perfect welcome-home present. We watched it together the night after I returned from 700 miles of hitchhiking and desert walking. I could not forget the look on his face after watching the gruesome death in widescreen format. Over the next sixteen months, I would dismiss McCandless as reckless and naive and not at all like me. But his story hung like a starving, bush-bearded spectre above my dreams and fantasies. And now, just a couple of hours after crossing the border into Alaska on a driftwood raft, the Magic Bus was back.

It was not the same bus that McCandless died in, of course. But it looked almost identical: an old green-and-white Fairbanks City Transit bus, dating to at least the 1940s. This one sat in a weedy trash heap outside Eagle, Alaska, a small town on the Yukon River a few miles inside the Alaskan border. The other one, the one McCandless called the Magic Bus, had been skidded into the bush near Healy during the 1960s. It was outfitted with a barrel stove so it could house construction workers on a temporary mining road, and subsequently abandoned. But forty-five years later, when it graced the cover of Jon Krakauer's book and the posters for Sean Penn's movie, the bus became an icon that transcended any one piece of industrial trash.

On closer inspection there were many differences. This bus had been filled with all kinds of garbage—old aluminum

chairs, mouldy foam mattresses, beer bottles, plastic bags—
and almost all of the windows had been smashed. The bus
number was different too, 156 instead of 142. And, of course,
beyond it lay the refuse of domestic life: heaps of old toast-
ers, washing machines, and ovens. The feeling of black magic
began to fade.

Lee and I laughed at the strange coincidence, posed for
pictures, and finally shouldered our packs and walked toward
the town of Eagle. Omens were things in movies and books,
not part of the world that we knew.

OUR JOURNEY had begun 150 miles upstream, in Dawson
City, Yukon. Like many things in Dawson, it started at the
bar. Dawson has a reputation for its bars. During the summer,
the town boasts ten of them, despite a population of less than
1,800. Caravans of RVs and enormous tour buses pass through
daily, injecting summer cash that pays for refurbished historic
sites, garish "Boomtown" facades, a huge museum, and a transient community of summer workers who for several years
formed an annual "tent city" where, legend has it, the parties
lasted for days.

Dawson's summer scene originates in one historic summer 115 years ago, when 40,000 transients stampeded what
was then a subarctic fish camp, seduced by news of gold. It
was a gold rush unlike any before it. For the first time in history a majority of North Americans now lived in cities. The
western frontier was closed. Unlike their predecessors in California fifty years before, many of the men and women who
converged on Dawson in 1898 were hardly prospectors at all.
They were poets, artists, and idealists from the city—aesthetic
voyagers of one stripe or another, searching for a disappearing
wilderness. Their spirit was immortalized by a young voyager

named Jack London, who travelled down the Yukon River on a log raft and whose classic novel *The Call of the Wild* was found inside the Magic Bus, right next to Christopher McCandless's deathbed.

It was inevitable that Lee and I would connect in Dawson. We hit it off immediately, chatting one evening on the bright-red ferry that bounces day and night between the banks of the Yukon River. This had a lot to do with a shared passion for expensive axes. I carried a well-oiled Gransfors Bruks in my pack, and I dropped this name the way a car collector might mention his Ferrari.

"Ah, balls," he said. "I wish I'd brought mine." Lee was from England, and had two Gransfors axes back home. We were brothers immediately.

We got to talking later that night over a couple of pints of Yukon Gold at the Midnight Sun tavern. A handful of local musicians were letting loose after a long, long winter, and the bar was packed. I leaned forward across my glass and hollered: "I've got this idea. I've been reading about the river, and I think it wouldn't—"

"What?" Lee shouted.

"I want to build a raft!"

Lee grinned, took a sip, and leaned back in his seat. "Fack it, why not?" he said.

A few mornings later, still tipsy and carrying rucksacks loaded with an axe, a week's worth of food, and a coil of rope, we left the hungover town. A few miles down the north bank of the Yukon River we found a huge tangle of driftwood piled on a gravel bar. Here we lashed together nine heavy logs and covered them with spruce boughs. To power the raft, we cut long poles and carved paddles out of a split spruce log, swinging the well-sharpened Gransfors until our arms ached.

Raft and paddles took just a day and a half to build. We launched, expecting to take another six days to drift the 175 miles to Eagle, but with the river roaring along at high water we found ourselves nearing Eagle after just three days on the water.

They were glorious days, full of long hours lounging on spruce boughs, daydreaming, dozing, and watching wilderness slip past. There was hardly a cloud in the sky, and hardly a cabin on the shore; just us and the current and the rocky bluffs of the Ogilvie Mountains plunging into the river, with the odd moose or bear on the shore. At night we tied up the raft and cooked bannock on a campfire, lost in a Jack London idyll. Or, at least, we would have been, if not for the Yukon Queen.

The Queen, a complement to Holland America Cruise Line's tour bus program, ran up and down the Yukon River between Dawson and Eagle every second day before protests shut it down in 2010. It averaged around forty miles an hour, with tour guides on board to interpret the wilderness that blurred past tinted windows. Locals complained about the hundreds of salmon left stranded above the waterline by the Queen's two enormous jets, and on the river they worried about getting caught in the backwash themselves.

Lee and I were lucky. We didn't meet the Queen at a bend in the river, and she had time to put on the brakes and slow to a crawl as she passed us. Dozens of passengers with white hair and white shoes—passengers for whom the Magic Bus meant (if it meant anything at all) Pete Townshend or a vw minibus painted with psychedelic swirls. They snapped pictures of us leaning on our paddles; shirtless, barefoot, pants rolled up like Huck Finns.

"Are you all right?" A man in a Tilley hat shouted. "Do you need help?"

ONE OF THE most disturbing details surrounding McCandless's death was the fact that a simple piece of paper might have prevented it. When he first crossed the Teklanika River in May, it was barely deep enough to flood his rubber boots. But two months later, when, weakened by starvation, he tried to find his way back to civilization, McCandless found that the trickle had become an impassable torrent. We know this from the notes he left behind, which tell a harrowing story of pain and desperation as he died slowly over the following days. If he had looked at a map, McCandless would have known that a cable car, left behind by a hydrologic survey, crossed the river only a mile or two downstream. He could have walked out alive.

Before leaving Dawson, I'd bought a coil-bound series of river charts, wincing at the thirty-dollar price tag. I'd also packed a GPS unit—a graduation present from my parents, one whose message was not lost on me. There was a SPOT emergency beacon, a first-aid kit, at least four ways to start a fire, and a bundle of warm clothes stuffed in the bottom of my backpack. At my insistence, both Lee and I also had life jackets.

I am reluctant to mention these details, because they reveal an embarrassing truth about our journey: I was scared. I didn't have the passion, or the hubris, to plunge completely into the wild like McCandless. The Yukon Queen and her bourgeois passengers presented an unsettling mirror, so that well before the Magic Bus made its ominous appearance I had decided I would go further, through the Yukon-Charley wilderness preserve to the town of Circle. "Fack it, why not?" said Lee.

Leaving the raft and the bus, we hiked into Eagle, looking for a grocery store where we could stock up for the 155 miles ahead. What we found was a pile of salvaged canned goods and jury-rigged refrigerators crammed into a former tire warehouse. Five-foot chunks of river ice had torn apart almost every riverside building that spring, including the only grocery store in town. The trickle of tourist traffic that usually came here—aside from the daily flush of the Yukon Queen—had all but disappeared. After lively Dawson City, it was eerie. The gift shops were closed. No one was dressed in 1898 costume. No one waved. No one asked where we had come from or where we were going. These were ordinary Alaskans, many poor, just trying to get on with their work in the face of an often hostile environment. In our search for the Wild, we had almost forgotten that real people lived here; people with lives of their own and, a few months earlier, homes of their own. Spooked, we hurried back to our raft.

We had almost floated by the last of the ruined buildings when a voice came thundering through a loudspeaker: "GET OFF THE RIVER NOW!"

Hearts racing, paddling as hard as we could, we just barely managed to jam the raft against a rock before the river swept under a cutbank. On the shore was a U.S. customs officer, pistol on his belt, looking very unhappy. Evidently, we had also forgotten that we were crossing an international boundary. I dug out my passport, suddenly very aware of the six days since my last shower.

The officer said nothing until he had our documents. "Where are you headed?" he demanded.

"Circle," Lee said, gesturing downstream.

"Do you have maps?"

I said yes.

"Good," he said after a moment. "People have had some problems before."

LEE AND I HAD just left Eagle and dusk was still hours away when the sun began to disappear. We hardly noticed it at first, but by the time we tied up our raft—now dubbed the *Alaskan*

Intruder—the sun had become a dull, red ball on the leaden horizon. The sky in front of us, we realized, was full of smoke.

That summer was one of the worst fire seasons in Alaskan history, with three forest fires burning a swath the size of a small country. Nobody had told us about this. The customs officer probably didn't know they'd spread this far; out here a fire might burn undetected for days.

Over the next couple of days, the smoke only thickened. Each night I woke up choking on it. On the third day, we saw an orange glow to the north and carried on nervously, late into the night, hoping to reach Circle as fast as possible.

By the fourth day, we knew we must be getting close but had completely lost our position. From our maps, we knew that Circle was on a narrow channel to the left, at the point where the river starts to braid into the Yukon Flats, a silty labyrinth of shifting isles. The customs officer had warned us not to get lost in the Flats; the current there almost stops, so it would take many days to get to Fort Yukon, 140 miles downstream. People had died out there, he told us, when they stepped out of their boats and into the quicksand that lurked everywhere. We took him only half seriously. But, judging by the smoke, the Flats were now on fire too.

The smoke was so thick that at times we could barely tell where the shore started. I dug into my pack and pulled out the GPS unit. I was checking the LCD screen every few minutes now, as the kilometres to Circle dwindled from thirty, to twenty, to two, to one. We stayed as close as we could to the right shore. If we didn't, we risked being swept into one of the four channels leading into the Flats.

Just before the last bend above Circle a sandbar appeared suddenly, forcing us to paddle hard to the right. Then a small island emerged from the smoke ahead. To our horror, the current started pulling us to the right, around the island, and our crude paddles did nothing to stop the drift. We passed over into the wrong channel and the current began to slow, signalling the start of the Yukon Flats.

For the next forty minutes, we paddled until our shoulders screamed, fighting our way left across the current, panting for each smoky breath. Finally, exhausted, we looked up as a few houses appeared through the gloom of the left embankment, a faint orange glow in the sky behind them. We'd made it.

We hiked up from the docks and down the dusty main street. Not a single person was in sight. At the gas station—the only building we could find that was still open—an attendant told us the town had been evacuated earlier that day. Only she and a few other locals remained to help the fire crews. Another woman, who had come to visit her firefighter boyfriend, was leaving late. We begged her for the last ride out of Circle, learning only later that the road was barricaded just a few hours after our escape. She dropped us off near Fairbanks with a couple of granola bars for the road.

LEE AND I HAD had enough. I had a job waiting for me, and Lee had met a girl in Dawson just before we left. We hitchhiked back to Canada as fast as we could. After two days on the road, we caught a ride with Diane, an Alaskan of fifty-five years who took us back across the border to Canada in her sixteen-passenger minibus. It was a long drive, and all the grand boreal vistas of the Top of the World Highway were hidden behind a heavy coat of smoke. There was plenty of time to talk.

Diane wasn't particularly impressed by our story. There were plenty of places to tie up downstream of Circle, she said, and, anyway, we probably could have found one of the fire crews. The conversation wandered elsewhere. She told us how she could land a plane on muskeg better than most people with those fancy pilot's licenses, how too many newcomers were making it hard to find big moose to shoot, and how she was so proud of the way her state had rallied behind "our hometown girl," Sarah Palin. Then she told us exactly what she thought about that movie, *Into The Wild*, and played us a song that was not on the too-familiar soundtrack—a honky-tonk parody written by "some local boys" and burned onto a cheap CD. It was called "Permafrost for Brains."

She also told us how devastating this fire would be. Out there in the Wild, fishnets were melting, cabins were burning to the ground, and livelihoods were going up in smoke. As acres of doomed forest rolled by, Lee and I sat quietly, buckled up in Diane's bus. There was nothing more to say.

Niall Fink

NORMAN AND
THE CROW

IT WAS shortly after his wife died that Norman started talking to the crow. She was an old bird who nested at the
edge of his trapline, and she told him where to find the rabbit
runs and marten. In exchange, Norman brought her jerky and
shared slabs of bannock.

"Sorry I burned it," he would say. "Myrtle used to do
the baking." But the crow didn't mind. Both were glad for
companionship.

The crow had her nest beside a small lake where the beaver
had built a single lodge. They met there for lunch every couple
of days that winter, even through the long darkness of January.

At first, Norman found it a bit strange talking to a bird. He
hadn't spoken with one since he was sent to residential school,
eighty years before. The crow was surprised at this.

"Were there no birds there?" she asked.

"Yes," he said. "But they stopped talking to me. I think
it was when I noticed the girls"—and they laughed at this,
though both knew it wasn't the girls that had changed things.

When spring came, Norman continued to visit. The days
were lazy and long, with lots of time to talk and tell stories. He
couldn't afford one of those new four-wheelers and he couldn't

ride his old mare as far as he used to, so they met halfway down the trapline, on a hill where a breeze kept the mosquitoes away. From the top, they could see the mountains in the east.

"I remember that one," he said, pointing to a snowy peak off in the distance. "They were going to put the road through there."

"What road?" asked the crow.

"The Canol. A big American pipeline back in the war days, when they needed oil to fight the Japs. The army bought four head of horse from me and shot them for dog mush. Then they told me and some boys to scout a trail to the Wells. It took forty days, and we had to hunt two moose when the horse meat ran out. They never even used our route."

"Why not?"

"I guess they found a better one. It was a rough trail. But I always wanted to go back, you know. That's God's country out there. No white men or Indians or government agents."

"Are there any crows?"

"Maybe. All I saw was a big black wolf and the two moose. Sometimes I think about how lucky he was, that wolf. The road would have changed everything."

In the fall, Norman shot a moose. The crow told him where a bull was feeding, and it was the biggest Norman had seen in many years. Years ago he would have hung the antlers above his cabin door, but he was too old for that now. It took him two and a half days to pack the meat out, and another three to make jerky.

One morning soon afterward, when snow covered the hill-sides and Norman knew that it would stay for good even on the south slopes, a government man came to visit his cabin.

"Hello Mr. Martindale," the man said. He had thick glasses and a clean blue parka.

"What do you want?" asked Norman, who had bannock waiting in the oven.

"Just to talk, sir. Please understand, I'm not here to take anything from you. I'm with social services. Your daughter, Mrs. McLeod, asked us to speak with you."

"What does she want?"

"Mrs. McLeod said she was worried about you living alone out here. She asked us to talk to you about the new seniors' centre in Whitehorse. You see, this is a very new facility, and I think you'll appreciate some of its benefits…"

"You tell Clare I'm just fine," he said, and turned back for the cabin door.

"Sir, please hear me out. This is a special facility for aboriginals."

Norman turned to face the man with his back straight like a gun barrel.

"I'm not an Indian, and I don't want your house or your talk," he said. Then he went back inside to pull his blackened bannock out of the oven.

When he was sure that the blue man had left, Norman saddled his horse and rode all the way to the little lake. His trail was not very long—it had shrunk every year for the last thirty—but he had not ridden that far in a long time now and it hurt him very much.

He waited below the crow's nest until the sun was gone and the snow was blue with twilight, when she came flying home on those big black wings.

"They want to take me away again," Norman said. The crow listened.

When he was finished, they were both silent for a while.

"I won't go."

When he had said this, he felt strong again. He noticed that it was getting cold and that he should build a fire, so he hobbled the mare and pulled his axe from his saddle roll and then set to work.

The crow watched him and helped as much as she could by bringing small twigs for kindling. Norman made a tall stack of logs and started a waist-high blaze, then settled into a bed of spruce boughs between the two, reclining on his saddle. His back hurt and he was tired, but the stars were out and he was happy to be beneath them. The crow sat on top of the wood stack, black as the night sky, and talked.

Norman did not want to think about the home in White-horse, but now it was on his mind and he could not think of anything else, even though it was the end of fall and the crow had many things to tell him about the rut.

"I told them I'm not an Indian," he said.

"Are you?" asked the crow.

"I think I was, once."

"Then what are you now?"

"I don't know," he said. "What are you?"

"I'm a crow," she said.

"Then I'm a man."

Soon they were both too tired to say anything more, and Norman began to doze. He would wake with the cold each time the fire died, add more wood, and then fall asleep again. Every time he woke, the crow was sitting there, watching him.

As the flames began to die for the third or fourth time, Norman had a dream. In it, he woke up by the red coals and was not a man anymore but a wolf, a big, black one. The crow was still sitting on the wood stack, and she greeted him.

"Hello, wolf," she said.

"Hello, crow," he said.

"It's getting light."

"We should be off now."

"Where to?" asked the crow.

"Follow me," he said, and started off east toward the snowy mountain, where a faint blue glow had appeared. The crow flew above his head as he loped along on four tireless legs.

When the searchers found him two days later, he was covered in a white blanket of fluffy snow. A crow was perched on the spruce beside him.

One of the men took a piece of firewood from the stack and flung it at the bird.

"Filthy animals," he said. "Can't leave the dead alone."

But the crow could not hear this. It was already above the snowy treetops, black wings whistling as it flew eastward, out of the forest and into the mountains where no roads are built and wolves are strong and black.

Andy Kirkpatrick

WRITING ON THE WALL

IN EARLY September of 2011 I packed up a lifetime's worth of climbing equipment, piled it high inside my tired green van, said goodbye to my two children, and set off alone to drive over 1,000 kilometres from the U.K. to Norway. I bought only one-way tickets as I boarded ferries and crossed toll bridges; I had no idea when I would be coming back, and had no intention of doing so until I had climbed the Troll Wall.

The Troll Wall is the highest big wall in Europe, higher even than Yosemite's El Capitan. But unlike El Cap, bronzed and perfect in the Californian sun, the Troll is made from darker matter. I joke that I never believed in God until I saw El Capitan, but when I first trembled up through the forests and mists, rocks whizzing down from above, and touched the Troll, I knew there was a devil.

Three times before I had made the long journey north to the mystical Romsdal Valley to climb the Troll: in summer and in winter, alone and with a partner. Three times I had been given lessons in fear and doubt like no other, then sent away to dwell. The poet-climber Ed Drummond called the Troll "the altar" and said only those who had climbed it would understand.

But at the age of forty, I had put away all ideas of climbing the Troll. It was a thing for the younger, more foolish me, a climb I would point younger, more foolish climbers toward, or even boast about: "Ah, yes—I tried to climb the Troll Wall three times."

Then it struck, as I sat at home looking at flights to America, dreaming of warm Yosemite rock, that it was not yet time to give up on the nightmare of the Troll.

And so I made plans to return that summer and attempt a route called Suser Gjennom Harryland, a 600-metre-high route named after a Swedish pop song. I also chose to blog every day, taking an iPad on the Wall. Perhaps, I thought, like a dieter who posts pictures of what he eats at every meal, that by sharing the experience I would gain some extra level of self-control, and lessen the weight of what I was about to do. Also, as a writer who had played about with Twitter, Facebook, and blogs on other climbs, I was fascinated by the rawness of what I had written on those trips—including some things I had never dared reread.

When you attempt to solo a route such as the Troll, you are very close to insanity—while at the same time possessing levels of self-discipline and awareness that are beyond anything you will experience anywhere else. You are hunting the lion. That's why I find what I have written during my climbs so hard to revisit: *This is not my voice*, I think; *this is the voice of someone unhinged.* Plus, the writer in me hates how rough and unedited it all is, like something a sixteen-year-old would write. But these are also the unfiltered words of a man who is struggling, with taped-out sore fingers and eyes dropping, relieved the day has ended and fearful of what the following will bring.

Although what follows might be the least polished prose in this collection, I suppose, in my defence as a writer, it is the purest form of mountain writing.

12TH SEPTEMBER 2011

I'm back in the campsite feeling well and truly wrung out. Today I had to carry the first of two loads up to the base of the route. A total of about 100 kilos. The way up is always a nightmare due to the awful state of the loose screes. Carrying a 50-kilo haul bag up such terrain just sucks it out of you. What makes it worse is that since my last visit the path that normally leads along a river to the screes has become an obstacle course of fallen trees.

So just getting to the scree was like some sick assault course, climbing over trees, crawling under trees, bushwhacking, and generally getting my ass kicked.

From the base, the route looked wicked steep, with one really nasty-looking first pitch: muddy, slimy, and green.

I sorted out the gear. I knew I should lead the first pitch before going back to my camp. But as I procrastinated, the mist came down and it seemed like it was almost dark. Very spooky, and I took it as a sign to leave the first pitch till my next visit.

I always forget (or the memory is erased) how much backbreaking work is involved in a big wall solo, and that anything beyond El Cap, with its short and easy approach, is a lot of work. I guess with this sort of climb, it's all about work, and the knowledge that you did everything yourself. My body already feels as if it's had a right good kicking due to the number of talus tumbles I've had over the last two days (hands, knees, and elbows have had a real bashing).

Onwards!

14TH SEPTEMBER 2011

"The rain continued. It was a hard rain, a perpetual rain, a sweating and steaming rain; it was a mizzle, a downpour, a fountain, a whipping at the eyes, an undertow at the ankles; it was a rain to drown all rains and the memory of rains. It came by the pound and the ton, it hacked at the jungle and cut the trees like scissors and shaved the grass and tunneled the soil and molted the bushes. It shrank men's hands into the hands of wrinkled apes; it rained a solid glassy rain, and it never stopped."
—"The Long Rain" by Ray Bradbury

Yep—it's raining in Romsdal.

17TH SEPTEMBER 2011

The weather cleared today and I finally made it up to the wall with the rest of my gear. I even had enough energy left to do the first pitch.

Think I'll make this my last trip where I carry a 50-kilo haul bag up a neverending scree slope.

First pitch (v) was a horrible slimy waterfall, and I ended up aiding half of it. Climbing above looks very steep and less wet.

I'm doing the route capsule-style (fixing some ropes from three camps) as this is much safer on such a nasty wall, and it allows me to zip back to my bivvy without getting caught out in a storm with no bivvy set up.

I'm sleeping under a slight overhang on the ground tonight, just under the wall, and have set up a tarp to keep the drips off, so pretty comfy. Tea was tomato soup with leftover bread dunked in. I've got ten days food with me, but I really hope the climb doesn't take that long!

Climbed two more pitches today—slow and careful (much of the rock is pretty fragile), a mixture of easyish aid and free climbing, but all done with ice falling from the summit, dripping water, loose rock everywhere. I would not recommend this route (or the Troll Wall) to my worst enemy, but it's not dull—I'll give it that.

Being camped on the ground is so much more civilized. Rapping my ropes and getting back to my bivvy (climbing kit off, into sleeping bag, book and tea and chocolate) was almost worth it in itself. Maybe I should just go camping more often!

Will keep this short as my back is killing me from carrying too much gear, plus my cup of tea is getting cold on the stove.

Had a bad night because the tarp was flapping, so I ended up having to get out of my sleeping bag to put it away. (Of course I only did that after having been kept awake for several hours trying to ignore it.)

Today was my big day—the goal was to haul all my gear on the wall. But it didn't quite turn out like that.

Hauled gear to the pitch 2 belay, then set off to climb the fifth pitch, which would put me on a sheltered bivvy. I spent all day climbing one bloody pitch—the last party to do it took ten days and I can see why. Ended up going off route (scary) and then finally got into the right groove system.

20TH SEPTEMBER 2011

Weather looked like it was taking a turn for the worse, and with my haul bags yet to make it to pitch 5 (my first wall bivvy), I've headed down off the mountain till Wednesday.

I'm set up in a little camping cabin with a bunk bed, kettle, and a table (even has a tablecloth)—and it feels like paradise. I was only camped out at the base of the wall for three nights, but it felt like a couple of weeks. The Troll is a strange place, where time and the intensity of most things is greatly magnified.

The best way to describe the experience is that it's a bit like going into a war zone. At any moment something bad could happen, but like a good soldier, you make believe it won't happen to you. Sleeping, climbing, just being there—you're always somewhat on edge. There is always the danger of being hit by a "bullet," a little stone tumbling down from the summit Trolls, not to mention the prospect of the BIG ONE, the nuclear option—a falling, hundred-metre pillar or flake that would probably get me with the impact blast alone.

But I'm a good soldier. I keep my helmet on tight and stay behind solid cover as much as possible.

I'm a little tired, and so coming down has been a good chance to rest battered hands, sore knees, and aching back, as well as get all those bits I forgot in the first place (watch, glasses cord, more pegs).

Also got to talk to the kids today. In a way I didn't want to, as I knew they would undermine my resolve. But I did, and they didn't.

21ST SEPTEMBER 2011

Been a very relaxing day—a bit too relaxing—spoiled by the fact the weather has been quite nice (think of a cold but clear autumnal day). Anyway, have spent the time well, sorting out gear and drying off my camping stuff that was festering in my car (although I am feeling a bit dizzy after gluing rubber dry suit cuffs into the sleeves of my jacket with seam grip). Last job was boiling all my eggs to take with me on the wall, so all very domesticated.

Cycled into the village to clear my head and bought a cup of tea (still have no idea about exchange rate, so it either cost 20p, £2 or £20). Åndalsnes has all the get-up-and-go of a Sunday in Cleethorpes, and seems to have closed down for the winter already. The number one fun activity is having a hot dog (they have three meat flavours) in the train station.

21ST SEPTEMBER 2011

Yesterday was by far the toughest day yet—and I came within a whisker of bailing—but now I'm lounging in my portaledge on the wall. I'm glad I didn't quit.

What made yesterday so hard was the hauling. It's always tough even when there are two of you, but alone it can turn into a real nightmare. The problem is that the terrain is very irregular, and every time the bag got stuck I'd have to rappel down and free it, then jug back and carry on. I seemed to spend all day jugging and rapping and hauling.

To make matters worse, just before I'd reached the ledge I watched a ship-container-sized block fall down the back of the Troll, 500 metres away. I heard it falling—imagine the sound of a small house tumbling half a mile—then saw the huge detonation as it hit the rock slabs. Very impressive, but it didn't inspire confidence.

23RD SEPTEMBER 2011

A good day today: two pitches climbed, no rain, and I finished in the light.

Woke up feeling as only a big-wall soloist can (I'd forgotten this part), with throbbing hands, tired muscles, but knowing you have to get up and get moving anyway. When you're solo-ing, if you're not climbing, you're not going anywhere. Had a nightmare that I was being crushed to death—which, consid-ering yesterday's traumas, doesn't surprise me.

The first pitch should have been easy, but I found it all pretty scary, due both to the bad state of the fixed gear and because I'm still not very confident about the rock.

Next pitch began with something I hate, a traverse under a small roof. The weather had also turned cloudy, and the route went up another big wet slimy patch. I really wanted to call it a day, intimidated both by the climbing and the weather. In the end, I told myself to get a grip. And I did.

25TH SEPTEMBER 2011

As usual it's been a long day on the Troll wall.

Had to haul my bag from pitch 5 to 10 allowing me to set up camp to climb the next eight pitches, and then descend.

Amazingly all the hauling went really easily, two 60-metre hauls, and a 30-metre one bypassing two belays.

The rock quality has suddenly improved dramatically, and is up to El Cap standard. Let's hope it lasts. The bivvy spot is good (four good bolts).

Really look forward to the end of the day, when I can sit on the edge of the ledge, take off knee pads, Russian aiders, boots, waterproofs, harness leg loops—shedding each little piece makes me feel normal again. After that I stick on my parka and fleece trousers and get a brew on.

My daughter Ella emailed and texted today, asking how long I'm going to be away, and so I'm feeling the pressure to get home. I was meant to be away for three weeks. Another limiting factor is that I only have a small amount of water left, and I'm using two litres a day.

The effort to stay safe up here is all-consuming; it's a relief to get back to the ledge at night and just let go of the paranoia that grips me every second when I'm leading. Only did two pitches today and don't think I can move much faster while staying safe.

Six more pitches to go and I have three days' worth of food and water left—so it could be close.

27TH SEPTEMBER 2011
Pulled out all stops today, alpine start in the dark, and climbed three pitches—including what was probably the crux.

The sound of the rain was amazing—the whole wall came alive with rushing water, and waterfalls, not to mention lots of rock fall. The mist also came in, and although it was very atmospheric (you could forget you were sky-walking 500 metres up), it also made the wall a lot spookier. Climbing up to the crux, the whole thing felt as if it could collapse at any moment. The rock became really strange—like alien, plastic rock.

The rain stopped by the time I got to the crux, which was only 15 metres. I'm glad it's over.

The worst thing about climbing capsule-style is all the jugging and scary abseiling, with my two static ropes spidering up five pitches—most without touching anything. It's funny, but after a while you can just switch off fear. You sort of say "Nah—can't handle being scared right now—I'll think about it later."

Keep waking up with a mind full of thoughts and memories and ideas.

Highlight of the day was getting back to the ledge and crashing out and listening to Dylan's *Blood on the Tracks*.

28TH SEPTEMBER 2011
Back in the ledge after a fraught descent. It took a brew, the rest of my chocolate, and the last of my couscous (plus a bit of Arcade Fire) to remove a mask-like grimace that had taken hold of my face all day. On reaching the ledge I was just utterly wasted—especially mentally.

Did I get to the top?

I free-climbed it up a pillar with good footholds and lots of loose flakes for hand-holds. I reached the top of the pillar, a little pedestal, expecting to find two bolts, like every other belay. Instead, all I found was a rusty wire clipped to a carabiner, sitting on the ledge. I stood there with the whole face below me and looked for a belay. There was nothing. Worse still, the climbing above didn't look easy, so I thought I must be off route. I stood there and didn't know what to do. The only thing I knew was that I wanted to get it over with, even if it meant climbing in the dark. I hadn't spent ten days only to get up here and fail on the last pitch.

But where was the belay?

I climbed back down a bit and looked around some corners, feeling increasingly rattled; you can't solo without a very good anchor. My options were to pull up my bag and try to create a belay with the gear at hand—which would take too long—or to just keep looking.

I climbed back up the pillar again, feeling very lonely, and sat on the top. Then I heard a voice.

As I'd been climbing up, my camera in my chest pocket kept switching on and off and beeping. I suddenly heard my son Ewen's voice, and thought I was going mad until I realized it was coming from the camera. It was replaying some film I'd shot before leaving, footage of my son as he was emptying bottles of lemonade in our car park, and spraying it at my feet. What I heard was Ewen saying, "Dad—get away."

Hearing his voice right then was pretty emotional.

It's best to try to block out such thoughts, as it just makes you weak. For three weeks that's what I had done. And it had worked. I was strong. But this morning I'd made the mistake of checking my emails and got this from Ella:

What day will you be home on? Realy Realy Realy Realy missing you

Xxxxxxxxxxxxxxxxxxxxxxxxxxxxxxxxxxxxxxxxxxxxxxxxxxxx xxxxxxxxxxx xxxx love ella

I switched off the camera. I climbed down again and looked at the same limited view.

Why did my camera play that clip just now? I wondered, looking for some guidance. Why now and never before on this trip? I took stock: I was wasted. Probably off route. Out of water. Out of food. Out of time. One more pitch hadn't put me on the top—just one more pitch away from the ground. Why did I want more?

I knew I'd found what I was looking for, and started making my way down. No regrets.

Karsten Heuer

FINDING FARLEY

A TATTERED PAPERBACK copy of *Never Cry Wolf* lay open on my lap as I steered our canoe across Nueltin Lake, which straddles the Manitoba-Nunavut border. Behind us, tucked into the twisted spruce trees along the shore, purple fireweed grew from the ruins of the trapper's cabin where Farley Mowat, then a young writer and naturalist just home from service on the battlefields of Europe during the Second World War, had stayed for two summers sixty years ago. Ahead, somewhere on the "yellow sand esker... winding sinuously away in the distance like a gigantic snake" was the Arctic wolf den he'd written about. We were paddling toward it to see if it was still in use.

Getting to Nueltin Lake hadn't been easy. Since leaving our Canmore, Alberta, home two and a half months earlier, my wife, Leanne, and I had paddled with our two-year-old son, Zev, and dog, Willow, across the prairies of Mowat's childhood. We had then dragged, lined, and otherwise struggled with our canoe up the northern Manitoba river he'd followed, humping loads over the same overgrown trails Mowat had portaged with his Metis guide in the late 1940s, and we'd negotiated the same "roaring torrents" of the Thlewiaza River down to Nueltin Lake.

But pilgrimages aren't meant to be easy. And a pilgrimage this was. Mowat's books were serving as our maps across Canada, and our purpose was to revisit their narratives as we travelled through the prairie, northern, and maritime chapters of his life. En route we'd write letters to Mowat, and the journey's end on the east coast would be an encounter with the author himself.

Like many Canadians, I grew up reading Mowat. *Owls in the Family,* his memoir of his childhood in Saskatoon, was the first chapter book I ever finished. I then dug into *Lost in the Barrens,* one of his first novels, and *The Dog Who Wouldn't Be,* a tender but lighthearted account of the Depression years on the prairies told through the eyes of a nature-hungry dog and kid. Under the tutelage of Mowat's carefully crafted sentences, my reading improved, as did my understanding of my own country. I learned about Canadian wildlife and threats to them in *Never Cry Wolf* and *A Whale for the Killing* and was exposed, through his encounters with starving Ihalmiut around Nueltin Lake, to the history and mistreatment of aboriginal people in *People of the Deer* and *The Desperate People,* both published in the 1950s. Few other Canadian writers were paying attention to such issues at the time.

These stories were, I suppose, part of what propelled me to study ecology at university and to become a wildlife biologist, working for Parks Canada in Banff and Ivvavik on the Arctic coast. Before long, I, too, began writing books about my experiences with wildlife and wilderness, telling stories that couldn't be shared through scientific data alone. The second of my books, *Being Caribou,* helped complete the circle. On the eve of its Canadian release, I sent a copy to Mowat, who was then eighty-six, along with a letter explaining the influence he'd had on my life. A month later, a one-page response, composed on a manual typewriter, arrived in our mailbox. "One of the best, most evocative, and hard-hitting accounts of man's inhumanity toward life," he said of my book, and then extended an invitation that would shape the next year of our lives.

I think Mowat expected that we would fly to Cape Breton Island to visit him at his farm, but given the adventures he'd had, jetting across the country in a few hours to meet him didn't seem right. So we decided we would do it in the style of the Viking Norsemen, old Newfoundland fishermen, inland Inuit, Arctic explorers, crusty sailors, and other characters that people his thirty-nine books. We would paddle and sail across the country to see him, covering its daunting distances in five months.

Such slow and deliberate travel has its challenges, of course, which were not made easier by the demands of two-year-old Zev plus a hyper border collie, along with our decision to shoot a documentary for the National Film Board as we went. What was barely manageable as we crossed the prairies in May and June became overwhelming in the boreal forest in July. No sooner had the river currents switched against us than the bears became numerous and more curious. Portage trails were elusive. Re-supply points grew farther apart. When the wind was blowing, it blew against us, and when it wasn't, the bugs made us wish it was.

Oh God, the bugs.

Three months after leaving Canmore, we finally had a little breakdown on the night we camped within sight of the old log cabin on Nueltin Lake. White-crowned sparrows trilled from the few spruce trees brave enough to poke north of the treeline, and in the distance a family of loons called from a tundra pond. Linking the two were the trails of the Qamanir-juaq caribou herd, smoothing an otherwise ragged transition between the forest and the barren lands with their graceful, curving lines.

In a state of cumulative exhaustion, we were eating dinner, a meal that was more blackflies and mosquitoes than beans and rice. Suddenly, the swatting and the gymnastics of dining with headnets on became too much. Grabbing Zev, we stormed off to the tent in a cloud of bugs, hurling curses that echoed through his two-year-old lips: "Ship." "Fruk." "Buggah oft!"

This episode lasted the two hours it took to kill the thousands of insects that came into the tent with us, and oscillated wildly between horror and glee. Then, a little more calmly, we began the nightly routine of doctoring the worst bites. In spite of our head-to-toe "bug-proof" clothing, all three of our bodies were covered in welts, including our crotches. Leanne didn't utter the question but it was certainly on my mind: Why had we embarked on this journey?

I reached for my bag of books, pulled out *The Desperate People*, and began reading aloud. It was a powerful passage about starvation, about true suffering in that very landscape only a few decades before. As images of dying Ihalmiut babies and contorted adults lifted off the page, what had seemed horrific a few minutes before suddenly became trivial. Throughout our journey, such Mowat-inspired moments helped us across the high points as well as the low. Once, while re-reading *Owls in the Family* halfway across the prairies, Zev and I climbed into a giant cottonwood tree and hooted so convincingly that a great horned owl alighted on a nearby branch. A crossover moment of timelessness. A gem held out to the pilgrim. It was the kind of moment we were searching for now, as we paddled our way down Nueltin Lake.

IN A LAND dominated by bogs and rock, we had no trouble finding the only sand esker for miles. And within minutes of coming ashore, we knew we were in the right place: the shoulder blades, shin bones, and vertebrae of wolf-killed caribou lay strewn across the old glacial riverbed, along with piles of hair-filled wolf scat. The signs were recent but not fresh; most of the scat had been bleached by sun and rain, and the few threads of sinew still attached to the bones were as brittle as twigs. By the time we found the entrance to the den we already knew what the lack of fresh tracks had told us: wolves still used the area that Mowat had made famous, but hadn't denned there that year.

Or had they? Later that night, after Leanne, Zev, and the dog were asleep, a wolf visited our camp. I was on a nearby knoll at the time, savouring a toddler-free moment of late-evening sunshine, when a whisper of movement caught my eye. It was a white wolf and it had already seen me, but nonetheless continued toward the tent with a relaxed stride. I prayed for everyone inside to stay asleep as it padded to within five metres of the thin nylon shelter. In a testament to the wolf's stealth, no one stirred, not even the dog. Without pausing, it continued up a nearby slope and, as fast as it had appeared, slipped into the shadows and was gone.

I wrote about the incident in my next letter to Farley, describing the wolf's creamy colour, regal size, and commanding demeanour as best I could. He replied with delight that it was likely one of the progeny of the alpha male and female he had spent so much time watching while researching *Never Cry Wolf* sixty years before.

That exchange of letters took more than a month. I couldn't send my handwritten message until we had canoed another 300 kilometres to the Inuit community of Arviat on Hudson Bay, and Farley's response didn't reach us until we had covered another 2,000 kilometres by train, ship, and sailboat and walked into the post office at the next major stopover in his life story, Burgeo, Newfoundland.

But standing there on the tundra, the thought of the time lag in our correspondence didn't matter. By then, I had a pretty fair sense of what Farley's letter would suggest: that attached to every landscape is an undercurrent of wildness, a story of geographic potential and biological belonging—the very kinds of stories he'd spent so much of his life articulating. Our gift back to him was a first-hand report that told him those stories were still out there among the owl-filled cottonwood groves of the South Saskatchewan River, with the wolves on southern Nunavut's tundra and, as we were soon to find out, among the great fin whales of Newfoundland's rugged southwest coast.

IT'S BEEN SAID that to gain the respect of its friendly people, the best way to arrive on the Island of Newfoundland is by small boat. Even better, we found out, is to arrive from Quebec in a gale-force wind and four-metre seas with freshly ripped sails. Throw in a blond-haired two-year-old stepping nonchalantly ashore while a wharf full of stormbound fishermen looks on, and you're certain to attract the attention and sympathy of the entire town. Or so it seemed. Within hours of blowing into the town of Burgeo, Leanne, Zev, our skipper Tam Flemming—an adventurous friend of a friend who took a month off work to sail us from Quebec's Magdalen Islands for the chance to meet Mowat—and I had enough offers of meals, beds, showers, and loaned vehicles to last us weeks, if not months.

This was the very sort of hospitality that had greeted Mowat and his new wife, Claire, forty-five years earlier. They, too, had put into Burgeo's sheltered harbour, in a thirty-foot wooden schooner, the *Happy Adventure* (the inspiration for Farley's hilarious book, *The Boat Who Wouldn't Float*). Their original plan was to stop only as long as it took to repair their engine, but they were so taken by the area's rugged beauty and the generosity of her people that they stayed for six years.

Part of the attraction, wrote Mowat, was the isolation. The small outport fishing community was a place where he could "escape from the increasingly mechanistic mainland world with its...witless production for mindless consumption; its disruptive infatuation with change for its own sake. . . "

But even isolated Burgeo succumbed to the "bitch goddess, Progress." In the four decades that separated Mowat's arrival and ours, a paved highway had linked Burgeo to the larger towns and cities of Newfoundland, and its mainstay fishing industry had collapsed, forcing many of its workers to commute to Alberta's oil patch for months at a time. Indeed, during the week we visited, more than thirty percent of the men in the community of 1,600 were gone.

Yet vestiges of the old ways remained. Each morning and afternoon the harbour around Tam's sailboat came alive with the comings and goings of small, open boats which, aside from the outboard engines and occasional depth sounder, differed little from the cod-fishing dories of 100 years before. These were the inshore fishermen who, unlike the purse seiners, bottom trawlers, and other modern monstrosities that Farley condemned in *Sea of Slaughter,* ply the narrow fjords and hidden backwaters of Newfoundland's convoluted coast with simple hook-and-line tackle that yield no bycatch and don't harm the sensitive ocean floor.

It was one of these fishermen, Max Strickland, who came alongside our moored sailboat one evening and shyly offered to take us to the site of the sad event that led to the Mowats finally leaving Burgeo.

"I knows you're 'ere because of 'im 'an what happened," he said in his thick Newfoundland accent. "I wunnit be sure you sees de place for yourselves."

The place was Aldridges Pond, a lagoon tucked into the rocky coastline just five kilometres from the small town, and the event was an eighty-tonne fin whale that had become trapped within its confines after chasing a school of herring over the shallow entrance on a high tide. For the next two weeks Mowat and a few friends had struggled to save the starving whale while other citizens of Burgeo had riddled it with bullets. The tragic story, told in *A Whale for the Killing*, is one of Mowat's most powerful and moving books.

The storm that had mired our earlier passage from Quebec had dissipated over the last few days and Strickland's motorboat skimmed across the calm ocean without so much as a bump. Tidal currents and hidden reefs riddled our route but he seemed oblivious to the dangers, steering with one arm while he held Zev, smiling, on his knee with the other. For a two-year-old accustomed to paddles and sails, the wide open throttle was pure bliss.

By the time we arrived at the pond's narrow entrance, Strickland had started to talk more freely, pointing out the cliff-lined coves where he fishes for lobster, cod, and halibut; the slopes where he and his wife go berry picking; the spots under the eagle's nests where he likes to drift in his boat and eat lunch as he guts his catch. His voice was reverent as he spoke, maybe even apologetic. Then, as he turned the boat around, lifted up the prop, and began backing up the shallow passage where the whale had chased the herring, I realized he *was* apologizing. He was trying to say that not all the people of Burgeo were whale killers.

Leanne, Zev, and I returned to the pond in the sailboat's dinghy the next evening, taking an hour to row a distance that the motorboat had covered in ten minutes for the privilege of being there alone. The lagoon isn't big—the size of just two Olympic swimming pools—and as we oared around its breadth we tried to imagine the chaotic roar, splash, and booms of motorboats running a great sea mammal aground in such a confined space while rifle fire ricocheted off the granite cliffs. After a few minutes Leanne asked to go ashore so she could film Zev and me floating around the liquid grave. I dropped her off on a ledge of wildflowers then slid back out onto the water and read from Farley's book:

> ... *As she moved slowly away from us she left ribbons of dark discoloration in the water. These were coming from the great swellings which had formed beneath her skin. I could see one of them pulsing out a dark flow of blood; and I realized that those swellings were vast reservoirs of pus and infection, some of which were breaking open to discharge their foul contents into the cold sea water.*
>
> *As I watched, stunned and sickened, the whale continued to move across the Pond. She did not submerge. I doubt if she had sufficient strength to do so. Almost drifting, she reached the opposite shore and there she rested her mighty head upon the rocks.*
>
> ... *and then I heard the voice of the Fin Whale for the fourth time... and the last. It was the same muffled, disembodied and unearthly sound, seeming to come from an immense distance: out of the sea, out of the rocks around us, out of the air itself. It was a deep vibration, low pitched and throbbing, moaning beneath the wail of the wind in the cliffs...*
>
> *It was the most desolate cry that I have ever heard.*

We sailed out of Burgeo the next morning, happy to be moving again but still saddened by the ghost of the whale. And the killing hadn't stopped. That morning, while listening to the CBC Radio news as we rigged the sails, we heard about the Japanese whaling expedition headed for the Antarctic Ocean. In addition to 850 minke and fifty fin whales, they planned to harpoon up to fifty humpback whales for the first time since hunting the endangered species was banned forty-four years ago. A quote of Mowat's from an interview I had once read popped into my head as the last of Burgeo's barrier islands slipped behind us: "God, I think I'll resign from the human race."

But there was hope, literally tons of it, and it came in the form of a pod of finners a few hours later. I pointed over the starboard rail to the great plumes of mist blowing out of the waves and Flemming shouted for me to push over the tiller as he pulled in the mainsheet. Armed only with binoculars, we too were off to hunt whales.

As we drew among the feeding pod, three of the great cetaceans pulled alongside the boat, their sleek, black backs arcing out of the water with each surfacing breath. There could be no doubt they were fin whales—the second largest animals ever to inhabit the planet—and as the great beasts sounded beside us I wondered aloud how one of their kind could have fit, let alone survived for more than two weeks, in that tiny lagoon.

"One of their kind or a relative of the one that was actually killed?" winked Leanne.

Another wild undercurrent. Another crossover moment. I made a mental note to tell Mowat, but this time I would do so in person. If everything went according to plan, we would cross Cabot Strait and sail right to the shore of his Cape Breton farm in seven days.

IT BEGAN like every day had in the previous five months. Shortly after breakfast, Zev's two-year-old mind demanded the outlines of a plan.

"Where are we going?" he began as we sailed out of Cape Breton Island's St. Peters Canal.

"To visit Farley Mowat," I answered, just as I had 150 times before. But from there on the conversation took a different tack. No more abstract explanations of time and distance. No more maps of provinces, river systems, and oceans hastily drawn on a piece of paper or scratched in the sand. I waited as his tiny lips wrapped themselves around the next question. "Today?" he asked. And then I pounced.

"Yes!" I cried as we rounded a forested headland. "There!" I pointed at an old two-storey farmhouse overlooking the water. "That's where Farley, Claire, and Chester the dog live!"

Zev was stunned. After 5,000 kilometres of paddling, lining, portaging, train riding, and sailing, we were now just a few hundred metres from Mowat's door. Zev studied the simple white clapboard home as we pulled into the shallow bay and dropped anchor.

"Oh, oh, I see them," he suddenly cried. "Persons and a dog!"

Indeed, two people had started down toward the beach where a small crew from the National Film Board had gathered. I looked through the binoculars and confirmed to Flemming that all his ocean navigation had been successful: one of them had a beard.

Flemming elected to stay on board and keep tabs on the sailboat as Leanne, Zev, and I clambered over the rail into the dinghy. It was a beautiful fall day, and a gentle ocean breeze pushed us toward shore. Yet for all its coolness, the moment had me sweating more than any midsummer portage. I took a few pulls on the oars then snuck a glance over my shoulder. It was Farley Mowat, for God's sake, standing on the shore to greet us! What the hell was I going to say?

As the oarlocks thumped-thumped against the gunwales I recalled the questions I'd left with five months before—about the power and persistence of stories in the landscape, and how they affected people's perception of the land. Like any good pilgrim nearing The End, I now realized the journey and Mowat's books had already provided most, if not all, the answers. The role of the wise elder was only to be a good friend.

The bow of the dinghy hit the gravel and I leapt into the gentle surf as Mowat walked toward us. I offered my hand but he scoffed at the formality and, instead, pulled me in for a hug.

Wayne Sawchuk

TOUGH LIVING, OH BOY

WHEN MY Uncle Norman offered to sell me the Gataga trapline, I didn't hesitate. Located in the far north of British Columbia, the Gataga River is true wilderness, where the tracks of another person rarely mark the winter snow. I craved the wilderness life, and it took only a few days before I was out of the logging business and into trapping. I was a happy man, but my decision certainly involved risk, and it sometimes kept me up at night. When the cheque came back from my first fur auction, I learned that fur prices in the 1980s were near all-time lows.

Money worries were the last thing on my mind as I gripped the handlebars and powered my snow machine around another corner on my first trip down to the thirty-mile cabin. The trail along the creek known as Swamp River parallels the much larger Gataga River for twenty miles or more. I was ready for a break when I glanced up and spotted a tall pine stump standing on a small flat above the creek. Curiosity piqued, I turned off the snowmobile and waded up through the waist-deep drifts to the flat above. There I found a few blazes on the lodgepole pines, a hump in the snow that looked to be an axe-cut log, and, beside that, a depression that seemed to indicate an old fire pit. The tall pine-tree stump I had noticed from below had been squared off on four sides. On the blazes I could make out the name, "Egnell," and the date—1943. I knew my uncle had purchased the trapline from Frank Egnell Junior. Judging by the date, Frank Egnell Senior had passed through here on his trapline rounds, likely many times, including his last.

Looking closer at the tall stump, I could just make out three more words—"Swamp River Post." I smiled at the pun.

It was hard work finding trail, cutting windfall, and snow-shoeing ahead in the rougher sections to pack a path for the snowmobile. The trail along the Swamp River followed curve after curve of the slow-moving tributary. The water in the creek was shallow and the ice thick. As I saw the Swamp River veering to the right and around the cutbank to join up with the main Gataga River, my heart sank. The plan had been to travel along the bank of the big river, but thick stands of spruce, alder, and pine trees choked the shore. I knew that beneath the deep, insulating blanket of snow that concealed the surface of the Gataga, strong currents were eating at the ice, and unseen holes could open anywhere. I paused for a long moment, then gunned the engine and sped out onto the river as fast as the machine could go.

The Egnell family, too, would have had to cross the river here when they came trapping. I could imagine the parents holding the hands of the kids, pausing now and again to tighten a snowshoe thong or adjust a dog pack. It would have been more dangerous for them, as they slowly made their way across the treacherous ice on foot, than it was for me on my machine.

Still, after several heart-stopping crossings, it was a huge relief to be able to steer the machine onto the riverbank and up through the trees. Before long I caught sight of the tiny cabin, almost lost beneath a heavy capping of snow, nestled among thickets of young, vigorous spruce trees jostling for space in what used to be a clearing.

Using a snowshoe as a shovel I cleared away the drifts from the door. At first it wouldn't open, bound by the great weight of snow pressing down on the roof. I bashed against the door with my shoulder until it broke free. Once my eyes had adjusted to the gloom, I made out a single small room with a pole floor and a roof of axe-split boards. A small rusty wood stove squatted near the centre of the room and a rough pole bed occupied one corner. A low wooden table nailed to the wall under the single window completed the sparse furnishings. Empty corn syrup and baking powder cans sat on a narrow shelf in one corner, and in a blue Player's tobacco can I found a box of .22 shells and a packet of Gillette razor blades. A few wooden stretchers used for drying hides leaned in one corner, and hanging on a nail from one of the low roof logs was a large metal kettle, possibly used for cooking meat for the pack dogs. The room was spartan, but ready for use.

I lit a fire in the stove, and when I had unpacked my sleeping bag and food and put on a pan of snow for tea, I took a closer look at the walls of the cabin. The scribblings of small children marked the lower logs, and there were many messages as well—"March 16, gone to Rabbit Lake, Frank." "Gone to Rat Lake to hunt beaver, back on the 5th." And, prominently, "Built 1938."

I spotted another note high on one of the logs. Peering to make out the words, I read, "Snow come, get deep. Tough living, oh boy."

I felt a jolt of recognition. Martha Egnell, Frank Jr.'s wife, had told me the terrible story of the thirty-mile cabin. Did this note refer to those events?

AS THE STORY WENT, in the spring of the year, in the late
'40s or early '50s, Frank Sr. and his wife, along with some of
their children, travelled down to the thirty-mile cabin to trap
beaver. Martha didn't say exactly how many children had
come along, but she did say one of them was Frank Jr.'s older
brother. All must have been old enough to snowshoe on their
own. Frank Jr., who was born in 1926 and would have been in
his early twenties at the time, stayed behind at Fort Ware, perhaps because he and Martha were newlyweds.

Martha told me that spring came late that year, and the
ice was thick. It snowed day after day, making trapping and
hunting impossible. In desperation, Frank Jr.'s older brother
waded across the river trying to find and kill a moose, but,
chilled by the frigid water, had to turn back. Soon after, he
caught pneumonia. With no first aid or medicines, his racking
cough could not be treated, and he died in the cabin. It would
have been a terrible death, similar to drowning, as his lungs
filled with fluid, choking off his breath. The ground was frozen hard as steel and so the family buried him under the floor
of a small cabin just upriver from the main building. It was
the only place where they could dig.

I had, in fact, noticed the remains of the smaller cabin in
the summertime. All that remained were a few rotten logs
almost lost in thick grass. There was nothing to indicate that it
was a burial site.

Fearing that the rest of his family might starve, Frank Sr.
set out to walk to Terminus, sixty miles downriver. Terminus
is slightly closer than Ware, and he must have thought that it
would be the fastest route to help.

Meanwhile, in Fort Ware, Frank Jr. was getting worried.
With no word from the family, and knowing the country as
he did, he feared that the deepening spring snows could bring
starvation for anyone caught out on the land. He loaded a

pack with food and set out for the thirty-mile cabin. It must have been an excruciating trip; as Martha told me, "the snow was over his knees every step."

Not far from the thirty-mile cabin, Frank Jr. met his mother and the kids. Driven by hunger, she'd decided to strike out for Fort Ware, a route she may have been more familiar with than the trail to Terminus. I could imagine the joyful reunion as Frank Jr. untied his pack and gave them food, dry meat perhaps, or maybe hardtack and lard. There would have been sorrow, too, as Frank learned of his brother's death, compounded by terrible anxiety, as he heard of his father's desperate departure.

As it wasn't far, they snowshoed back to the thirty-mile cabin, and with the food Frank Jr. had brought, the family soon revived. Now Frank had a difficult choice to make. He couldn't have brought a lot of food with him, so the family would have to go back to Fort Ware. Would he accompany them, or should he go look for his father? If he did strike out downriver, it would mean that his mom would have to set out alone with the kids; in deep snow, that would be a grim task. No doubt he weighed the possibilities, questioning his mother about his father's condition at the time he set out, wondering how far Frank Sr. might have made it and whether it was worthwhile to set out after him. Finally, he made his choice. Packing up what food was left, he and his mother and the kids set out once again for Fort Ware.

When Martha reached this part of the story, she paused and looked down at the cracked linoleum. After a few moments, she said, "Frank still thinks about that."

When the family arrived back at Fort Ware without Frank Sr., a ski plane was chartered and Frank Jr., the priest, and an RCMP constable flew north and landed on the far end of the Pike Lakes. They walked down the creek, and in a little camp by the river, they came upon Frank's father. He had tried to make a fire, cutting alder sticks for fuel. Weakened by hunger, he had been unable to chop through a small, dry tree, something he could have done with one stroke had he been well. He died there, and beside his frozen body they found his axe and the partly chopped stick.

Frank must have known then that had he gone downriver those seven miles instead of taking his mother back home, he might have saved his father's life.

EVERY FEW DAYS throughout that first winter, I made the snowmobile trip to thirty-mile on the trapline rounds. No sign of the second cabin could be seen under the unmarked snow upriver.

Often, as I sipped my tea or finished up a meal, my eye drifted to the cryptic inscription lit by flickering candlelight, high on the wall behind the stove. *Tough living, oh boy.* Were they written that tragic spring? And if they were, whose hand had held the pencil? Was it Frank's mother's, while she waited, or his brother's, before he died? Or was it his father's, before he snowshoed into the silent, snowy forest?

And as the months passed, I began to understand the land in a whole new way, not as a visitor, but as someone to whom it was home. During the long nights at the thirty-mile cabin, stars glittered over the frozen river and above the line of serrated, icy peaks beyond. All was still. The land was wrapped in profound silence. As the hours passed, the temperature plummeted to -40°C, then -50°C, and lower. From time to time a crack rang out in the darkness as another tree exploded under the grip of the cold. The tiny tin wood stove fought a losing battle and the frost line hovered at knee level. I huddled in my sleeping bag on the spruce-pole bunk, the same one the Egnells had used so many years before. I listened to the small pops and whispers from the stove and watched the firelight flicker on the logs. I thought about the life-and-death choice that Frank Jr. had made. I thought about my own life and my choice to take up trapping. It seemed that Frank Jr. had made the best decision he could have, given all the factors he'd had to weigh. And so, I thought, had I.

Bruce Kirkby

MUSKWA-KECHIKA

"Did you hear that?' Wayne Sawchuk whispers, freezing mid-stride. For the past twenty-four hours we have tracked a lost horse through dense woods cloaking British Columbia's northern Rocky Mountains.

Well, more accurately, Sawchuk has tracked the young horse, and I have followed Sawchuk, who is making me feel like a neophyte in the wilderness for the first time in decades. The logger-turned-cowboy-turned-conservationist stoops often, finding clues that I would have missed, running his hand over blades of bent grass and scuffs on rocks, changing direction, retracing his steps, muttering, and all the while deciphering the mystery of the horse's flight. Scars in alder bark show where the frantic horse smashed his panniers. Prints of elk, moose, deer, caribou, and galloping horse litter the thick carpet of moss underfoot, and Sawchuk patiently points out the differences. Despite such tutelage, they all look the same to me—as if a drunkard hopped through the forest on a pogo stick.

Watching Sawchuk walk through the woods, or sit motionless atop a horse while scanning the horizon, offers a rare glimpse of a man utterly and entirely in his element. Every summer since 1989, Sawchuk has mounted gruelling (upward

of ninety days) horse journeys through this vast and virtu-
ally forgotten corner of Canada—and brought commercial
clients with him. These are no run-of-the-mill eco-tours. "Par-
ticipatory expeditions" is how Sawchuk describes the experience. The guests who join him for two-week stints, flying in
and out of remote lakes on float planes while the pack string
continues its relentless march over the rumbled landscape, are
expected (and desperately needed) to pitch in with saddling
horses, loading packs, cooking meals, gathering wood, and
setting camp.

Two days earlier, an eighteen-wheel transporter unloaded
twenty of Sawchuk's horses at Summit Lake on the Alaska
highway: eight for riding, twelve for packing. After a fitful
sleep under the midnight sun and the usual "rodeo and yard
sale" that comes with the first day of any horse trip, our nascent
team of strangers leapt atop their saddles and the excited
pack string thundered up a steep trail leading to alpine table-
lands above.

Sawchuk's string is comprised of proven, trusty mounts.
Hazel, the patriarch, is the veteran of twenty-seven expeditions. But each year, a handful of new horses are broken in. It
was after a lazy lunch on the banks of a clear creek that Buddy,
one of three novice pack horses, panicked and bolted. Maybe
it was a gust of wind, or just his reflection in a puddle, but
by the time we realized something was amiss, Buddy had vanished into the tangled choke of trees that rise steeply above
the north fork of the Tetsa River.

Dismounting, we followed on foot, retracing Buddy's trail
through a maze of trunks and fallen trees. "Poor horse was
out of his mind with panic," Sawchuk noted. "It will be a miracle if we find him alive." Every bash and bang of his hard plastic panniers would have added to Buddy's terror; his unabated

full-out gallop was evidenced by all he'd left in his wake. Tent poles, cans of beans, and fluorescent jackets were strewn through the forest, leading us in an enormous loop. Eventually, we found ourselves lost in a confusion of hoofprints going every which way. Riding our horses to the top of the mountain, we scoured the upper limits of the forest to ensure he had not crossed into the next valley, but found nothing.

"He's still down there somewhere," Sawchuk declared at day's end, "and we'll find him." I did not share his confidence. We were travelling at a snail's pace, trying to find a charging horse with a full day's lead on us, amid a wilderness so large that Ireland could fit within its borders. It felt like the proverbial search for the needle in the haystack.

The next morning, as we prepared to resume the search, Sawchuk slipped a lever-action .308 Browning rifle into his backpack. (This rifle, along with a mirror-polished axe, is always slung from Sawchuk's saddle, within arm's reach.) It was a reminder of the grim reality: if we could not find Buddy—who might already be dead, or lying stricken with a broken leg—he would surely perish in the days ahead. Sawchuk's pack horses are fitted with a muzzle each morning to prevent grazing on the trail. If bears and wolves didn't get him, starvation would.

NOW, AFTER SIX painstaking hours of following whispers of Buddy, Sawchuk—who auditioned for the part of Mantracker in the popular television show—has heard something. We stand motionless. Clouds of mosquitoes press around our faces and ears. A squirrel screeches in protest at our presence. A chipping sparrow flits past, and on a nearby snag, a pair of hairy woodpeckers dance in circles. Then, hidden amid these gentle sounds, comes a faint grunt.

"That's the sound of a struggling horse!" Wayne exclaims, and strides off at a near-sprint. Soon Buddy is before us, standing motionless in a cluster of pines. The remains of a saddle and rigging hang in a tangle beneath his belly. Sawchuk approaches slowly, steadily, whispering encouragement. The horse is exhausted but unharmed. Gently wrapping an arm around Buddy's neck, the normally stoic Sawchuk turns, with misty eyes, and asks me to snap a picture.

IF YOU SPREAD a map of North America across a table and then poured an entire bottle of red wine upon the heart of the continent, the subsequent stain—soaking the high mountain cordillera to the west, drenching the Prairies, engulfing the Great Lakes while seeping southward toward Mexico and north to Alaska—would represent the historical (or "pre-contact") range for most of the New World's large carnivores and ungulates.

With time, that spill has been steadily mopped up. A recent study by the American Institute of Biological Sciences shows just a splash survives today. Plotting the current populations of North America's large species (ten carnivores and seven ungulates) reveals that in one—and only one—spot on the entire continent does the full palette of original wildlife remain: the sprawling wilderness straddling the northern spine of British Columbia's Rocky Mountains known as the Muskwa-Kechika. And arguably no one has played a bigger role in protecting and preserving the Muskwa-Kechika than the misty-eyed man with his arm around the neck of Buddy.

In the early 1990s, British Columbia set the ambitious goal of developing a comprehensive land-use strategy for the northern half of the province. Early processes on southern lands had proven bitterly fractious; determined to find a better way, the provincial government gave a unique directive to northern stakeholders: find consensus. No votes, no split decisions; policy must address and satisfy all concerns. And everyone was invited to the table: forestry, mining, oil and gas, recreational users, organized labour, guide outfitters, trappers, conservation groups, hunters, first nations, and local government.

Sawchuk—who knew the wild lands of the northern Rockies intimately and understood what was at stake—leapt headlong into the process. It may seem contradictory that a man equally comfortable behind the wheel of a logging skidder or guiding a big-game hunt has become one of Canada's leading conservationists, but that is exactly what Sawchuk is. The seeds of his environmental ethic were sown during his youth in the 1950s and '60s, when he watched his father raze forests, farms, orchards, and entire towns in advance of dam construction. The loss of so much beauty felt wrong, even then, and he wasn't about to stand by and watch it again.

The solution the diverse group of stakeholders eventually arrived at represents a unique attempt to find balance between the competing needs for wilderness protection and industrial activity. Ultimately, 6.4 million hectares—an area ten times the size of Banff National Park—was set aside: 1.6 million hectares in a constellation of twenty protected areas, and 4.8 million hectares in a special management zone where, although industrial use is permitted, wilderness and cultural values are factored into all operations, and the land is returned to its previous state when they are complete. An advisory board—with members representing every interest—reviews all plans and proposals, offering its opinion to the provincial government, which makes the final decision.

With timber prices at record lows and significant gas discoveries just outside the boundaries of the Muskwa-Kechika, fate has admittedly played a hand in keeping demands and tensions low. Nonetheless, approaching its fifteenth anniversary, this groundbreaking experiment in the co-management of wild land continues to provide hope that a successful balance can be found.

When asked why it works, Sawchuk is unequivocal. "Consensus. If the board wasn't obliged to consider every view, it would all fall apart." One recent example: when shale gas deposits were found in an area designated as critical stone sheep habitat, the board ordered a detailed population survey. The sheep, it was discovered, utilized only half the zone set aside for them. So development proceeded in the other half—during winter, when the footprint was almost nil—while the sheep population remained protected.

Despite its size and success, you'll be excused if you've never heard of the Muskwa-Kechika: it may be one of Canada's best-kept secrets. A recent study showed that only sixty percent of area residents recognized the name. Awareness plummeted to five percent in British Columbia's Lower Mainland, and while the poll did not cross provincial boundaries, it's easy to guess where the numbers head as one travels east. Which is a shame, for the lessons of cooperation the Muskwa-Kechika affords, both on a national and international stage, are desperately needed today.

Even more regrettable is that the British Columbia government has made no commitment to fund the Muskwa-Kechika advisory board beyond this year; this delicately balanced solution is in peril of collapsing before its lessons can spread.

WITH BUDDY safely back among the pack string, our party continues south, travelling against the grain of the land, rising and falling as we cross the rumpled foothills of the front ranges. The desolate alpine grasslands are spotted with the purple and white of spring—avens and lupines which our horses greedily nibble. Far to the west, snow-capped peaks crowd the horizon. Aspens cloak closer hillsides like summer grass, their leaves rippling in waves with every passing gust.

The rivers draining these peaks—impossibly clear and the colour of Bombay Sapphire—have carved narrow canyons, begging exploration, through the limestone bedrock. Not one prone to frantic hydration, I find myself guzzling litre after litre of the clear stuff. It tastes that good.

We follow whispers of ancient trails carved by outfitters, guides, explorers, and first nations long before us. Some wind through ghost forests of burnt spruce, others beneath sheer rock faces, thousands of feet tall. The pack string acts like a Rototiller, eighty hooves pounding into the soft earth exposing rich, brown soil whose aroma mixes with the scent of the horses. In places where the trail has been dug into a trench, the horses prefer to balance on the edge, perched—perilously, it feels to the rider—on the narrow ribbon between gulch and forest.

One of the grand luxuries of horse travel is not having to perpetually stare at your feet, or "push bush." This lends itself to constant observation—a good thing, as there is plenty to see in this "Serengeti of the North." One day alone we spot 160 elk, thirty-five caribou, a dozen stone sheep, two moose, and a black bear. As hunters have long known, wildlife that would flee a walking human does not vanish at the appearance of a mounted rider. The mountain caribou are particularly curious, running toward our horses, sniffing the air, sprinting away, and then returning to tail us.

"I WANT TO show you something," Sawchuk says after dinner, rising from the campfire on one of my last nights in the Muskwa-Kechika. We set off together down a faint game trail near camp. A nighthawk calls, and to the east, a waxing moon rises in a purple sky. After several hundred metres, Sawchuk drops to his knees and begins combing the gravel.

Then he finds it: a tiny piece of black chert, no larger than a dime. I turn the piece in my hand and the smooth face of a conchoidal fracture glistens in the fading light.

"That was knapped by someone hundreds, if not thousands, of years ago," Sawchuk explains.

A tingle passes over me as I ponder the history of the flake. Chert does not naturally occur in the area, and whoever brought it here almost surely was shaping a weapon where I now stand. My eyes stray over the land, sitting silent around us. Little if anything has changed in the centuries since the flake landed amid the river-smoothed gravel.

"Why do you leave it here?" I ask.

"Why would I take it away?" Sawchuk counters. "I worry a horse may step on it one of these years, but this is where it belongs."

He pauses for a bit. "Far too many people today are thinking only about feathering their own nests. If we could just see beyond that, and leave things the way we found them." Then he is silent again, and we listen to the nighthawk.

Bruce Kirkby

WALKING OFF THE
EDGE OF THE WORLD

IT TOOK several days for the true extent of our isolation to become apparent. In that time, we'd trekked inland from the coast, past desiccated gypsum hills and along the shores of Buchanan Lake, where towering cliffs soared up into the blue Arctic sky and hinted of peaks to come. Then came a labyrinth of braided rivers and narrow canyons, leading steadily upward. Emerging at last atop a vast interior plateau, we stared across unremitting plains of burnt-red rock and mocha-brown earth. A few wildflowers were sprinkled about, but nothing that could assuage the mood of desolation.

In four days, we hadn't seen a single human footprint, nor any sign of humanity at all except a dilapidated cache and bronze plaque commemorating a 1959 scientific expedition. Apart from Arctic hares—which bolted across the tundra on their hind legs, like figments from *Alice in Wonderland*—we'd seen no animal life, either. Which isn't to say there wasn't any. Muskox trails wove across the landscape. There were plenty of wolf and fox prints, and countless caribou droppings. But how did they survive? We'd passed not a sprig of vegetation taller than my big toe. That animals endured in the face of such scarcity seemed miraculous.

A biting wind swept down from the west, so the four of us sought shelter beneath a silicon tarp held up by ski poles, gnawing on a scant ration of Landjäger sausage and smoked cheese. In the distance, the peaks of Axel Heiberg's central spine heaved upward, glaciers oozing from rounded valleys like soft tongues of white toffee. Though they appeared close in this surreal landscape, they lay a day's march away.

The inevitable hunger of backpacking had set in, and as I mentally inventoried the food supplies buried in our packs, accounting for all eight days ahead, a sense of precarious-ness set in as well. If the plane scheduled to pick us up on the other side of the island never arrived, if the world changed in our absence—planes were grounded, say, or av-gas ran out—I doubted we could save ourselves. It wasn't a feeling I was accustomed to. Even in the depths of Burmese jungles or lost on the plains of Mongolia, I'd always had the option of escap-ing under my own power, by harvesting wild food or seeking the help of wandering nomads. Such surety does not exist here, in a land teetering on the edge of nowhere.

A RASPY, broken voice on my answering machine offered the first tantalizing hint. It was Dave Quinn—good friend, veri-fiable dirtbag, and life-long wilderness guide—calling from God knows where on a cellphone that kept cutting out. All I could make out was "Axel Heiberg," "July," and "kinda heavy pack." But that was enough. I immediately cancelled my other plans.

Despite persistent rumours of its rugged beauty, Axel Hei-berg Island is one of the least visited, least livable, most mys-terious corners of the world. It's easy to miss when scanning maps of the Arctic, for it huddles against Ellesmere Island's western coast. Just next door, Vilhjalmur Stefansson filled in

the last big blank space in the Canadian atlas with his sighting of Meighen Island in 1916. Not until 1927 did a Canadian
explorer actually set foot on Axel Heiberg. It is the third-larg-
est uninhabited island on the planet, as empty today as it was
a century or a millennium ago. By comparison, Ellesmere—
with its national park, army outpost, research base, and Inuit
village at Grise Fiord—feels positively pedestrian.

Eric Walters, a well-heeled European Arctic-phile, was
financing a personal expedition to Axel Heiberg. Dave, who'd
travelled with Eric before, was arranging logistics, and I was
happy to tag along when invited, even if that meant hauling a
hundred-pound pack loaded with food, a perimeter-fence to
warn off bears, a shotgun, and a small raft.

We met Eric in Ottawa. Short, with a shaved head and
wireless spectacles, he looked like he could fit in my backpack.
He proudly patted his flat stomach. "Nine stone!" he said—
just 125 pounds. A corporate banker originally from Britain
who now split his time between a castle in France, a home in
Zurich, and a flat in Davos, he seemed an unlikely devotee of
the North. But it was clear a part of his soul resided there. He
came every summer, and his journeys, although grand, were
never for glory. Even at home, his mind constantly wandered
to the cold wastes, and he wrote endless letters to Ottawa and
Iqaluit bureaucrats on themes ranging from hunting practices
in national parks to unusual wildlife observations.

Accompanying Eric was his regular Arctic travel companion, Brian Keating, the Calgary Zoo's fountain of energy and
interpretive information. Two days and two long flights later,
the four of us arrived at Ellesmere's Alert military base.

Our plan was to explore the southern valleys around Axel
Heiberg's Wolf Fiord, but the Twin Otter pilot we'd hired
to ferry us there dropped a bombshell: there was no chance
of landing in the island's southern reaches. Earlier in the

summer he'd spent two days and burned thousands of dollars of gas searching fruitlessly for a gravel strip. Suddenly we were scouring a map on the wall of the officers' mess for options.

"What about Mokka Fiord?" Dave asked, pointing to a long indent on the eastern coast, where a saddle led west across the central icecap toward Strand Fiord. "What about attempting a traverse of the island?" It was a massive change of plans, and we didn't even have correct maps. When the base commander discovered Dave photographing the wall map—planning to navigate the 125-kilometre route by studying the pictures on his digital camera—he took pity on us and handed over a topo. Minutes later we clambered aboard the Twin Otter and buckled in.

LATE ON the fourth day of our trek, a deep canyon suddenly appeared before us. From its depths, we heard the roar of a torrent that boiled over drops, careened around bends, and tore straight down through the soft tundra. It blocked our intended path, but by hugging the bank, we could still gain Axel Heiberg's central icefield and make our way to Strand Fiord Pass—which looked, from where we stood, like a gentle ramp into the sky. Just then, three slender Peary caribou materialized from the mist on the other side of the gorge. A hundred feet away but unreachable, the curious animals skittered closer and then melted away.

After a cold and fitful rest, we were hiking by five A.M. the next morning. As we stepped onto the glacier and began our ascent, ominous clouds began rolling in, obscuring the peaks and bringing flurries. The route appeared simple on our maps, but we edged forward cautiously, ever-watchful for crevasses.

We were soon disoriented in a complete whiteout. We thought we were still climbing the snowfield when Dave suddenly shouted with glee: "Look! Look! We're going down!" Rivulets of blue meltwater were now flowing in the direction we were headed. The pass comprises two bumps, like a Bactrian camel's back, and we were over the first.

Soon the tiny streams coalesced into larger meltwater rivers that carved down the icy slope at a furious rate, then vanished into the black depths of the glacier. Slipping into one of these sapphire flumes would have been fatal. When drifting snow began concealing them beneath a thin crust of white, our progress slowed and we probed every step.

"Break time," Eric would announce every hour. A man of discipline, he favoured the British Army style of travel: one hour of work followed by a five-minute snack break, repeated ad nauseam. His notepad was always in hand, filled with distances walked, rates of progress, wildlife sightings, and weather reports. "I doubt anyone will ever read these," he confessed, chuckling. "But it's a habit I've had since youth, and I simply can't stop."

We fell wordlessly into the routine of walking and snacking and then walking some more. Disrobing almost entirely to cross a pool of meltwater atop the glacier, we clambered over piles of loose moraine and pressed on. Far ahead, three muskox skulls sat alone and sun-bleached on the snow, and Brian veered towards them. "Can you believe this?" He practically bounced with excitement. "An entire family has been slaughtered by wolves. Look at how they've chewed the noses and licked the marrow. Why did they ever wander onto this expanse?"

Eleven hours and twenty-one kilometres later, lost in a meditative state, we reached the far side of the glacier. Picking our way down the steep ice to terra firma, we collapsed into tents, nursing mug after mug of tea and sugar.

TAKE A PIE-SHAPED slice out of the High Arctic, running north and west from the town of Resolute, and you have what's been dubbed "the Barren Wedge." The continual press of pack ice against the western shore of the Arctic Archipelago brings fog, wind, and a constant chill. Plants struggle to grow; game and marine mammals are unusually scarce. Axel Heiberg straddles the edge of this desolate zone; the western shores we were headed toward lie in this "Empty Quarter," while the eastern coast we had come from hugs the relative lushness of Ellesmere.

The snows continued for three damp days, until at last high pressure moved in. We were following the Strand River west, winding between high ridges and globular glacial toes, swaddling ourselves in every garment we had. Then, suddenly, T-shirt weather graced us. Flies and bees appeared, flitting across the tundra, buffeted by steady winds. Entire hillsides shimmered with blooms of yellow arnica. Cotton grass and pale yellow Arctic poppies pressed up toward the sun. A chocolate-brown fox visited camp, rolling in the grass at our feet, sniffing every tent and then bounding away. We stumbled upon a field of perfect ammonite fossils. Day after day brought the joy of discovery and solitude. Unbeknownst to us, the only other people on the island, scientists at a McGill University research camp, had evacuated following the recent storm, leaving us alone. Yet as blessed as the warmth was, it felt thin, illusory, and not to be taken for granted.

Environment Canada employs the Climate Severity Index to rate the relative comfort of the nation's communities, with one being the most mild and 100 the most severe. At 13, Victoria ranks among the most pleasant of Canada's climes. Toronto lands at 36; Whitehorse 46; Alert, on Ellesmere, 84. The most inhospitable of all? The former Isachsen weather station, located on Ellef Ringnes Island, not too far from our destination. It earned an atrocious 99.

Inuit call this part of the extreme High Arctic *Inuit Nunangata Ungata*—"the land beyond the land of the people." Despite that, occupation sites have been discovered on Axel Heiberg dating back almost 5,000 years. These sparse settlements of one to four homes employed bowhead whale bones to support roofs of sod and skin. Before the advent of seal-oil lamps, it's postulated that the precursors of today's Inuit survived the winter here by entering a state of torpor, moving only occasionally to nibble food or urinate.

"*Berg heil!*" Eric shouted as we clambered atop a high summit adjacent Strand Fiord. Amidst swirling snows we looked out over a medieval scene of peaks, ice, and great, braided rivers, the entire panorama a palette of only black, brown, and white.

Later at camp, Dave called the pilot on a satellite phone. We were due to be picked up early the next morning, but a surprising message came back. They were already in the air, racing our way. With the good weather expected not to last, they wanted to get us out while they still could.

Author's note: Last November, just four months after visiting Axel Heiberg, Eric Walters tragically passed away while hiking in Oman. The Canadian Arctic lost a champion.

Bernadette McDonald

SEARCHING FOR HUMAR

I OPENED THE email and my stomach dropped. "Tomaž Humar trapped on Langtang." Oh, no, I thought—not again. And the situation was even worse than I imagined. Tomaž was solo climbing a ferociously dangerous route on the north face of Langtang Lirung in Nepal and was trapped on the wall. It was unclear what had happened: either he had fallen, or he had been hit by falling rock. All we knew was that he was injured, unable to move, and had called out on his satellite phone. The email was from our mutual friend Viki Grošelj, alerting me that he had initiated a rescue operation but wasn't very hopeful because the weather was worsening. The date was November 9, 2009.

I thought back to another message, four years earlier, when Tomaž was desperate for help on the Rupal Face of Pakistan's Nanga Parbat. Indirectly, I had been part of that incredibly complex and infamous rescue. When I'd heard the news, I had contacted a friend in the helicopter rescue business, who called his Swiss colleague, regarded as the top rescue pilot in the world. The colleague had flown to Pakistan, only to be scooped at the last minute by a daring Pakistani pilot under direct orders from President Musharraf himself.

As I reread Viki's email, I remembered coming across a photograph in Tomaž's book, *No Impossible Ways*, a self-portrait that had haunted me. The photo revealed a face deep red from the cold, swollen with edema. His eyes were rimmed with ice. His headlight was so caked with snow that only a small pool of light illuminated the dark night of May 6, 1995. He was on the summit of Annapurna I, alone. "I was so happy," the caption read. "Because I had absolute faith, I was rewarded with the answer. The Himalayas love me."

But as I stared at the image, I didn't see happiness or love—I saw primal fear.

I FIRST MET Tomaž in May of 2000 at a film festival in Trento, Italy. When Mexican climber Carlos Carsolio introduced us, I naively offered my hand in greeting. Tomaž's famous bone-crushing handshake both amused and irritated me. It was soon obvious that his high-voltage personality lit up every room; he was the man of the hour. "Let's have another drink," he insisted. "It's liquid oxygen, you know." His overwhelming charisma won me over and I invited him to come to Banff. As director of the Banff Mountain Film Festival at the time, I knew he would impress the discerning audience.

Months passed and I heard nothing. Finally, Silvo Karo, a mutual climbing friend from Slovenia, tracked him down in a German hospital. After years of climbing on steep unconsolidated rock and fragile ice pillars at extremely high altitudes, Tomaž had sustained serious, multiple compound fractures—by falling from the floor joists into the basement of his unfinished house. He'd undergone a series of botched surgeries and had been told he would never walk again. He called his new wheelchair "the red Ferrari." It appeared that a home construction project had ended the climbing career of one of Slovenia's finest alpinists.

But after several more operations and months of physiotherapy, Tomaž began to ride a bike and then to walk with crutches, albeit with a lurching gait. As soon as he could, he began to wheel, walk, and bike to the Kamnik Alps near his home, drawing physical and spiritual strength from the mountains that he loved and found "holy."

He came to Banff a different man than the one I had met in Italy. His face still radiated joy and the handshake had not changed, but his body was seriously compromised. This didn't prevent him from discarding his crutches at the festival wrap party and dancing like a madman, however. "Lazarus rises," wrote one British journalist in *Climbing* magazine. But the journalist was still on the dance floor when I half-carried Tomaž up the hill to my office to collect his things. Still, he enthused about what fun he had had, how beautiful the Canadian women were, and how grateful he was for this visit to the Rocky Mountains.

We met again in 2001 at Paklenica, the Croatian climbing paradise. He still stumbled on level ground, but up on the razor-sharp limestone walls he moved like a dancer—fast and light. We climbed long, finger-shredding routes at what felt like breakneck speed during the day, and at night Tomaž told stories. Together with a roomful of friends and countless bottles of crisp Croatian white wine, he held court, regaling us with tales of desperate bivouacs and German physiotherapists. One of the most memorable—Hilda—had connected him to some kind of high-tech contraption that provided him with a remote control to manipulate the height of his suspended, heavily casted, and recently rebroken leg. It looked like fun at first, Tomaž said, but the horrific reality soon hit. "It was a kind of a perpetual-motion machine, with weights attached to my leg," he explained. "The only way to make the pain leave was to keep moving the leg, yet each time I moved the

leg, another wave of pain would come, over and over and over."
Afterward, Hilda would wheel him to the pool and yell from
the edge: "Schwimm, schwimm, schwimm!"

"You should be writing this story," I told him.

"Yeah, good idea, Bernadette. We will think on it. Let me
read your aura . . . okay, it looks good, you can help me."

DESPITE MY prodding, the next few years produced nothing
more than vague promises. In fact, Tomaž had no time to
write. He was a climber, and his life was full. He was focused
on the mountains: Shishapangma in Tibet in 2002, where
he tested out his newly minted, steel-reinforced and slightly
shorter leg; a new route on the south face of Aconcagua in
2003, where he teamed up with Aleš Koželj for the first time;
back to Nepal for Jannu in 2004, when he came tantalizingly
close to soloing a new route on its east face; and Cholatse in
2005, where he, Koželj, and Janko Oprešnik climbed a new
route on the northeast face. The climbs didn't capture the
attention of the mainstream media, but they were noted by the
cognoscenti—and acknowledged as fine accomplishments for
anyone, let alone someone with a bionic leg.

All the while, he had an even bigger plan—to solo climb
a new route on the Rupal Face of Nanga Parbat, Pakistan's
second-highest mountain. The 4,500-metre Rupal Face is a
formidable place—the highest rock and ice wall in the world.
He went to the base of the Face in 2003, just to take a look.
Back again in 2004, Tomaž made an attempt, but warm temperatures had created a death trap. In the summer of 2005, he
returned.

His original plan was low-key, with a minimum of fuss. But
all that changed when his sponsor pulled out, leaving him
with a big bill. He solved that problem by bringing together
a combination of media sponsors that would fundamentally

alter the experience. Now he would be expected to provide regular online updates, newspaper and television stories—*plus* climb the Rupal Face. He arrived in July and acclimatized on the easier Messner Route in wet, stormy weather. Then he waited. And waited. The storms rolled through and conditions on the mountain worsened. Finally, a three-day window of decent weather was forecast. Meanwhile, American climbers Steve House and Vince Anderson had arrived in the area and were planning their own new route on the Rupal Face. The pressure was fierce.

Tomaž left his base camp and climbed alone to a point at around 6,300 metres. Then the weather closed in completely. Day after day of snow and rain and continuous avalanches followed. Tomaž dug into a slot in the icy slope and hunkered down, unable to move in any direction. After four days in his ice coffin, out of food and fuel, he was forced to do the unthinkable—call for a rescue.

Asking for a rescue is difficult—even shameful—for any serious alpinist. But at over 6,000 metres on the Rupal Face of Nanga Parbat, with the entire world monitoring his website, it was tantamount to treason. American climber Mark Twight commented on National Geographic Adventure's website, "Now every ill-prepared sad sack whose ability falls short of his Himalayan ambition can get on the radio, call for help, and expect the cavalry to save the day."

The rescue was an epic in itself, featuring political intrigue, the presidents of two countries, villains, and heroes. After a couple of false starts and increasing pressure from President Musharraf to succeed, two Pakistani helicopter pilots managed to perform the highest high-angle technical rescue ever done. It was a happy ending for Tomaž, his family, the brave Pakistani pilots, and the team at base camp. But Tomaž was vilified by climbing journalists and by his peers. He had transgressed, broken the code of alpine honour. He should have been braver. Dying would have been the honourable thing to do.

Back home in Slovenia, the reaction was completely different. For ten days, Slovenian citizens had been glued to their television sets, watching the evening news to see what was happening to their favourite son. When he was plucked from his ice coffin on the Rupal Face, he became a national hero. Many Slovenians urged him to run for president. He probably could have—and won.

In the meantime, North American journalists kept calling me, asking for his cellphone number. I reached him in Croatia, where he was recovering from the ordeal.

"Do you want to talk to the media?" I asked.

"Absolutely not. Now it's time to write the real story. If you can find a publisher, you should do it, Bernadette. I will talk with you openly and freely."

And so began a two-year odyssey. Somehow I had to discover the truth about this man who elicited such strong emotions within the climbing community. Of course I was impressed with Tomaž as a climber, but I was even more intrigued by his character. Despite his public persona—the overconfident superstar—I sensed greater complexity. What sort of past had created this passionate, focused, spiritual, and incredibly funny alpinist? When I talked with friends about the idea, their responses were polarized. Some encouraged me, but many told me not to waste my time: he would never open up. They pointed to a quote from the Slovenian newspaper *Delo*: "I will not let anyone know me completely." Yet I was hopeful. Tomaž seemed to trust me. I knew that writing his story would be an adventure, but a personality this volatile could also explode, destroying everything in its presence. I would be in that line of fire.

ON MY FIRST visit to Slovenia to interview him it looked like my chances of getting to know the "real Tomaž" were slim. He had offered me ten days of his time. I had anticipated quiet hours sitting together with a tape recorder, capturing stories with specific dates and places. Instead, I waited patiently while he lived his frenetic life. Not satisfied to work on one computer, he navigated three—at the same time. He would check his email on one, and do some research on the second while organizing his slides or videos on the third. Phones rang, the fax machine purred, printers printed and scanners scanned. From his tiny corner at the foot of the Kamnik Alps, he connected with the world of climbing as well as with his crew of workers out painting the telecommunications towers of Slovenia—Tomaž's business and main source of income.

The days passed. I continued to wait.

Gradually, I became part of the Tomaž whirlwind, racing around the country in his car while he inspected his towers and took phone calls, interspersed with stories told—frighteningly—with both hands. On foot, I chased him up trails at speeds my lungs couldn't quite handle. I got the stories, but they lurched drunkenly from his youth to Ganesh V to gossip about the labyrinthine Slovenian Mountaineering Association, all within the distance of one switchback. I went back to my room after a day of chasing Tomaž around the mountains, intent on transcribing the hours of tape I had recorded. To my horror, the most audible sound was my own rasping breath. He was uncapturable.

But slowly, as we spent more time together, a picture began to emerge. Tomaž's first climbing experiments had taken place at the age of eighteen—in the basement of the family home, where he leapt about from beam to beam. Soon he was venturing out to the local crags near his Kamnik home, clad in his first harness: a discarded Fiat seatbelt. He joined the local mountain club in 1987 and within that highly structured system he trained to become an elite alpinist—one of the world's best. But there were occasional clashes with the club, usually because of Tomaž's disregard of the Climbing Commission rules.

But it wasn't until a warm sunny day on my second visit to Slovenia that he described an experience that had changed his life. We had been out climbing on a local crag and I had backed off a route, unable to finish leading it. He lowered me down to the ground and climbed it with no problem, but reassured me (and my bruised ego) that it was difficult for its grade. We climbed a few more routes and returned to his car. "Now I will tell you about Kosovo," he said. Out came the tape recorder. And for the next two hours, sitting on the tailgate, he unburdened himself of the horrors of war.

He took me back to 1989, when Slovenia was still a part of the former Yugoslavia, a country which did not die a natural death. Rather, in Tomaž's view, it was systematically and brutally destroyed by ambitious men who had everything to gain and nothing to lose from thwarting a peaceful transition from socialism to democracy. Of these men, it is Slobodan Milošević who is most often blamed, for deliberately harnessing the rise of Serb nationalism in the mid-1980s to prevent that transition. He wanted to create an enlarged Serbian state, swallowing as much of the former Yugoslavia as possible. Kosovo was his launching pad, the place where Tomaž served when he was conscripted into the Yugoslav People's Army. Alongside Serbian soldiers, Tomaž's job was to guard ethnic Albanians trying to escape Serbian rule in order to create their own republic. Countless people died, on both sides, and there were systematic rapes and other brutal atrocities.

"I discovered the bottom of humanity," he said.

After Tomaž had tried to desert several times, his disgusted superiors finally released him, with nothing more than the rags on his back and an empty Kalashnikov over his shoulder. "I returned home less a person than an animal," he said. His belief in the goodness of humanity was shattered. His behaviour changed; he alienated his friends and shunned his family. He became suspicious of his fellow climbers and authority figures alike, a trait that only intensified throughout his life. He lived alone; he lived rough, and he spoke even rougher. Almost certainly, he was suffering from post-traumatic stress disorder.

He coped by fleeing to the forests and the mountains. And he climbed. His emotional and spiritual lifeline was climbing—facing risk, head-on. He became increasingly bold, soloing routes that many referred to as "sick." He began making waves within the Kamnik Club, climbing in a style that was frowned upon by the club elders: winter climbs, solo climbs. Inevitably, his boldness aroused envy amongst his peers.

I listened silently to this tale of horror. Later, back at his house, we sat at his kitchen table with a bowl of pistachios between us. As the shells flew from his restless hands, Tomaž talked, faster and louder as his enthusiasm grew.

Tomaž was twenty-five when he was invited on his first Himalayan expedition to Ganesh V. Stane Belak, known by all as Šrauf, was the leader, a legendary veteran of the highest peaks: Makalu, Dhaulagiri, Everest, Gangapurna, Aconcagua, and K2. Tomaž admitted that, "for me, it was like climbing with a god." But it was Tone Škarja who had actually orchestrated the invitation. Škarja was the single most powerful man in Slovenian climbing and was head of the Mountaineering Association's commission for expeditions. He was the one who decided which climber went where, and with what funding. Škarja was considering Tomaž for Annapurna the following year and, curious about how he would perform at altitude, had offered Ganesh V as a test.

Tomaž and Šrauf succeeded in reaching the summit, although Tomaž very nearly died on the descent. Ganesh V was deemed a success, and Tomaž was on for Annapurna in 1995. Škarja's vision was to place Slovenian climbers on the top of all fourteen 8,000-metre peaks, by new routes as often as possible. His record was impressive, but now he needed Annapurna.

It was clear to everyone (except Tomaž) that Tomaž was not regarded a likely summiter. He was there to carry loads, to break trail, and to help set up the camps. Tomaž put his head down, worked the route, and bided his time. He felt sure he would summit. Finally, he was at Camp 3 at 6,500 metres, together with three team members and the Sherpas. Radio messages flew back and forth to base camp; the others were instructed to continue up and Tomaž was ordered to descend. A very bitter Tomaž headed down.

By the middle of the next afternoon he reached base camp, where Škarja greeted him.

"Tomaž, great to see you. What a fantastic job you have done in breaking trail and helping to set up the camps. Here— take some tea." Tomaž threw the cup on the ground. "Why did you order me to descend when I was climbing so strongly?"

Škarja was shocked at this insubordination from a junior climber. He was behaving like a spoiled brat. The next day, the others summited and Slovenia had successfully completed all fourteen of the 8,000-metre peaks: the expedition was an unqualified success. But not for Tomaž—not yet.

Together with Sherpa Arjun, he disregarded orders and climbed back up to Camp 4 at 7,500 metres in a full-blown storm. They hung on through the night but, in a terrified state, called base camp to explain the situation. They were ordered down at the first opportunity. Tomaž refused, and turned off his radio—for six long hours. This single act of defiance forever altered Tomaž's relationship with the Mountaineering Association of Slovenia. He later understood Škarja's motivation for ordering him down; but as a climber, not the leader, his mind was set on the summit.

The next day Arjun turned back but Tomaž plowed on alone through deep snow—sometimes waist-deep. After five hours he reached the base of the summit couloir and called base camp. When they realized where he was, and that he was alone, their tone shifted from anger to concern, for he was still at least two hours from the summit. He continued up. At seven P.M. he called again, to report that he was very close to the summit and that he was surrounded by an absolutely splendid sunset; the clouds had lifted, revealing a magnificent view to the west. Base camp thought he was hallucinating. But he managed to make those last steps to the summit, where he was quickly overtaken by darkness. He stayed just long enough to take some photos, including the self-portrait that had first caught my attention, that image that had seemed so infused with terror.

Despite his subversive behaviour, his Himalayan career was launched.

IN 1996, Tomaž's wife, Sergeja, was expecting their first child, but the Himalaya was calling. He went back to Nepal and, together with Vanja Furlan, climbed a difficult new route on the northwest face of Ama Dablam, a beautiful peak on the way to Everest. Their climb won both of them the prestigious Piolet d'Or—the Academy Award of climbing—but, tragically, Furlan wasn't there to celebrate. Just three months after the expedition, he fell to his death in the Julian Alps.

The climb and the prize catapulted Tomaž into alpine prominence. But, as the French say, *il faut payer*. Tomaž summed it up succinctly: "Ama Dablam gave me the chance to become a Himalayan climber, but the cost was my family. That was the deal. I didn't know it at the time . . ." Sergeja's delivery had been difficult, and she had been alone, something for which she never completely forgave Tomaž.

Less than six months later, Tomaž was back in Nepal, this time for a 6,808-metre peak named Bobaye. The idea had originated with Šrauf, but now Šrauf, too, was dead, killed in an avalanche the previous Christmas. Furlan and Šrauf—in less than a year. It would have given other climbers pause, but not Tomaž. The following year he was back again, this time with popular Slovenian climber Janez Jeglič on Nuptse, a spectacular peak in the Everest group. Many would eventually regard it as his finest climb. It was certainly tragic.

Jeglič and Tomaž began climbing Nuptse on October 27. On the night of their third bivouac, Jeglič confided: "If we climb this, Tomaž, we'll be happy the rest of our lives, and if we don't, we'll make half of Slovenia happy!" This statement, from one of the country's top alpinists, summed up the highly competitive state of climbing in Slovenia. They were back at it by four A.M. on October 31. At one P.M., Tomaž saw Jeglič waving, apparently from the summit. He waved back, and fifteen minutes later stood on the summit ridge—where he was assaulted by a gale-force wind. There were Jeglič's footprints in the snow, leading in the general direction of Peak WI. Tomaž followed them a bit, and then they ended. All that remained was the radio that Jeglič had been carrying. He had simply disappeared.

It was three P.M. before Tomaž calmed himself sufficiently to begin his descent. First he lost his goggles. Then his

headlamp batteries failed. He fell repeatedly and began to hal-
lucinate. Upon finally reaching his bivouac tent, he accidentally set it afire. By the time he stumbled into camp in the early
hours of November 2, he felt like he'd returned from the dead.

Back home in Slovenia he was praised for the climb, but
something else was brewing—blame. Jeglič had been close to
other climbers, much more so than Tomaž. Emotionally and
physically crushed, Tomaž came to feel that "the wrong man
came back from Nuptse."

Soon he was planning his biggest project yet—a solo climb
of the south face of Dhaulagiri. The plan was super-sized in
all aspects: big mountain, big route, and big media partner,
one which expected daily—even hourly—updates on his website. He began climbing on October 25, 1999. The conditions
were bad, with seracs breaking above him, pummelling the
face with ice, rock, snow, and water. Tomaž climbed mostly
at night, so as to minimize the danger as best he could. But
he also believed that he could communicate directly with the
mountain and that the mountain, in its turn, would keep him
safe: one more idiosyncrasy about Tomaž that fascinated his
supporters and irritated his detractors. After eight days he
was high on the face, dry-tooling up the shattered, steep rock.
Then, with obvious signs of frostbite setting in, he was faced
with an open bivouac, equipped with neither stove nor tent.
He survived the night, and decided to traverse to the ridge
and descend rather than attempt the final bit to the summit.

"Dhaula had let me have the face," he said, "but not the
summit."

Yet Dhaulagiri had catapulted Tomaž to a level of fame
almost unheard of for a climber, and the speculation and
debate were unprecedented. Some said he had overstated the
difficulties on the route and, worst of all, that he had sold his

soul to the media devil. The facts were somewhat simpler. He had soloed a new route (yet to be repeated) in the central part of the south face of Dhaulagiri, up to 8,000 metres. He had become a national folk hero and the darling of the international climbing media.

Life after Dhaulagiri was different: more attention, more money, more fun, more pressure. And certainly more criticism.

Tomaž responded with wild emotional swings. He would rant his distrust of the climbing community and then shower the people close to him with acts of kindness and love. He would take his young son mushroom picking and have long, serious talks with his teenage daughter but refuse entry to his house to a climber he didn't like. He would fly into a rage at a disparaging comment about him on some climbing website and, in the next moment, dismiss the media as completely irrelevant.

One of the most consistent criticisms about Tomaž was, indeed, his use of the media. But in this regard, Tomaž himself was anything *but* consistent: one climb would be broadcast on an hourly basis, and the next would go unreported. As he pointed out, "I decide when to have media. I'm the switcher guy."

After the Nanga Parbat rescue of 2005, many climbers dismissed Tomaž as a has-been who had disgraced himself and the entire climbing community. Mark Twight was quoted online saying, "Personally, I think this rescue fucked the evolution of alpinism in a way that no other single act could have done." Tomaž responded with a biblical reference: "The person who is innocent should cast the first stone. These people are trying to eat my soul. They can eat my body, but not my soul." He added, even more dramatically, "The alpine world is much clearer now. There are no more masks." But what I saw in Tomaž was not increasing clarity, but greater murkiness. His distrust of other climbers, his doctors, even his closest friends, was approaching paranoia. I found him terribly difficult to connect with and, in frustration, began to wonder if I was becoming as mad as he was. Capturing Tomaž was as elusive a goal as one of his crazier climbs.

After Nanga Parbat he retrenched, alone, in his spiritual centre—the forest—and in the Kamnik Alps. He tended his wounds and gathered his strength. In a strange way, Nanga Parbat had freed him: it brought him so low that he could finally begin to live without media hype or sponsor expectations. He could now do what he did best—climb.

And so he did. On October 29, 2007, a rumour circulated that Tomaž had reached the east summit of Annapurna the previous day, after soloing the south face. Nobody had known of his plans; many were skeptical of the news; everyone wanted to know more. Tomaž remained silent. He finally tried to explain what motivated him: "I carry out a climb for my soul. Every climb is a story in itself. You come back changed from each one. Your consciousness grows; this is the most important thing. And if you enjoy each journey, then all the rest is superfluous." It seemed that alpinism could still provide Tomaž those rare moments of grace.

THERE WERE OTHER Himalayan summits. I knew about them only because he told me, in confidence. He had taken on a new persona—private climber. He was preparing for a landmark climb, something that would secure his place in history. But he planned in silence and in secret. And in the meantime, he went to Langtang Lirung.

His first Sat call from the Langtang Face wasn't for a rescue: it was to his girlfriend. Alone and in trouble, he needed human contact, and to say goodbye. There was one more call: to his Nepalese cook, waiting at the bottom. "I am near the end," he said. The rescue effort took on a life of its own despite a stretch of terrible weather, but Swiss rescuer Bruno Jelk didn't spy Tomaž through his helicopter window until Saturday morning, five days after the first call. Of course, he was dead.

I sat, stunned with the news, remembering the last time I had seen Tomaž. It was in Dundee, Scotland, a couple of years earlier. He had arrived in that northern city on a drizzly December day looking worn and tired. His eyes were sunk more deeply than before and the lines on his face were more pronounced. It seemed to me then that a part of Tomaž—the most important part, his soul—was in trouble.

After the initial shock of his death wore off, I realized that this was a message I had always been expecting. I remembered an earlier conversation, when I challenged him on the dangerous nature of his climbs and asked him whether he was courting death. "Do you have any intention of growing old?" I asked. He became angry. "You know how I love my children," he yelled. "I want to be a grandfather."

Maybe. But his actions didn't match his intentions. As always, he seemed at odds with himself. Sometimes a party animal, sometimes a mystic. He rarely spoke straight; more often in parables. He was either in love with the public or a complete loner. He yearned for recognition but refused to conform. He courted journalists but, when his mood shifted, would simply shut off his phone and go mushroom picking. He could be cruel, as well as kind and generous. As he freely admitted, "I'm only predictable in my unpredictability."

Searching for Tomaž had been a wild ride. His personality was explosive and I often caught the shrapnel. During one long, frustrating Skype call, he yelled that I was no better than Margaret Thatcher, but moments later, he fondly called me "Lady B." Throughout it all, I remained convinced that Tomaž had a huge heart—at least as big as the south face of Dhaulagiri. And despite the risks and setbacks that had come with the task of writing his life story, I'd survived. I only wish he had.

Christian Beamish

UNDERWAY

An extract from the memoir, *The Voyage of the Cormorant*

I HAD TO tack a few times to work my way out of the cove at La Bufadora, but once in the open water I ran free and swift before a good and helpful wind. I set the next headland off the bow and let *Cormorant* ride the swells, and sailed on for two or three hours until at last the point at Santo Tomás was less than a quarter-mile off the port rail. As I came on to a port tack to sail in to the cove, the wind swung before me and gusted, suddenly much stronger than it had been all day. I sailed on, as close to the wind as I could get, but the daggerboard and rudder got fouled in thick kelp outside the anchorage, holding me fast.

I first dropped the main, then furled the mizzen and shipped the rudder. The last step before going to oars was to pull the daggerboard in, but when I did, the wind took *Cormorant* swiftly across the water, the daggerboard having been our last hold on the kelp. We were in open water in less than ten seconds and heading seaward fast. Even pulling with everything I had, I could make only the barest movement windward, but I managed to edge into another stretch of kelp and grabbed at a handful of strands and wrapped the bow line around to hold us steady. The little pangas and a lone house on the point looked far away in this blow, the water a series of tight rows of ripples driving at us from the shore. *Cormorant* strained at her kelp tie as if the wind were leaning against her, forcing her bow upward in an effort to pry her free.

I put all three reefs in the main, unfurled the mizzen and re-hung the rudder, then undid the kelp tie and sheeted in the sails. The wind took us tearing off across the bay. I put the daggerboard down and came about to try to tack against the wind and regain the cove. We made progress, fully reefed and sailing close-hauled, bucking through the chop, through two or three tacks. But closer in to the cove, between the outer bay and where the pangas lay at their moorings, the kelp once again seized *Cormorant* by her daggerboard and rudder, putting me right back in the fix I was in before.

A bow wave appeared inside the cove, close to shore, then closer to me, more distinct—it was a panga, with three men motoring out. I had just cut my way free of the kelp, and was again fighting to windward and making progress, when they reached me. The pilot put his boat about and came across to my bow and the men in front motioned for me to throw a line. They caught it and tied *Cormorant* off, but the panga hit my bow with a splitting sound, and one of the men in front made a wincing face as he glanced at the stem of my boat. From where I sat amidships, I could see a thick, ugly splinter sticking sideways out of the stem like a badly broken finger, but that was the price of the rescue.

The men hunkered in their boat, motoring back to the cove with *Cormorant* in tow as plumes of spray shot overhead off the bow. They were nearly expressionless as they pointed out an empty mooring can that I could tie to. I thanked them profusely and called them *hermanos del mar*—brothers of the sea—as I shook their hard, work-scarred hands. They nodded as if it had been their duty to help me and that was all, and then motored the last fifty yards to shore.

I sat and felt *Cormorant* pull to the solid hold of the mooring in the strong evening blow.

AFTER THE MEN left me on the mooring I set up the boat tent, and then put a pot of rice on the stove to boil. Retrieving the burlap sack with the bass I had caught that morning (and which I'd swept overboard from time to time throughout the day to keep cool), I cleaned the fish and fried the fillets and head in a pan with oil, onion, and garlic. I chopped a yam and put the works in the half-cooked pot of rice with a bouillon cube, and covered it to cook a while longer.

The stew was hearty and tasty, the best meal of the trip so far, and I felt re-energized for the journey—warm food so essential to one's sense of well-being. An orangey glow came over the cove and the rock-strewn hillsides, but even so it was a somewhat dust-filled and desolate-feeling place. The transistor radio did not pick up any signal, and the dial moved stiffly, salt crystals already accumulating under the face. Once the sun went down, I snuggled into my bag and started in on *Leaves of Grass* by the light of my headlamp, Walt Whitman an appropriate companion for my nineteenth-century mode of travel.

I made coffee in the morning as I do every day, and these cups aboard *Cormorant*—fine grounds boiled straight in a pot of water, cowboy style—have been the best cups of my life. The men who had given me a tow the evening before motored past and idled for a minute to say good morning. They were divers also, like the men up at Punta Banda the previous morning. The oldest fellow had a coarse black beard and a boxer's scarred face creased by sun and salt air. He smoked a cigarette and nodded sagaciously when I admitted that I had gotten myself in a bit of a fix the night before. *"Que te vayas bien,"*—go well—he said to me, which, with its quality of a blessing, is always heartening to hear, and they were off.

The morning unfolded slowly, the sun warming the cove as it rose higher. I hung my damp sleeping bag from the halyard on the main mast after folding and stowing the boat tent. Getting underway each day involved a precise system of shuffling, repacking, and then restowing my gear, since in such a small craft each space had multiple uses. The sleeping platform had to be taken down to place the packed dry bags, the pots washed before I could stow them away with the stove.

I gave the divers a beach towel I had brought; it had been soaked from the first day out and I saw that it would never dry out enough to serve its purpose. The radio no longer even registered static, the dial refusing to turn past 103.9 and the little screws holding the body in place already encrusted with rust. I wanted to pitch it overboard, but my conscience wouldn't allow it, and I packed it deep within one of the dry bags.

By mid-morning I was hungry again, and with the boat pretty well squared away, I heated the rest of the fish stew and finished it off, enjoying it even more this time as the flavours had settled throughout. With a quick scrub out of the pots over the side, I finished stowing my sleeping bag and galley. I untied from the mooring, stood up and waved to the empty houses on the beach and then bowed in thanks, and set off under oars through the thick kelp for the open water beyond.

A light wind had already started up and my best guess was that the time was near eleven as I hung the rudder and hoisted sail, running about a mile off the coast and keeping an eye out for kelp beds that would impede our progress. Not two miles on we got mired, which forced me through the awkward process of first cutting away the kelp and then bringing the rudder aboard, switching to oars, and then redoing the process in reverse once free.

The afternoon turned out to be another day of gentle sailing, the rolling hills leading down in ravines to wide, sloping beaches. The winds were steady and light enough to allow reading; holding the tiller under the crook of my knee, I continued with Whitman, channelling him to the occasional pelican or gull—"Swift wind! Space! My Soul!"—so consumed that I sailed right past the cove I had thought to shelter in.

With a sailing guide for Baja, I had some information on good anchorages—or anchorages that would serve—and I regularly spread out my charts and noted my location off the more prominent headlands and points. But as night began to fall, I realized that I had still to push on through twenty-five miles of darkness to the next possible anchorage. This loose reckoning was not at all in keeping with my generally focused approach to my journey. I had been lulled into complacency by Walt Whitman, the fine breeze, and soft winter sunshine.

I sailed to the edge of another vast kelp bed that looked to be three or four miles long and two miles across and surveyed my situation. A little town was perched on a rocky bluff, and although I scanned the coastline carefully through my binoculars, I could not see any place that seemed like a landing—no place where pangas sat in rows on the beach, no obvious ramp down to shore. I was not overly concerned at first, and decided to sail on into the night, as I was running easily enough before a twelve-knot northwesterly breeze and keeping well offshore.

A FULL MOON rose over the *arroyos*, the desert held a pinkish glow, and stars shone down like a complement in a million points of light all across the water. I sailed along, swaddled against the cold in a parka and outer shell, drifting in my thoughts deep into the night. Eventually, the wind fell away, and the ocean settled into a broad, glassy sheet. I smelled the clean desert scrub on the suddenly warmer air. The lines and sails and my outer jacket seemed to crackle in the dryness.

I knew that this was all the warning I would get.

Lashing the tiller in place with a bungee, I scrambled forward and dropped the mainsail. Not one minute later, I saw and heard the wind line across the water behind, roaring down and tearing at the surface like a swarm of locusts: the dreaded *Norte*. People call it the Devil Wind because of the fires it breathes to life, and, I suppose, for the madness, too; it is a terrible, mindless thing.

The wind did not slam into us so much as gather up and consume us, then sling us forward with spindrift and foam flying all around. Both hands on the tiller, I pulled hard to keep *Cormorant* running before the short and steep waves, surging ahead on the bigger swells with a strange vibration shuddering throughout the hull. A couple of steep lurches put us right on the beam-ends—the very scenario of capsizing in a raging sea that I had imagined—cold water slurping in over the rail and filling the boat to her bilges with a frigid footbath. But the danger was too immediate to think of anything beyond keeping the boat upright, even if somewhere in my consciousness lurked the image, inevitable it seemed, of going over.

How long did I run like this? It seemed a lifetime, as the intensity of the flashing spray, the points of starlight dancing weirdly, and the moon gleaming off the waves kept my gaze locked just ahead of the bow—the steeper swells catching my peripheral vision as they swept alongside and hurled us faster on.

My hands ached with the strain of holding the tiller, and then my upper arms and shoulders began to burn. There was no opportunity for relief. Steering through the steep troughs was the only way to remain upright, and although I was sailing on the small mizzen alone, it seemed even bare poles would have been enough for the wind to drive us dangerously fast.

I had come in closer to the shore and found myself a few hundred yards off a wide sandy beach. The wind here blew straight offshore over what appeared to be a series of dunes, and lumbering swells rose up with spray sheeting off their tops like fireboat hoses in full harbour display.

In the blue dark of the night, which, for all its violence, had a magical quality, I thought I saw a light in the dunes. The surf was well-shaped and eight to ten feet. I imagined a long-time surfer set up here in a camper, and the thought of an old bro and his dog made me smile. I was so sure he was there that I considered making for the beach through the big surf. But I read the conditions for a moment longer and realized I would lose everything if I tried to make it in. I sailed on.

The wind still hurled us down the coast, the occasional tendril of kelp wrapping the rudder blade like a tentacle and then breaking free with the inexorable force of our momentum. Though my hands, arms, and shoulders were knotted with fatigue, I was prevailing in the fight to keep the boat steering in line with the waves. I even got the hang of riding out the bigger ones, and actually hooted once with the fun of linking one wave with a second, and then a third, steep swell for a *shooshing* toboggan-slide of more than 100 yards.

I recognized that *Cormorant* was handling herself, and that her pointed stern split the waves like cordwood, allowing them to roll off to either side. I had only to maintain my course, and if I managed to avoid running up on a reef I would eventually make the sheltering cliffs of Punta Colonet. It was an absurd situation nonetheless—the roaring wind and desolate shore, this long winter night and the ghostly moonglow illuminating the whitecaps off into the distance, and me, completely alone in my open boat, 250 miles down the coast.

Then I sang. For the ridiculous peril I faced; for my folly; for grace and for a prayer. I sang an old Anglican hymn in praise of creation, and the wind became almost funny at that point—the absolute opposite, the utter rejection, of morning and calm. The fact that no one in the world had a clue about my predicament, or even knew, precisely, where I was—let alone that I had put myself here—struck me somehow as humorous. "Blackbird has spo–ken" I belted out in the rage, "like the first bhir-hi-hi-hirrrd!"

I had come in close now, spray blowing back off the crashing surf just a few hundred yards in and the high cliffs of Colonet looming ahead. As I had hoped, when I sailed to the base of the sheer walls the wind passed overhead, 300 feet off the mesa, and left the water calm and strangely still, even as the ocean went ragged not 100 yards outside.

I could have scrambled up the boulders to kiss that old cliff face for the shelter it provided.

I set anchor and then put booties over my wet wool socks, slaked my thirst with deep draughts of fresh water, and mashed handfuls of trail mix into my mouth. My body shook with fear, exaltation, and relief. I wrapped myself in the mainsail, too exhausted to arrange the boat tent and sleeping bag.

The moon and stars had burned into my irises, and light patterns swirled hypnotically behind my lids. With these strange points of light in my vision, I wondered if this was what dying might be like.

Helen Mort

NO MAP COULD
SHOW THEM

Six Poems

How to Dress

"A lady's dress is inconvenient for mountaineering."
— MRS. HENRY WARWICK COLE, 1859

Your fashionable shoes
might be the death of you.

Your hemline catches stones
and sends them plummeting.

Below the col, set down your parasol,
put on the mountain's suit—

your forearms gloved with permafrost,
your fingers lichen-light,

your mouth becoming fissured
and your ankles malachite.

Slip on a jacket made of scree,
cold stockings from a forded stream.

Take off the clothes they want
to keep you in. The shadow of the hill

undresses you. The sky
will be your broad-brimmed hat.

An Easy Day for a Lady

"The Grepon has disappeared. Of course, there are
still some rocks standing there, but as a climb it
no longer exists. Now that it has been done by two
women alone, no self-respecting man can under-
take it." — ANONYMOUS CLIMBER, 1929

When we climb alone
en cordée féminine,
we are magicians of the Alps—
we make the routes we follow
disappear.

Turn round
to see the swooping absence
of the face, the undone glaciers,
crevasses closing in on themselves
like flowers at night.

We're reeling in the sky.
The forest curls into a fist.
The lake is no more permanent
than frost. Where you made ways,
we will unmake:

give back the silence
at the dawn of things.
Beneath your feet,
the ground
retracts its hand.

Tilberthwaite

"We had not known steepness 'til now" — DOROTHY PILLEY, 1929

I.
We dragged ourselves from an afternoon wrung dry
by heat and climbed into a darkness so complete
we couldn't dream of climbing out of it.

The rocks became a mirror for the night
and soon our bodies were as well; the colour gone
from clothes and skin and hair and boots,

nothing left but this reflection of our element.
You moved invisible above. I took in slack,
your weight tightening the rope, the only proof

I wasn't here alone. When you paused,
I could believe you'd climbed out of the quarry,
up and out of Cumbria,

lithe on a ladder of old clouds,
as easily as you stepped
out of your shoes and left them here below.

At last, you switched your headtorch on.
The world came back, encircled, pale.
Its light became a moon high on the slab.

II.
With a coffin-sized stone for a bed,
a coiled rope for a pillow, I slept
and dreamed I was already dead,

my stiff limbs cooling where I lay,
the breeze lightly inspecting me, closed eyelids
down to painted fingernails and toes,

running an idle hand over my hair,
down over my neck, belly, and thighs,
filling my coat as if my lungs still worked,

then the same breeze curling under my arms
and feet, finding it could grip, and lowering me
down into a hole, patting the soil.

I woke up with a start. The ceiling wasn't
made of earth but numberless, huge stars
though, in my dream, I'd say that's just

the light that filters through the soil,
down from a world that can't be reached
for all I climb towards it, reaching up with calloused hands.

Ode to Bob

"Then there is 'Bob,' the imaginary character invented
by women climbers tired of hearing unsolicited advice
from male passersby..." — DAVID MAZEL, 1994

For he never calls to us unkindly
from a ledge, voice like an avalanche.

His feet dislodge no flat-backed stones.

For when he drinks, he leaves the whisky
undiminished in the flask.

He never steals the morning
with a story of a pitch he climbed
one-handed, wearing boxing gloves

and never casts his shadow
on the path, dark as a winter coat,

nor whistles like a postman
from his belay stance.

For, when he has advice
he will not offer it

and when we have advice
he takes no heed.

The rain stitching
the valley does not trouble him,

the wind can never peel his body
from the crag.

For I will not have to
love him,

watch as he threads
a way through limestone,

finding the day's vanishing point.

Above Cromford

For Alison Hargreaves

Your body tight against the cold
inside a tent high on K2

you dream about Black Rocks:
squat monoliths, tattooed with names,

routes so graffitied
that you'd sink your fingers

into letters, pull
on the initials of the dead.

You didn't need to carve your own.
Your signature was grip and lift,

partnerless dance that left
no mark, and as you moved

the sequences spelled out
your name. And it was

unrepeatable. And gone
when you looked back.

Prayer

"HAPPY" — entry in Alison Hargreaves's diary,
early 1979, after Scottish winter climbing

Give us good days.
Days unspectacular but adequate:
the weather neither calm nor wild,
your coat zipped nearly to the top,

a silver thermos cooling in your bag,
the sky at Bamford reddening, as if
embarrassed by its own strange reach
and day-old, pipe-smoke clouds.

Above the Hope Cement Works,
crows wheel arcs of undramatic flight
and when you touch the rock
your fingers hold.

Katie Ives

TRANSGRESSIONS

WHEN I WAS ten or eleven years old, my father and I stood at the edge of a sea cliff, watching the waves strike the rocks below us in starbursts of white foam. On impulse, I asked for permission to leave the path and climb partway down by myself, past steep and broken ledges to a small alcove. I thought he'd refuse. I don't remember whether I was surprised when he allowed me to go—or whether I was afraid. I only remember the sudden solitude as I began to descend, the way the world seemed to crack between each handhold and the next. When at last I reached the alcove, I sat there, still and quiet, enfolded by air and stone. And then I scrambled back up toward the sounds of tourist voices and the fading of the day. For a moment, the sunlight dazzled and the dried sea salt sparkled in all the crevices around me. Each crystal was as bright and luminous as frost.

IN MY MID-TWENTIES, I finally asked my father why he'd let me climb down that cliff. He said, "I was watching you." At first, I thought his answer made no sense: my father had been standing too far above me; there was no way he could have caught me if I'd fallen. Later, he added that he thought it was important for children to have a sense of independence, to explore their surroundings, to take minor, controlled risks. Although he had a Ph.D. in educational psychology, his theories might not have accounted for the realities of height, gravity, and a child's body.

I was a graduate student, by then, at the University of Iowa. Soon after that conversation, I transformed the scene into a story for a fiction class. In that version, I described the stone as red. And when I try to recall it now, I imagine a rust-coloured precipice above sharp, black rocks. But I could be wrong. We'd spent so many days at different places along the New England coast. Over time, the separate landscapes blurred: the stone might have been ashen yellow, the beach sandy and flat. I can't say for certain, anymore, how high the cliff actually was.

Around the time I tried to put that memory into words, I'd already started learning to climb with traditional gear on the limestone bluffs near my school. There, as I searched for holds, my fingertips traced the relics of long-extinct sea creatures, the smooth arcs of shells encrusted with frost-white crystals, the intricate hollows of lost exoskeletons. Reflections of rivers flashed across the cliffs like the ghosts of ancient oceans. With each route, new layers of sensation accumulated between me and that original experience, until the sea cliff became more and more faint—the flicker of a distant shoreline beneath the edges of a dark fog.

"Her fear subsided," I wrote about this child who was no longer myself, "and she felt something between pain and joy in the light on the waves and the rock, the water and the ledge reflecting and absorbing the warmth of the sun, a feeling of all-encompassing and incongruous safety."

WHATEVER REALLY happened that day, these fragments of memory have lingered in my mind: inexplicable, ominous, radiant. When I began working on the fiction story, I wasn't planning to climb ropeless again. Lead climbing seemed dangerous enough: I was still a novice, struggling to place protection in the rippling cracks and rain-filled holes of Iowa's brittle limestone. One late-autumn morning, I put my writing aside and hiked with a friend through dry, yellow fields into the leafless woods of Indian Bluffs. At the base of a cliff, he opened his pack and realized he'd forgotten to bring any gear. We sat for a while, sharing a single cup of warm, sweet tea.

He asked me if I'd ever wanted to "free solo"—to climb without a rope. His face trembled a little as he smiled. He didn't know that I already had. The sunlight spilled, pale and almost silver, across the fallen leaves. The rock shimmered in the still, cold air. In retrospect, I think he expected me to say no. By the time we finished the tea, however, it seemed inevitable that we'd both solo the route, one by one. I went first. Stone features separated into disjointed images: a dusty overhang; a narrow ledge. Dead plants crackled under my hands. Dirt filled the empty spaces in the rock. Fear descended and then drew back. Blue sky rushed down a stone chimney like a tide. Some light seemed to explode within me, shattering everything that was not itself. At the top, I held on to a tree, waiting for my friend, while the forest reeled.[1]

Back in Iowa City, I walked downtown alone, staring at the ginkgo leaves that swept like yellow paper fans across the sidewalks, forming and unforming tessellated patterns as wind and feet displaced them. It was like learning to see again. Shapes and colours lost their dulled, familiar meanings. Sunlight paled across the storefronts. Brick walls shone like the backs of oak leaves. Through the windows of restaurants and bars, the hunched forms of other people wavered, dim and luminous, as if underwater. I felt an expanding tenderness toward everyone and everything. It was as though I'd broken through into some secret, more essential and more beautiful world.

IN THE CLASSIC book *Climbing Ice,* the American alpinist Yvon Chouinard declared, "Most climbers are a product of their first few climbs."[2] Over time, my memories of those two initial solos transformed into a kind of personal myth, at once alluring and unsettling. Long after I left Iowa for bigger cliffs and real mountains, I found myself returning to easy, unroped, solitary climbs. Along golden alpine ridges or in shadowed blue-ice gullies, I've chased that brief, sharp sense of joy like the receding eddies of some vast and oceanic light.

Like most climbers, I've listened to endless debates about the morality of our pursuit. Often, the matter gets reduced to the same contrasts between selfishness and self-discovery, responsibility and freedom, ordinary existence and transcendence. Of all the justifications for climbing, I'm most drawn to the argument that "it's not a sport, but a spiritual experience." Yet I hesitate to use the word *spiritual* for actions that place my life at risk. And I wonder whether my early solos provided only an illusory shortcut, a trespass into a realm more genuinely and more respectfully reached through years of meditation or prayer.

During the late twentieth century, the American alpinist Gregory Crouch spent several seasons in Patagonia, revelling in the eerie music of storm winds, the fleeting pulse of sun on rime, the "full power of desire." At the end of his memoir *Enduring Patagonia,* he asked: "Does alpine ascent have value? Is it a noble endeavor honored by the gods, or a sin against the will of God?" He concluded, "*I do not know.*" Perhaps, he added, "I have made an intellectual choice for sin, for by climbing dangerous mountains, I do not honor the divine sanctity of life."[3]

Nonetheless, in many cultures, the impulse to climb strains with metaphysical longing. In 1977 an Italian Catholic priest, Don Arturo Bergamaschi, led the first ascent of Latok II, a 7,108-metre tower in the Karakoram Range of Pakistan. Gradually, his expedition left behind the last apricot trees and stone villages for an isolated realm of hanging glaciers, violent avalanches, and shining walls. There, he felt small and vulnerable—and yet deeply at home. In an article for *Alpinist 30*, he wrote, "Something [about the high peaks] attaches itself to us, inside. It's a feeling we will never conquer."[4] He told one journalist, "To seek after the soul of a mountain means to seek God."[5] That same year, Ashraf Aman became the first Pakistani to climb K2. "Mountains are my soul," he later told me. Atop the world's second-highest mountain, he remembered a passage from the Koran: "O ye mountains! Sing you back the praises of Allah." Below him stretched an immensity of bright mountains and winding glaciers. Everything, he said, seemed "busy with meditation and constant praise of their nurturer."

As the mountain writer Maria Coffey researched her 2008 book *Explorers of the Infinite*, she became "increasingly convinced that extreme adventurers break the boundaries of what is deemed physically possible by pushing beyond human consciousness into another realm. Their experiences give a glimpse of those unimagined levels of existence."[6] Around the turn of the last century, the Canadian climber Barry Blanchard spent years attempting the Emperor Face of Mount Robson, which the Texqakallt people named *Yuh-hai-has-kun*, "the mountain of the spiral road." High on its walls, he gazed at the frozen wave of a cornice and for an instant he found himself transfixed, dreaming of some "underlying pattern of existence: the plumed whorl of a storm, the snail-like shape of the inner ear, the trail of stardust whirling into a black hole; structure and chance; aspiration and destruction; hidden unity; increasing chaos."[7] In 2002, when he finally climbed the face to the summit, he howled.

If mountains can represent our inmost selves, as the psychologist Carl Jung once said, then how many climbers start up their flanks hoping they might see into the heart of life, into the unconscious universe itself? How many of us feel that the consequences of never seeking that vision could be worse than the chance of death?

EVEN IN backyard wild places, the line between the sacred and the forbidden seems to blur. To *transgress*, in English, doesn't only mean to "violate a law." It can also signify "to go beyond a boundary or a limit."[8] In *The Solace of Fierce Landscapes*, the Protestant theologian Belden C. Lane describes high peaks as "dream symbols" of moments when people "transgress the limits of culture, language, all the personal boundaries by which their lives are framed . . . In stretching the self to its edges, the geography helps in forcing a [spiritual] breakthrough."[9]

When I was a teenager, my mother, my little sister, and I trespassed for several winters on the large frozen reservoir near our house. A year or so earlier, a woman had drowned after falling into the cold water. Ever since, the local authorities had stopped people from approaching the shorelines. For my mother, it was as though a glass barrier had sealed off her favorite landscape. My father had recently left, and her days were filled with traffic-jammed commutes, bleak office work, and relentless bills. Gliding across the immensity of the ice provided rare instances of escape. And so, well after dark, when we were least likely to be caught, we packed our skates and stumbled along the forest paths toward the pond.

One evening, the temperatures dropped to an arctic cold. Under the full moon, the black ice shone like the night sky. Trapped far below the surface, air bubbles gleamed like galaxies of stars. Cracks spread in filaments of white. Midway across the pond, my sister and I looked back: my mother's shadow swooped toward us in the silver air, her arms outstretched to the wind. "I never wanted that night to end," she said, years later. "It was so vast and wonderful, so freeing. That pure joy of a child. You don't forget those moments, and afterward, they become a part of who you are."

CLIMBING WRITING is full of allusions to crossing thresholds: from tales of early explorations on imperial frontiers to modern catchphrases like "the cutting-edge" and "the limits of the possible." A long tradition of lawlessness also exists within the margins of its history: trespassing, unpermitted ascents, drug use. In *Straight Up*, James Ramsey Ullman describes how the American mountaineer John Harlin II became obsessed with Aldous Huxley's book on mescaline, *The Doors of Perception*: "The expansion of experience, and resultantly of consciousness, was precisely what [Harlin] considered the living of life to be all about." Instead of using psychedelic drugs, as many of his peers did, Harlin relied solely on immersion in the natural world to push his mind past ever-farther boundaries—until, at last, he could emerge "from a sauna bath into the winter landscape and . . . [hear] the snowflakes falling around him."[10]

After Harlin fell to his death on the Eiger in 1966, his friend Ted Wilson summed up his life: "Whatever [Harlin] was trying to be, always, was something he *was*."[11] If there is a peculiar redemption for climbers and adventurers, it may exist along those narrow borderlands between the audacity of our presumption and the humility of our awe. It may echo within us, in such bright and imperceptible sounds as the falling of the snow, in such moments when we truly *are*—a state too intimate to be expressed, justified, or understood.

In seventeenth-century Japan, the Zen poet Basho set off, one day, to climb Mount Gassan. Around his neck, he wore

a bleached-cotton hood and a ritual white paper rope. Afterward, in *The Narrow Road to the Deep North*, he recounted miles
of scrambling through cloud layers, up glassy slopes of ice and
snow, "till at last through a gateway of clouds, as it seemed, to
the very paths of the sun and the moon, I reached the summit." He recorded only pieces of what he saw there in a series
of haiku: the wan sliver of the moon, the black shadows of the
peaks, the disintegration of the clouds. Unable to reveal any
more of the "holy secrets" of Mount Yudono, he burst into
"reticent tears."[12] Again and again, his mountain stories broke
off. He could merely take his readers to the limits of the say-
able—and then into wordless light.

DURING ONE of the workshops of the 2005 Banff Mountain
and Wilderness Writing program, a participant pointed out
that when climbing writers turn dangerous adventures into
art, we commit another transgression: we encourage readers
to take part in activities that might kill them. One woman
replied that an author's most important duty is simply to
tell the truth, whatever it is, regardless of the consequences.
Today, as I approach my forties, I've become increasingly
aware of how elusive that truth can be; of how much is
refracted by time, memory, imagination, and desire. I believe
that children shouldn't climb steep cliffs without a rope, that
beginners shouldn't solo technical routes. My only defence
lies in the absurdity of beauty, a force that seems, at times, as
unpredictable and overwhelming as grace.

The shape of my life still grows out of these transgressions.
I don't want my parents to regret what their actions have
taught me: that in certain instants, wonder and joy take pre-
cedence over security and rules. In choosing beauty, thus, am
I honouring or dishonouring life? The euphoria of adventure
spills over into daily existence. The blue spark of a snowflake

ignites on a driveway. A yellow band of evening light hovers on a neighbour's wall. A stranger looks at me with a soft and weary face. All this, too, blazes with unveiled intensity.

With each climb, I feel a spreading calm, a growing quiet, binding me deeper to moss and stone, frost and ice, starlight and shadow. A hint of that incongruous safety still enfolds me on frozen waterfalls between the full moon and the snow, on those winter evenings when the rhythmic swing of an ice axe seems like meditation, and mere breathing feels like prayer. I clamber over the last narrow ice bulge through the thickening trees. A branch snaps, and the smell of pine fills the air, sharp and green. Something vast and inchoate flows through my mind like a faraway sea—full of so much yearning, so much love. And yet, like Gregory Crouch, in truly honest moments I have to admit: *I do not know.* And I'm also aware that I might be crossing yet another, more ambiguous boundary, in sharing these childhood secrets, with you, Reader, now.

1 Ives, Katie, "Afterimage," *Alpinist* 11 (Summer 2005).

2 Chouinard, Yvon, *Climbing Ice* (San Francisco: Sierra Club Books, 1978).

3 Crouch, Gregory, *Enduring Patagonia* (New York: Random House, 2002).

4 Bergamaschi, Don Arturo, "Home: The First Ascent of Latok 11," *Alpinist* 30 (Spring 2010).

5 Bergamaschi, Don Arturo. Email message to author, February 7, 2010.

6 Coffey, Maria, *Explorers of the Infinite: The Secret Spiritual Lives of Extreme Athletes— And What They Reveal about Near-Death Experiences, Psychic Communication, and Touching the Beyond* (New York: Penguin, 2008).

7 Blanchard, Barry, "Dragons in the Mist," *Alpinist* 29 (Winter 2009–2010).

8 *Merriam-Webster Online.* merriam-webster.com.

9 Lane, Belden C., *The Solace of Fierce Landscapes: Exploring Desert and Mountain Spirituality* (New York: Oxford University Press, 1998).

10 Ullman, James Ramsey, *Straight Up: John Harlin: The Life and Death of a Mountaineer* (Garden City, New York: Doubleday & Company, 1968).

11 Ibid.

12 Basho, Matsuo, *The Narrow Road to the Deep North and Other Travel Sketches*, Trans. Nobuyuki Yuasa (New York: Penguin Books, 1966).

Erin Soros

SURGE

An extract from *Hook Tender,* a novel in progress

THE BUS windows rattled as the engine farted and sputtered to life. Olaf plunked down next to his sister, Greta. The leather seats smelled of old man. The big boys sat together in the back of the school bus where they were shouting now about how they were going to climb the surge tank all the way to the top, this time they wouldn't turn chicken and creep back down.

Olaf knew only one other boy who had climbed the surge tank. Now that boy was overseas, fighting in the war.

They called at Olaf. Someone tossed a roll of caps at his head. His friend Ralph was back there with the teenagers even though he only had six months on Olaf. Ralph was imitating the guttural noises Greta made when she was trying to talk. He got all the boys laughing. Olaf pretended he couldn't hear. The wet splat of a spitball caught his neck. He pulled at the collar of his shirt, as if the fabric was scratching his skin, and then opened his book to stare at the lines of black on white. The bus was a cage full of noise. Greta stretched over his shoulder to look back at the older boys, but Olaf knew they'd be talking too fast for her to read their lips.

She slipped back into the seat. Each time the bus rounded a corner, her hip dug into his thigh.

He turned to face her, stretching his lips into huge ugly shapes. "What did you do at school today, Greta?" he asked, taunting her by exaggerating each word. Before she could respond he began to sign. This time he wasn't making words. He was fluttering his fingers as fast as the wings of an insect. Greta stopped swinging her legs. Her mouth formed a small knot.

"It's a bee," he said, his voice warmer now, as if he'd been waiting all along to share this trick with his sister. "Just a bee. See Greta? The letter *B*." He pinched her under the arm until she squealed and pulled away. She giggled. Even her laugh sounded wrong.

The driver soon dropped off most of the children, who lived near town. Only Ralph was left. The bus creaked and huffed up a hill and around the next bend. When it braked, metal joints complaining, Ralph walked to the front, saluted the driver, then was gone. The bus rocked over gullies and bumps, deeper into the woods, Olaf and Greta its only passengers. They sat with their hands in their laps, surrounded by the rows of green seats.

Olaf stared out the window. Greta's breath had clouded the glass so the trees were smeared into an unbroken green wall. *Skirt tree*, Olaf signed in his lap as they passed the giant red cedar that marked the halfway point to home, its base stretching out like the sweep of a lady's skirt. His hands took the shape of what passed: the abandoned truck, the white pine burned black by lightning, the break in the woods that showed a slice of ocean, the pile of rocks where Greta scarred her knee. Each landmark he signed and Greta matched his sign.

Behind these trees, closer to the shore, were the houses the Japanese families had been forced to leave. Beside the busy stink of the mill town, beside their own lives in the boisterous logging camp he knew so well, the woods were full of people who were gone. From here no one could see the empty build-ings, but he still felt uneasy whenever he passed this part of the road, as if the houses themselves were what had made the families disappear.

Greta gestured in their sign language to ask him what was inside—beds and tables, like their own house? But Olaf just shook his head. He didn't want to imagine the rooms, each one dim as a shadow.

The houses were perched on the rocky bank right next to the ocean, where the air was damp and cold with sea spray— closer than any white person wanted to build. Each building was as small as a fishing boat, and the Japanese took small steps when they walked, or that's how he remembered them. The children were quieter than normal children, at least they were quiet when they were in the mill town with their parents, the summer before they were carted away. If a storekeeper shouted at them—*get off the railing, put that down*—they did what they were told. They didn't say a thing. Greta used to stare at them and smile and even wave, but without lifting her arm, like she didn't want her and Olaf's mother to see. Some-times a child waved back.

The whole lot had lived near the beach, boys and girls and parents and grandparents all together in their own houses as if they were innocent—and yet at any moment one of them could have jumped onto a boat to take secret information out to a Japanese warship. That was the threat. Olaf was old enough to know all about it. They had been living right there, separate from the camp but so close. Any one of them might betray the whole country. You couldn't tell but even the children might be dangerous, all of them with their shiny caps of black hair like matching helmets.

One of the houses was off on its own. By the door stood two small trees, round trees that lose their leaves, the kind people plant on purpose. He'd only seen those kinds of trees in schoolbooks. With Ralph he'd stood right outside that house and he told Greta to keep back, no telling what they might discover. It was no place for a girl. So she went to find a turtle on the beach while he and Ralph launched pine cones at the roof. The house had shutters—the white paint scabbed off—and matching chimneys on either end. It looked surprised. He was sure there would be guns in the rooms and maybe even battle plans written in code. But he and Ralph never went inside to look. Through the glass the kitchen was just a kitchen. One window was blocked by a white shirt. The mother must have washed and ironed it, and then it had hung there, waiting, tinged green with mildew, still neatly buttoned. The outside walls were growing moss and the shutters were loose so he and Ralph tugged a couple of shutters free and ran around holding them like shields, brandishing sticks for swords, and they shouted the metal sounds of Jap talk. For some reason they avoided breaking the windows. It seemed important to keep the glass intact.

Ralph wanted to go back to that house with matches and buckets of oil and set it on fire. They'd have to wait until the summer, Olaf said, when the wood would be dry as kindling. You're scared, Ralph said, you'd never. I dare you. Olaf said he'd do it. And maybe one day he would, and then the Japs couldn't return and frighten his mother with more of their plans for war. Really it was Olaf's responsibility, since Ralph wasn't even from around here and he had straight black hair just like the Japanese children. Olaf planned to sneak out at night and leave Greta at home. It wouldn't be safe, for her. One of the Japs might still be there in hiding.

Before the families were taken away, Greta had given one of the Japanese boys a ball of red yarn, just like that, something she'd stolen from home. That boy could speak English, Olaf had heard him, but he'd just stood there grinning at Greta. Then he said a gruff word that Olaf couldn't understand. He said it again and Greta matched the shape of her lips to the boy's lips as if she knew what he meant when she didn't. Then they both nodded. What would he need yarn for, Olaf had asked her—a boy? The Japanese boy had held it tenderly, away from his body, the way one would balance a full bowl of soup. Olaf remembered his cupped hands, the knuckly fingers that were calloused from fishing like a man's would be, not just sweaty and dirty from games of Run, Sheep, Run.

Greta did that kind of thing. She did it without thinking who was the enemy.

Now Olaf didn't sign their word for house. He looked up the road to find something else he could name.

The road narrowed and branches scratched at the windows, trying to speak. Greta leaned her head on his shoulder. They rode higher for three miles, the trees getting closer, the road darker. Then the bus stopped and they climbed out. The driver told Olaf to look after the little girl.

No buildings lined this road—it was just a strip of dirt splitting the forest in two. They rustled under the scrub where they'd left their bikes. The logging camp was two miles farther, up the mountain on a road too steep and rough for the school bus, a single lane used for empty trucks heading up and loaded trucks heading down, the vehicles blasting warnings with their air horns at each bend in the road. Greta couldn't hear their horns. His mother always warned him that Greta should never be left to do this stretch on her own. The children pushed their bikes a bit, then they got on to pedal, Olaf listening for oncoming trucks.

In the summertime, they stopped for huckleberries, squirting them between their teeth. They sat at the crib dam and spat the sour ones into the tumbling water. But today the cold air bit their knuckles. He needed to get Greta home. He tried to yank his sleeves down over his wrists. Greta followed him a few yards back, moaning at the wind. When they reached the hill, she climbed off her bike to walk.

"I'm not walking with you," Olaf twisted around to say. "You've got to pedal." He kept his grip tight.

She propped the bike against her hip so she could sign that she was tired.

"Keep going," he said. "Get back on."

He was not going to get off to push both their bikes, not this time. There was nothing wrong with her arms.

All the way to the crib dam she trailed behind him, walking her bike with one hand. He pedalled as slowly as he could. His bike rocked side to side, and he had to keep dropping one foot to the ground to keep it steady.

"It's getting dark!" he shouted, turning back to her, even though she probably couldn't see his lips in the dusk. Soon they wouldn't be able to talk at all.

He crossed the crib dam ahead of her. The water clamoured far below. The concrete buttress was smooth under his tires and he could have raced ahead if he were with one of the boys. By now they were all down at the beach. Even Ralph would be with them and he'd climb to the top of the surge tank and then tell Olaf about it, or maybe not tell him, just nod a bit if he asked, as if someone like Olaf wasn't even worth the bother of the whole story.

He stopped to let Greta catch up. Then he ducked into the bush where she couldn't see him. At first he planned to jump out and scare her. But as she trudged along he stayed where he was. When she passed him, she didn't look up, just kept her gaze on the slow spin of her bicycle's wheel. She started humming that deep-throated noise like a grouse.

She turned the bend. She must think he was up ahead. He had never left Greta on her own. But it was only another half-mile or so before she'd be safe home. Instead of following behind, he turned his bike around and pedalled back down the logging road, away from her, his legs spinning as furious as the sound of the water. He would be at the bottom of the hill by the time she turned around to look. The bike picked up momentum as the wheels skidded over pebbles that flew into the brush. He was going too fast for the brakes to work and he knew he'd spin into whatever truck was coming his way. He soared past the last clump of trees, then, with a quick shove, he pushed the bike out from under his body, the metal clanging and the handlebars twisting as he dove and landed on his chest.

His lungs clenched at nothing. He gasped for air, coughed, then rested his lips and forehead on the cold damp earth as he felt his wind return.

He rolled over, sat with his knees up. He brushed the rocks and dirt from his trousers and shook his feet—he was fine, not even a twisted ankle. Trembling, he got up to check the bike, straddled the frame to twist the handlebars into place. He got on, moving slowly to test it, then faster, turning south onto the main road. He wondered how close Greta was to their home.

When he reached the dirt bank, he found a tangle of bikes where the boys had tossed them aside. The twilight made the chrome glisten like a clump of metal bones. He dragged his bike up the bank and dropped it on top of the pile.

Olaf ran into the trail that led to the beach. Pine gave way to the stench of seaweed. He could see the tank, the metal tower rising 300 feet. Under the darkening clouds it was whiter than usual. Down by the boom the boys were tossing rocks into the ocean. Not skipping them—just lobbing handfuls of rocks into the air and letting them drop. The boys made bombing sounds.

"Hey," Olaf called out as he ran to meet them.

At first the five didn't move.

"Hey," he called out again, relieved when Ralph gestured for Olaf to join the group. Ralph walked ahead and stood on his own, arms akimbo, surveying the shore. Ralph's dad had died last spring and now he didn't need anyone.

"Let's go," said Joel. The boys scrambled up the beach single file, each kicking rocks ahead, trying to hit the boy in front.

Ralph found a good flat stone, and they all waited for him to skip it. They counted as it bounced off the water.

"Nine," Karl said, and whistled. They started walking again, crunch of mussel shells under their soles, none of them willing to try to beat Ralph. Olaf slipped his boots into the others' footprints, his face hot against the cold air. He could see the surge tank clearly now. Against the night sky, the white paint glowed like phosphorescence.

"Climbed it before?" Ralph asked in a loud whisper. Olaf hated him for asking in front of the other boys. "With Greta? You climb with your little sis?" Even in the dark Olaf could tell he was smirking.

The wind rose up from the ocean and twisted past the surge tank's slick surface, making the metal ring out. Sometimes the tank was full of the river. The men could stop the turbines at the dam by funnelling the water into this tank where gravity absorbed the surge. But now the tank was empty. A great blank dividing the sky.

Once, last summer, Olaf had walked up to the base of the tank with Greta, and they'd touched it to see if the metal was warm or cold, but they never even tried the ladder. It ran from the height of the tank and then stopped eight feet from the ground.

"To the very top?" Olaf asked.

"You climb the tank first, you get to drop out of school," Ralph said.

He bet Ralph had at least climbed part of the way. Maybe his father had taken him, before the accident. But Ralph was the kind of boy who could spring up that ladder without anyone urging him to do it.

"You can't look down," Ingmar yelled. "That's what kills you."

The boys all jumped onto a line of rain-wet logs and walked along them, silent again, hands in their pockets to prove they didn't need arms to balance. The rotting wood crumbled under their steps. When they reached the tank, they crouched together and pulled a small log under the ladder. One by one they balanced on the log and pulled themselves up to the first rung, scurrying fast so the next boy could join them.

Ralph stood back, picking up rocks. Olaf nodded toward the tank. Ralph tossed a rock at it, a high ping. The boys above them stopped, looked down, then started again. Olaf and Ralph eyed each other awkwardly, Olaf tearing at a fingernail with his teeth, Ralph sliding his tongue along the cracks in his bottom lip.

Olaf was the youngest, so he should be the last. He cupped his palms together to offer a holster for Ralph's foot. With a grunt Ralph ignored the gesture and hoisted himself up onto the log, leaning over to grip the ladder. He started to climb.

Olaf wanted to shout something out to his friend. He scrambled until he had his own feet on the ladder. Salt air pushed open his lungs. Then he peered down. It was dark already, only the moon casting pale light across the beach where they'd left their prints in the sand just minutes ago.

He'd been up ladders before. The first forty feet were easy. He felt a burst of energy as his boots pattered from rung to rung with a hollow clang. Olaf knew his father could climb up this thing easier than walking into his own kitchen.

But halfway up, the surge tank flared like a goblet, the top wider than the bottom. The sides jutted out at a thirty-degree angle. Olaf had to climb not just up, but out. With his arms stretched above him, his back hung parallel to the dark sea that crashed on the shore a hundred feet below.

The weight of his body pulled at his hands. His fingers were raw. He glanced down at the water. The view swayed too fast, lurching forward then retreating as his stomach turned. He clenched his eyes shut. His left foot slipped from the ladder and flailed. This leg suddenly felt longer than the other, heavier, the muscle pulling as the foot dangled in the air. He swung forward to hook the wayward heel over the rung, found his footing, pressed his face against the ladder's cold metal edge. He breathed. The rung of the ladder felt good under his boots.

If Greta were with him, she'd want to go down. But she was home by now, warm and safe.

Someone up above was laughing. At first Olaf thought one of the boys was laughing at him. Ralph had almost reached the section of the ladder where it ran vertical again. But he was clinging to the ladder without moving. It was Ralph who was laughing, only it didn't sound like Ralph. The laugh was high-pitched and fast, and it echoed off the surge tank's metal walls.

There was something wrong with Ralph. The laugh got sharper. He screeched like a crow. Olaf's arms started to shake, air rippling through his chest.

Olaf was not going to laugh.

Ralph's arms were going to loosen. Laughter slackened his muscles.

"Keep going," Knut shouted to them from somewhere above.

"I can't. It's not me," Olaf said. "Ralph stopped. It's not me."

Ralph had swung to the side of the ladder so Olaf could pass. Ralph was giggling quietly now. His feet were jammed tight together and he was hanging on with one arm. His body swayed out like a cupboard door.

Olaf clawed his fingers around the ladder's rungs, one hand over the next until he was sharing a rung with Ralph. He could keep only one boot on the ladder, tucking the other as close to the rung as possible. His left hand began to spasm. Just a few feet above, the ladder straightened and their ascent would become easier. Olaf opened his mouth to explain, but something about Ralph's laugh made him stop. He wanted to climb away from it.

"Wait here," Olaf said. "Wait and we'll get you on the way down."

He climbed ahead. Looking down, he saw that Ralph was gripping the ladder again with both hands. Olaf felt lighter. The laugh coming out of Ralph faded.

Olaf was stepping into the sky. The half-moon lit the edges of the surrounding clouds. Beside him a seagull rolled on the air.

He curved around the tank where the ladder straightened, his arms reaching ahead to find the rungs. When he got his grip, he had to let both feet hang out free before he could swing them back onto the ladder as he pulled himself up. His sweating palms squeaked on the metal. He climbed another eighty feet. A cobweb caught his cheek.

In the last stretch of the climb, the ladder narrowed, the rungs not rounded but flat. Their edges dug into his palms. Bits of rust stuck to his hands, flaked into his eyes. He tried to keep climbing with his eyelids clamped shut, but the surge tank started to tip.

The ladder seemed too narrow for a man. Olaf wondered who had to climb up here and why. A seagull swooped and cawed. Olaf waved at the too-close flap of its wings.

Above him the other boys had reached the top. Olaf couldn't hear Ralph at all.

He grabbed the last rung, swung himself up and folded his body over the edge of the roof, his arms dipping into shallow, stagnant water.

The other boys watched him, Joel's face as white as the tank.

Three hundred feet. Olaf stood up.

The roof of the surge tank was flat and white and the boys scattered like five peas on a plate. Rain had pooled on the surface. The boys all kicked at it—small explosions of water. They whacked their boots into the metal to hear it clang.

Ralph would feel that from far below.

The wind answered. It sounded different than it had on the ladder, low and hollow, it didn't thud against the roof but whipped and whined across the surface as it tried to slide the boys right off.

Olaf leaned into this wall of wind pushing at his chest. Gusts fattened his jacket. He couldn't believe he was up here, a hundred feet taller than Ralph.

There were dead birds. A seagull, dark grey and rotting, its wings splayed out in a puddle. The feathers shimmied slightly as wind raked the water. And smaller birds, a blackbird, and what he thought were chickadees, although it was hard to tell in the dark. Their bodies were clumps. They reminded him of the mice trapped in the cookhouse, the cook walking to the woods with a dustpan full of eyeless tufts of fur. Did the birds fly here to die? Or was there something on the roof that killed them?

Olaf looked across the water at the lumps of islands, darker black than the black of the sky, each island rimmed in purple. He was higher than any tree. His father had never been this high.

The boys airplaned past him, arms stretching into wings,

their lips whirring the buzz of a high-pitched motor. *Raven One*, they shouted, *come in Raven One.*

Olaf curved his hands into imaginary binoculars and scouted the landscape for signs of enemy invasion. Up the coast the electric glow of the Powell River mill cast an eerie light that was as yellow as the stink of sulphur. It lit the smoke pouring into the sky in four iridescent columns. Right now men wearing masks were scurrying inside that box. He could reach over and pluck it from the ground.

He turned to the south. A mile down the coast the moon caught the powerhouse's grey roof. That would be a good place for his air force to land. He signalled and pointed it out to the older boys who were busy chasing each other and howling at the moon like coyotes.

From up here Olaf couldn't see more of that powerhouse than the roof, but he knew the entire front of the building had been painted like a huge picture to match the shore and trees, camouflage against attack. A warship could pass by and never know it was there. Every day the powerhouse greeted the ocean with this false face.

Karl started shouting cuss words upward into the wind and the other boys tried to be even louder. Ingmar balanced near the edge and spat over it. He said his spit smacked Ralph right on the head, and they all knew it didn't.

But if the Japs attacked now, Olaf could watch the planes swoop down and the incendiary bombs fall. The vibrations would rattle the surge tank and shake Ralph off the ladder.

The Japs wouldn't bomb the ocean, he knew, they'd bomb the mill. And the camps. Olaf spun around and beeped his own made-up signal of Morse code. Tin Hat Mountain stretched out behind him. The mountain was a black mass, something inked out.

He imagined his mother and sister alone in the wooden house. They were sitting by the stove and worrying about where Olaf had gone. Across the table they passed his name back and forth. *What I'm going to do to that boy*, his mother said. She couldn't see him, way up here. Greta couldn't watch his hands. He stretched them up in the air.

"What's that ball for?" Joel asked him, pointing at a metal ball the size of a crouching man. It lay on top of the tank like a giant's toy.

"Lightning," Olaf said right away, and the boys nodded. His words lifted in the dark wind. "It captures lightning. It protects the surge tank." Olaf wasn't sure if this was really what it did, but the boys looked convinced. He could say anything up here and it would become true.

The others were kicking the birds off the tank, waiting to hear the splat and not hearing the splat so shoving at each other and asking who was scared, who was scared now, until one of them finally marched toward the ladder.

Olaf watched each head disappear.

He wondered if another boy would help Ralph down or if he'd still be there, his body blocking the way. Olaf didn't want to have to stop.

He tried not to look at the smashed birds the boys had left lodged on the edge. He grabbed the ladder. It was trembling. The wind and all that space down to the ocean dragged him forward and urged him to fall. He backed away from the ladder. And since he was sure that the others couldn't see him, he got on his hands and knees and crawled. He turned to nudge his foot down until he could feel the third rung. The wind pulled at his clothes. If he let go now, he would float.

It was harder going down, his arms and legs awkward with each backward step. His hands were growing numb. He counted as he descended. The seagulls had gone. What time was it now? His mother would be furious. He kept his eyes on his hands, dizzy with the effort not to look below.

The rungs of the ladder thickened. He reached the bend where it began to run diagonal. He had to curl himself around the corner, boot searching for a rung. He hinged from the hips, kicking his feet forward so they could catch the ladder while he kept his right hand on the straight section above. With his left hand he grasped the lower part of the ladder. The rust made his grip slide. To continue down, he was going to have to let go of his upper hand. He hooked his feet, released his fingers, each one still frozen around the shape of the rung. He reached below for the ladder. His hand opened and closed on air.

He was falling backward. Then his fingers smacked the metal and he clasped the rung tight. His whole body began to shake.

Ralph was still there. As Olaf climbed slowly toward him, swaying his feet forward with each step so he could catch the next rung, he could see Ralph's arms rigid against the ladder. The laughing had stopped. Olaf swallowed a flake of rust and it tickled his throat.

Olaf coughed. It sounded like a laugh.

Ralph hooked one arm over the rung and one arm under it and leaned closer in.

"Ralph Forrest," Olaf said. The name ricocheted off the surge tank.

The wind tugged at Ralph's hair and flapped his jacket open. Olaf wondered if he had seen the birds the boys kicked off. Ralph squeezed to one side of the ladder so Olaf could pass.

Olaf stepped down until the two boys were perched on the same rung, boots cramped in a line. Ralph pressed his cheek against the ladder.

"Go on," Olaf said. Below them there was the steady clatter of boots hitting metal. The other boys had climbed right past Ralph. Were they going for help? The wind whistled through the ladder and whipped Ralph's hair across his eyes.

"Go on."

Ralph didn't move. The boys were nearing the bottom. Olaf dropped one foot to the next rung.

He waited. Ralph glanced down, snot running into his mouth. He wouldn't let go of the ladder long enough to wipe it away. His sleeve slipped to the elbow. His arm was taut with muscle and veins.

Olaf could still reach out and rest his palm on the nape of Ralph's neck to coax him down, but he didn't want to touch Ralph.

"Say something. Ralph. Talk. It will make it better." Bits of his words were torn by the wind.

Olaf waited.

Even the jaunty under-the-breath comments Ralph always made, even those he'd take.

"Come on."

"Go on."

Ralph was not going to move.

Olaf took another step down. He felt Ralph watch him. Three more steps, four, and he looked up through the black shapes of Ralph's boots. If Ralph let go without leaping free of the tank, his body could tear Olaf from the ladder and they both would drop to the earth.

He climbed more quickly, careful not to look down until he was close enough to jump. Three yards from the ground, he leapt free with a high-pitched yell. He cleared the logs, landed on the balls of his feet, then rolled into the familiar crunch of sand and shells. He lay there for a moment, feeling the moist sand flat between his shoulder blades. Above the clouds, the stars looked as if someone had thrown a handful of rocks across the sky.

Ralph was small, way up there on the surge tank. He hadn't moved. If Olaf hadn't known Ralph was there, he wouldn't have realized the dark speck was a boy.

Olaf scurried to his feet, rubbed shells and pebbles off his knees.

"You coming?" Karl yelled as he ran toward the water. The other boys ran too, jumping up and down on beach logs. The salt air was sharp on Olaf's face. Down by the ocean, the boys began to shout.

"Dumplings and gravy! Right now a whole plateful of dumplings and gravy!"

"Roast beef!"

Olaf couldn't tell who was saying what. His stomach spasmed. It was long past supper. Greta and his mother would eat without him. Greta would ask if she could have his portion and his mother would blow cigarette smoke across the table, then slide his plate to Greta.

"No, flapjacks. A foot-high stack of flapjacks!"

"And bacon!"

"And bacon! Hey Ralph! We're going to have bacon!"

"Pork and beans!" one of them bellowed over the noise of the waves.

That's what Olaf wanted. They could stay out here all night and sit around a bonfire like the men did in the summer, heat a can over the flames. Ralph would climb down, shoulder Olaf for a space, grab a spoon. They wouldn't say how long he'd been up there.

Olaf missed his tin lunch box right now, its slim black handle. He'd unfold his mother's wax paper and pass her bread pudding to the boys.

"Salmonberry pie!" Olaf heard his voice toss the words out

into the wind. He was suddenly giddy. "Salmonberry pie!" He yelled up to Ralph as if he had a piece to offer. He could do this. He could just shout out what he wanted to eat.

The boys scampered back up from the ocean. Ingmar said it was too bad they didn't have a tarpaulin—then Ralph could just jump down and they could catch him. Knut said he was too high up for that. He'd need a parachute from up there. "That's right, a parachute!" they shouted. "Hey, Ralph, you need a parachute!" Olaf said he knew how to get him down. You bunch are just making him nervous, he said. I'll get him down, he said. You head on back. We'll catch up.

Olaf waited until the boys were out of earshot then yelled up that Ralph's mother was waiting for him at home.

"You don't want to scare her. She's alone now, Ralph. She's kept dinner warm for you."

But Ralph stayed where he was.

Olaf turned around to see how far the boys had got. Maybe they were going for help. They'd reached the trail that led to the road. If he didn't go now, he'd lose them.

"Salmonberry pie!" he shouted at the surge tank before breaking into a run.

Steve Swenson

THE TELEPHONE POLE

I HAD NEVER paid particular attention to the fifty-foot-high telephone pole that towered above me at the bottom of our driveway. It was an old pole, full of splits in the wood, and it had two wooden crossbars bolted to the top, with ceramic insulators that held overhead power and telephone lines. I was sixteen and had been climbing for a couple of years, and I had studied books on how to rock climb up cracks similar to those in the telephone pole. I desperately wanted to put my book-knowledge into action, but I couldn't yet drive to real rock cliffs. So I started looking for things to climb in my neighbourhood, and there was the pole. I decided to climb it.

Just up the driveway from the pole was the house in Seattle that I shared with my parents and four siblings. My father worked as a mechanical engineer for Boeing and my mother managed the household. My parents were devout Catholics, and family activities revolved around their parish church and the Catholic schools we all attended. It was a healthy and loving environment, but I felt hemmed in. I was much more interested in exploring and having adventures in the natural world. I joined a local Boy Scout troop to hike and explore the Cascade Mountains. One of the dads in our troop, a climber, started taking a few of us on trips where we learned basic mountaineering skills. My earliest obsession was Mount Rainier, a peak that dominates the skyline south of Seattle. I reached its top with my Boy Scout group when I was fourteen, in an experience rich with excitement, fear, and wonder.

By the time I noticed the telephone pole, my friends and I had already started teaching ourselves the basics of technical rock climbing. My parents didn't understand the dangers in what we were doing and, later on, when I'd drive away to go climbing, my mother would call, "Have fun hiking with the ropes!" To them it seemed like a wholesome outdoor activity that I would probably outgrow. So they let me pursue my climbing, so long as it didn't interfere with Sunday church-going. They were more concerned with familiar issues, such as my brothers and sisters driving the family cars and dating— activities they saw as more dangerous, both physically and morally.

Around this time, a UPS truck appeared in our driveway, and the driver unloaded a heavy box addressed to me. I ran to the door so full of excitement I collided with my mother, almost knocking her over. Inside the box was a mound of different sized pitons, the metal spikes used for rock climbing. I signed for my new prized possessions, paid for with money I'd earned doing odd jobs. Now I was equipped for the telephone pole.

My plan was to climb the pole during the day, when my dad was at work and my mom was running errands. One afternoon during summer vacation, that moment arrived. I quickly called Gordy, one of my Rainier climbing partners, to come over and help. We eyed the equipment. Each piton had a thick metal ring—the "eye"—forged at a right angle to a tapered metal blade similar to the business end of a table knife. The blades came in different sizes—thin, medium, and thick. My safety depended on handling these correctly: I knew I had to place the right size piton into a crack and hammer on the end of the eye until it was firmly wedged in the wood.

It was time to go. I started up the pole using direct aid, a technique I had studied in my rock climbing books. This involved reaching as high as I could to hammer in a piton. Then I clipped a short rope ladder to the eye of the piton using a carabiner and clambered up to the highest rung. Perched there, I reached up higher again to place another piton and repeated the process. It worked, and soon I was fifteen feet up the pole.

My climbing books had taught me another important lesson: how not to hit the ground if a piton pulled out of the wood when I weighted it. I accomplished this by tying the end of a climbing rope to my harness, and now, after placing each piton, I clipped the rope into the carabiner attached to it. Gordy stood at the base of the pole and fed the rope through a braking device. If one of the pitons pulled out as I moved up, Gordy would hold the rope firmly to keep it from slipping through the braking device. The rope would then come tight where it ran through the carabiner on the piton below and stop me after I took a short fall.

I tried with each placement to choose a piton whose blade was thicker than its destined crack, but thin enough to be pounded all the way in to where the eye was flush with the outside of the pole. Yet as I got higher, I became afraid that the soft wood might compress on both sides of the crack and the pitons would not be wedged tight enough to hold my weight. One of the safety measures I had read about was to gently step into my rope ladder, once I'd clipped it to the newly placed piton above me, and give it a little bounce. It was less scary and more secure to commit my weight to the new piton placement if it passed this bounce test. As I gained more confidence in my system, I began to enjoy my position high off the ground. Looking down on the familiar neighbourhood that I had never seen from this perspective, I felt free. But how much more liberating would it feel to be on a real rock wall hundreds, maybe thousands, of feet above the ground!

Of course, I'd never done direct aid climbing before, and I was slow. I had planned to finish before my parents came home, but by late afternoon I was only three-quarters of the way up the pole, and there was my dad, home from work in his old brown Studebaker pickup. As he stopped at the bottom of our driveway, a wave of fear swept over me, greater than any anxiety I'd felt in climbing. I'd been discovered, and there would be consequences.

Dad looked up and walked to where I was swinging forty feet above him. "What kind of stupid stunt is this?" he yelled. What could I say? He didn't know anything about climbing; it was going to be difficult to convince him that I was following all the proper safety techniques practiced by adults on big walls in Yosemite. To him, climbing a wooden pole topped by power lines was stupid and dangerous.

I worked up enough courage to call down, "I'm being very careful! My technique is safe!" My dad shouted back, "I don't *care* what you're doing. Come down immediately!"

I was faced with a dilemma. I didn't want Gordy to lower me, which really *would* be dangerous. But my dad expected me to obey his command. We had a common interest in science and technology, so I knew the best way to get him to listen was to provide an engineered solution. And so, perched high on the pole, that's exactly what I did.

"Dad," I called down, "it isn't safe for Gordy to lower me with the rope running through these pitons. The wood's too soft. If they pull out, I could fall. But I can build a safe anchor if I climb up another ten feet and tie a loop of nylon webbing around that wooden cross-bar bolted to the pole. Then I can feed my rope through the loop and I can rappel safely to the ground."

My dad calmed down, listened, and understood the merits of my explanation. And he let me finish my climb. What I didn't tell him was that rappelling would also allow me to retrieve my precious pitons on the way down. I would need them for future climbs on real rock.

I was later punished, but finishing my climb up the pole was worth any penalty. And even more satisfying was my dad's first-ever acknowledgement that I knew more about something than he did. Through books and now through direct experience, climbing had introduced me to a world where possibilities seemed infinite. This was my secret. There was no going back. At home, when I began to feel out of place, I would look out the window and see my loop of webbing high up on the pole. It became a symbol, there to remind me that adventure and exploration were waiting in the mountains.

Steve Swenson

PIONEER RIDGE

I T STARTED so innocently, with a call from Bill Joiner. Bill, a college friend, had recently graduated and moved to Juneau, Alaska, where he and three local friends were planning a summer expedition to climb Pioneer Ridge, a route on the north side of Mount McKinley that had only two previous ascents. Would I and my climbing partner Bruce like to join them? I was twenty-two and had a solid resumé of climbs in the Cascade Mountains near my home in Seattle, and a few ascents in the Canadian Rockies. But this was an altogether more serious undertaking: climbing a remote route on the highest mountain in North America was the kind of adventure I craved, and it would be a rite of passage to bigger things. I accepted without a second thought.

In our climbing permit application to the national park, Bill's friend Joe Ebner took on the role of expedition leader. I spoke to Joe on the phone and he said, "We're Alaskans and we want to climb the mountain like the sourdoughs did in 1910. They headed up with no special equipment from their mines on the north side of the mountain and made the first ascent of the North Peak. All these climbers who come up from down south use bush planes that land with skis on the glacier on the south side of the mountain. We want to do it like the pioneers did."

Making a human-powered ascent from the road involved hiking twenty miles across the tundra through mosquito-infested grizzly bear habitat. I said to Joe, "I think it would be a great adventure to walk in from the old mines near Kantishna, but I think we should hire a horse packer to carry our supplies so we only have to make the trip once. If we try to do all this work ourselves we will spend three weeks ferrying loads across the tundra and we won't have enough time or energy to climb the mountain."

The Juneau contingent resisted my suggestion and finally I had to threaten to drop out if we didn't use the horses. They needed a team of six climbers to share the work, so eventually they relented, and I flew to Alaska with my partner from Seattle, Bruce Blume. On June 21, 1976, Bruce and I, along with Bill and his friends Joe, Dick Rose, and Larry Fanning, hiked across the rolling tundra toward Mount McKinley.

We waded several rivers and trekked past grizzly bears lounging on hills across from us while trying to protect ourselves from swarms of giant mosquitoes. The tundra ended and the mountain began as we hiked over McGonagall Pass onto the mile-wide Muldrow Glacier. After a week of ferrying loads up this crevassed river of ice, we established our base camp at 10,000 feet in a giant amphitheatre of ice and rock. Ahead of us was the Harper Icefall, a jumbled mass of ice towers tumbling 5,000 feet down a steep rock wall from the glacier above. On our left was Karsten's Ridge, a steep snow arête that goes around the Harper Icefall onto the Upper Harper Glacier. It was named after Harry Karsten who, along with Hudson Stuck, Walter Harper, and Robert Tatum, climbed this route on the first ascent of the mountain in 1913. Pioneer

Ridge, our objective, towered above us on the right, beckoning toward us in the clear Arctic air. We would reach it from base camp by climbing a spur called the Flatiron, and then follow Pioneer Ridge to the top of an exposed promontory, Taylor Spur, at 15,000 feet. Above Taylor Spur a knife-edge snow ridge led to a series of steep ice gullies that cut through several rock bands just right of the ridge crest. This would be the most technically difficult section, but above it there were easy slopes back to the crest of Pioneer Ridge. From there it looked like a beautiful walk in the sky to the summit of the 19,470-foot-high North Peak. Overall we planned to go in a big circle by gaining 9,500 feet of elevation along four miles of Pioneer Ridge, traversing over the North Peak to Denali Pass, and then descending back to base camp via the easier Harper Glacier/Karsten's Ridge route.

Pioneer Ridge protrudes from the mountain more than any of the adjacent ridges or faces, so we would be very exposed to the weather. Mount McKinley is subject to frequent storms with heavy snowfall and hurricane-force winds. If we were hit by a storm high on our ridge, there would be no place to hide: we would suffer its full fury. If it lasted for more than two or three days, it would be hard to survive. Everyone knew that launching onto Pioneer Ridge would be truly committing, and that our safety depended on being able to move quickly.

But already there were worrying signs. Bill's friends were slow carrying loads up the Muldrow Glacier. I could see they were struggling physically and that Larry had little or no experience with a climb of this magnitude. At our 10,000-foot base camp they seemed tired and intimidated by the challenge we had ahead of us, but they insisted that they still wanted to climb. While they rested in base camp, Bruce and I broke trail up the Flatiron to the crest of Pioneer Ridge, where we dug a large snow cave for our first camp. The group did manage to join us the next day, but I was concerned about whether we could move fast enough to be safe. However, my overwhelming desire to climb the mountain prevented me from acknowledging our team's problems. I convinced myself that we would be okay if Bruce and I just worked harder.

On the Fourth of July we moved up to the top of Taylor Spur, where we would place our second camp on the ridge. Soon after we'd left our snow cave above the Flatiron, clouds blew in from the southwest. Once again, Bruce and I left the Juneau contingent trailing and stubbornly pressed ahead. As we approached Taylor Spur, a savage storm broke, with winds over eighty miles per hour and stronger gusts that made it difficult to stand. We placed our camp on a large flat area on the top of the spur, but we couldn't set up our tent because it would be destroyed by the wind. So we built a small igloo using an aluminum saw to cut snow blocks. We arranged them in a six-foot-diameter circle that spiralled upward and inward to where we capped off our dome when it was about five feet high. Before we got inside, we weather-sealed our igloo by packing snow over the entire exterior and into all the cracks between the blocks.

We were relieved to be out of the roaring gale. But our respite was short-lived. The wind-driven snow and ice worked like a sandblaster against our shelter and was soon eating holes in its six-inch walls. We waged an unending battle to plug the gaps, and we were unable to cook inside the igloo because heat from our stove would have melted the snow blowing onto us through the holes. If we got wet in these conditions, we would freeze to death—but without food and water, we were getting progressively weaker.

Fortunately, the storm abated after about thirty-six hours and was a harsh reminder that we needed to hurry. On this mountain it was only a matter of time before we would be hit by another storm, and once we were beyond Taylor Spur it would be almost impossible to retreat. At that point, whatever the conditions, the easiest way down would be up and over the top.

We'd heard the Juneau contingent arrive while we were busy battling the storm inside our igloo. The wind prevented us from communicating with them, but we could hear enough to know they had built some kind of temporary shelter. We'd learn later that they'd been out in the storm for several hours longer than we had, and survival had been an even greater ordeal for them. Larry suffered frostbite blisters on a couple of fingers when he lost a glove and didn't replace it with one that was warm enough. They were equipped with thick parkas and sleeping bags that helped protect them in the severe conditions, but they were very heavy to carry, contributing to their exhaustion and slow pace.

After the weather cleared, we took a day to dry things out and recover from the storm. Everyone still wanted to continue, but the unease I had felt when leaving base camp persisted. Our teammates had taken far too long to reach Taylor Spur, and despite the storm they seemed content with their progress and saw no need to move faster to get off this ridge. My fears about getting caught in another storm grew.

On the evening of July 7, Bruce and I took advantage of good weather to climb the steep ice gullies above Taylor Spur, place some fixed ropes, and return to our camp. We traversed a horizontal snow ridge just beyond the camp, and from there we headed for the ice gullies that penetrated the steep rock wall above. We kicked the front points of our crampons and swung the picks of our ice axes into the steep, hard ice as we worked our way to the top of the gullies at 17,000 feet. From here, easier snow slopes angled up to the summit ridge that led to the top of the North Peak, now 2,500 feet above. Before heading back to Taylor Spur, we also spotted a flat place 500 feet above us as a good site for our next camp. We had just completed the most difficult section of the route, and we anchored 600 feet of rope in the ice gullies on our way down. Back in camp, we were exhausted but satisfied. Getting beyond the difficulties to within easy striking distance of the summit boosted our morale.

The next day, the rest of our team carried a load of supplies to our high point while Bruce and I rested at the Spur. Then, on July 9, we set out with Bill, and the three of us reached the final campsite we had spotted two days earlier. From our eyrie, the Wickersham Wall fell 11,000 feet below us to the Peters Glacier, and beyond that, flat tundra stretched away as far as we could see. The rest of the Juneau contingent had agreed to join us later that day, but they didn't arrive. Where were they? I fumed over having to waste a day of perfect climbing weather.

The next day, the others finally showed up. "Before leaving Taylor Spur we saw some threatening clouds and decided to stay put in our igloo," Dick explained. As far as I could see, the weather had been fine, and by making Bruce, Bill, and me wait an extra day in our more exposed and precarious camp, they had been jeopardizing our safety. The group dynamics were failing. I felt that while Bruce and I were working hard to keep us moving safely up the mountain, Joe and Dick would follow only when they felt like it. Larry would do whatever his friends from Juneau decided, and Bill seemed caught in that same group while trying to mediate between us. But the mountain was unforgiving, and so was I. The stress of not working effectively as a team made me irritable and impatient. I knew I would feel better the next day, when we all got up and over the north summit and down to the relative safety of Denali Pass.

On the morning of July 11 Bruce and I fought our exhaustion to break trail in the deep snow that led to the final summit ridge. We had been operating as separate groups for weeks, so Bruce and I continued to the north summit at midday, well ahead of the others. We waited there for a long time, watching a large lenticular storm cloud brewing over the south summit about two miles away. We wondered, should we go back and look for them? Or should we descend to a safer and more sheltered spot at Denali Pass between the north and south summits and wait for them there? I assumed that they would have retreated to our previous campsite after seeing the clouds, just as they had done two days before. If we waited for them any longer we'd get engulfed by these same clouds and risk getting lost descending to Denali Pass via an unfamiliar route in a whiteout. We felt we'd already taken enough risks on this mountain, so we decided to head down to the Pass.

The storm hit, but fortunately not until that night, after we had reached Denali Pass. The wind was strong enough to keep us in our tent all the next day. We figured the Juneau contingent would also have stayed put in our previous camp. But July 13 was a beautiful, windless day, and Bruce and I decided to use the time waiting for the others to climb the higher south summit. It was an easy walk to the top, and from there we looked down on a sea of clouds with only the higher summits like Huntington, Hunter, and Foraker poking through. It was an exhilarating achievement: the view, the success after all our difficulties, and my first major world summit. We lingered at the top taking photos, relaxing, and eating. We weren't in a hurry, as we only had to return to Denali Pass. I was surprised we had the summit to ourselves on such a beautiful day; it seemed no one had climbed even the more popular West Buttress route. It was more of an adventure for us to be here alone in such a vast landscape.

As we came down, I could see the summit of the North Peak, from which we had descended to Denali Pass a couple of days earlier. But I didn't see the others coming that way, and when we got back to our camp, there was still no sign of them. Then I spotted a C-130 military airplane further down our descent route on the Harper Glacier. I said to Bruce, "Now I'm worried—those guys should have been here by now and that plane must mean there's a rescue operation."

We packed up quickly, and as we headed down we met two members of an expedition on the Karsten's Ridge route who were coming up the Harper Glacier.

"There's been an accident," they told us. "The other members of your team tried to descend a snow gully from Pioneer Ridge down onto the Harper Glacier, but they all fell. Two of them were killed and two are badly injured, but we don't know their names. We were walking up the glacier from our camp and just found them there, lying in the snow at the base of the snow gully. We're taking care of the injured climbers and we've notified the park. They're planning to land a helicopter near our camp at the top of the Harper Icefall, and the C-130 is doing reconnaissance to tell them when the weather is okay for the helicopter flight."

We were stunned. As we followed them back down to their camp, my heart was pounding and questions raced through my mind. *What were they doing? Who was killed and who is alive? What are their injuries? How could this happen?*

When we arrived at their camp, we learned that it was Joe and Dick who had been killed. Bill and Larry were the ones seriously injured but still alive. Bill had suffered a head injury from hanging upside down on the slope and was incoherent, his head swollen to the size of a basketball and his fingers badly frostbitten after losing his gloves in the fall. Larry had what appeared to be a broken femur.

Later that day, as I was stomping out a helicopter pad at 15,000 feet on the Harper Glacier, the midnight sun traversed the horizon just above the tundra, painting the mountain a soft orange. I shuffled sideways in the dim light, boot packing the snow in concentric circles. With each revolution, I passed the two frozen bodies that lay at the edge of the pad.

Soon the cold, clear quiet was disturbed by the lumbering twin-rotor Chinook helicopter as it climbed out of the dark Muldrow Glacier valley. Struggling to land in the thin air, it touched down and the rear door dropped slowly, with a deep mechanical whine. The crew was anxious to leave immediately. Bruce and I hurried up the ramp into the belly of the machine bearing stretchers, first for Bill, and then for Larry. We then carried the bodies of Joe and Dick into the cargo bay and ran clear as the door closed. The snow was whipped in every direction as the chopper blades revved up, and I crouched down, pulling my hood tight around my face. The helicopter rocked slightly to break free of the snow, climbed a few feet, and then slipped sideways beyond the edge of the ice cliff and dropped into the shadows. The evacuation had taken only a few minutes and we were left behind to descend the mountain on our own. I pulled the hood away from my mouth and vomited into the snow.

Bruce and I made the descent down Karsten's Ridge and the Muldrow Glacier, then across the tundra back to the road. At the hospital in Anchorage we learned that Bill was recovering from his head injury, but would lose all his fingers to the second knuckle from frostbite. Larry's prognosis was for a full recovery.

Both Bill and Larry had gaps in their memory of the accident, but we learned that Larry had gotten sick climbing the final summit ridge and so they couldn't follow us up and over the north summit down to Denali Pass. They tried instead to descend a snow and ice gully onto the Harper Glacier. They had their ice axes, but lacked equipment to build snow and ice anchors for lowering Larry. Most of that gear was with Bruce and me, since we had been using it while doing all the leading.

I had never experienced death and injury in such an intimate way. The loss of life was appalling, but I still felt that climbing was intrinsically valuable. I didn't know how to respond to the expedition members and their families, and I became defensive when questioned about my decisions. Over the following months I struggled to understand the reasons why such a terrible tragedy had occurred. Without the answers I needed, I felt empty. Climbing had been my spiritual and emotional refuge, but now it left me frightened and uncertain.

That winter I and three partners traversed the three summits of Mount Index in the Cascades. It was a route that had never been climbed in the winter and it was a difficult one, requiring commitment. We were a compatible team with similar experience, fitness, perseverance, and trust in each other—qualities we had lacked on Mount McKinley, with grievous consequences. I came to realize that these qualities kept us safe, strengthened our friendships, and helped us to be successful. Knowing this, I was able to overcome my fear and accept my climbing life with all its joy, hardship, and tragedy.

Maria Coffey

SPIRIT FRIENDS

THE LITTLE black elf was sitting on the wing, facing him. With one hand it was playing with the canard, threatening to pull it in the wrong direction and send the plane into a downward spiral. Don't worry, it assured Dick Rutan. You've already died. You fell asleep and crashed into a mountain. You're in transition between life and death; this is normal. Relax, go to sleep now, come with me.

Rutan had been flying for over twenty-four hours, shuttling back and forth over Owens Valley in the Sierra Nevada in a tiny experimental plane, trying to set a closed-course distance record. It was his first long-range flight. After working on the plane for most of the night, he had set off at dawn. The plane had no autopilot, so he was required to maintain a state of constant concentration. He had ten more hours to go.

Part of his brain urged him to lay his head on the control panel, close his eyes, and let the elf take over. Another part ordered him to take control. He wiped his face with a cold rag, he sniffed smelling salts, but the elf remained. And soon he had more company.

"I saw a spacecraft," recalls Rutan in our conversation. "It was big and complicated with little grey men looking at me from its windows. When I turned my head to see it better it would pull up and go away. If I looked straight ahead I could see the spacecraft in my peripheral vision, with all its intricate details. There were airplanes as well, dogfighting me from behind, and a big battle going on down on the ground. I could hear beautiful loud organ music. I had no idea what the hell was happening."

This occurred in 1979. Has he come up with an explanation since then?

"I don't believe in any spiritual crap," he says bluntly. But his journey, he notes, took exactly the same number of hours as Charles Lindbergh's 1927 non-stop transatlantic flight, which he describes in his book *The Spirit of St. Louis*. During that solo flight, Lindbergh was also visited by what he described as "phantoms."

"When I'm staring at the instruments," Lindbergh writes, "during an unearthly age of time, both conscious and asleep, the fuselage behind me becomes filled with ghostly presences—vaguely outlined forms, transparent, moving, riding weightless with me in the plane... These phantoms speak with human voices... they are friendly, vapour-like shapes without substance, able to vanish or appear at will, to pass in and out through the walls of the fuselage as though no walls were there... I feel no surprise at their coming... Without turning my head I see them as clearly as though in my normal field of vision."

Lindbergh believed these visions were "emanations from the experience of ages, inhabitants of a universe closed to mortal men." They spoke to him, helped him with his navigation during the hardest part of the flight, then disappeared.

It turns out that many explorers and adventurers, pushed to the edge of their limits, have had experiences they find difficult to explain once they return to their ordinary lives. And that such experiences are more common than people—or science—imagine.

One of the earliest accounts of a spirit friend was penned in the fifth century BC by the Greek historian Herodotus. He wrote that when the Persians invaded Greece, landing at Marathon, an Athenian herald called Pheidippides ran for two days to Sparta, a distance of 150 miles, to request help against the enemy. Near the top of Mount Parthenium he saw an apparition of the god Pan, who told him to remind the Athenians of how he had assisted them in the past, and to ask them why they had forgotten him. This vision spurred Pheidippides to run even faster to reach his destination and deliver Pan's message.

Long distance runner Marshall Ulrich has covered a similar distance—135 miles, on the Badwater Ultramarathon across Death Valley and up Mount Whitney, California—thirteen times. He's run it in daytime temperatures that hit 130°F. His fastest speed, in 1993, was thirty-four hours. During that race, as he neared the top of Mount Whitney, he saw hundreds of green lizards flowing down the path like a river. In 1999, on the second day of the race, he saw a woman rollerblading a hundred feet ahead of him.

"She was wearing a sparkling silver string bikini," he told me, "and she was skating her ass off. She kept turning to wave at me—she was gorgeous. I didn't even blink—I was thinking, *I'm liking this!* I kept that hallucination going for over ten minutes."

His attempts to conjure her up again failed, but two hours later a one-winged 747 airplane pulled up so close to him that he could see passengers waving at him through the portholes.

Hallucinations and visions are usually attributed to some kind of temporary or permanent neurological malfunctioning.

People who suffer seizures within the prefrontal or temporal lobe sometimes report "sensed presences" or flashes of mystical rapture. Medical historians have suggested that religious visionaries such as Saint Teresa of Avila, Joan of Arc, Saint Paul, and Joseph Smith, the founder of Mormonism, suffered from seizures. The Russian novelist Fyodor Dostoevsky has written about a rare form of temporal lobe epilepsy he suffered from termed "ecstatic epilepsy." During the last twenty years of his life, he kept detailed records of 102 seizures, describing the ecstatic feeling of being in "full harmony" with himself and the whole world that he experienced a few seconds before each attack. Such ecstasy came at a cost, as his post-fit symptoms, which lasted up to a week, included pains in the head, "nervous laugh and mystical depression."

The Canadian psychiatrist Dr. Michael Persinger, head of the Behavioural Neuroscience Program at Laurentian University, has tried to prove the connection between hallucinations and temporal lobe activity. He developed a helmet that shoots electric currents into specific regions of the brain, generating a low-frequency magnetic field and creating micro-seizures. When currents are aimed into the temporal lobes of his research subjects, they sometimes report dreamlike hallucinations and sense a "spectral presence" in the room.

In his original experiment, conducted under double-blind conditions, forty-eight men and women were subjected to partial sensory deprivation and exposure to weak, complex magnetic fields across the temporal lobes. Subjects who received greater stimulation over the right hemisphere or equal stimulation across both hemispheres reported more frequent incidences of presences, fears, and odd smells than did the subjects who received greater stimulation over the left hemisphere.

As the left hemisphere of the temporal cortex is, according to Persinger, the seat of our sense of self, he posits that the spectral presence is actually a transient awareness of the right hemispheric equivalent of the left hemispheric sense of self. While such a "transient awareness" is rare in normal life, he believes it might be caused by periods of distress, psychological depression, and certain drug-induced and meditation states. The experience of a presence, he has stated in one scientific article, is "a resident property of the human brain, and may be the fundamental source for phenomena attributed to visitations by gods, spirits, and other ephemeral phenomena."

IN 1989, Lou Whittaker, a veteran North American mountaineer, was leading the first American expedition to climb Kanchenjunga in the Himalayas. At base camp, he told me, he kept getting the feeling that someone was in his tent with him.

"I'd look around and think, *Who's here?* Then I would feel the presence of a Tibetan woman. There were no Tibetan women at base camp. But she was there every night. She was middle-aged, and dressed traditionally. It wasn't a strong image, more a sensation. There was nothing sexual about it. She was a friendly spirit, able to share my concerns. I felt she was communicating, without words, that everything was okay."

While he was on the mountain, his wife, Ingrid, was also in the area, leading a trek as far as his base camp. Eager to see him, she persuaded her group to skip the last resting stage of the trek and go straight from 12,000 to 16,000 feet in one day. It was a mistake. By the time they reached the base camp, Ingrid was suffering from altitude sickness. For the next three days she had such an appalling headache that she never left Lou's tent. But she wasn't alone there. In the daytime, when Lou was climbing, she was kept company by a Tibetan woman.

"I always felt this local woman with me," she recalled to me. "She was wearing a headscarf and a long dress. She was shadowy and two-dimensional, like a silhouette. It was a good presence, very comforting. She would put her hand on my forehead and help me roll over. She was just kind of hovering around and helpful the whole time. She didn't speak but there was always a feeling of kindness, that this was a good person who was going to take care of me. It was like we were communicating mind to mind, without words. I thought, *Oh my God, I'm really sick, I'm hallucinating, I'm losing it, I'll probably die.* I didn't tell Lou about it; I was in such a lot of pain, we hardly spoke to each other the whole time I was there."

Once she managed to stagger down to a lower altitude, her symptoms abated. Two months later, when Lou returned to North America after the expedition, they talked about her visit to base camp. Hesitantly, Ingrid told Lou about the presence in the tent.

"That's weird," he replied. "I had the same feeling. This woman was there with me in the tent for the whole three months."

They are both convinced that it wasn't a hallucination. It was a real presence. Nothing like this has ever happened to them again and they have told few of their friends about it.

"Most of them would think we were making it up," says Lou.

HEARING THE Whittakers' story, Dr. Pierre Mayer shrugs and says, "Hypnagogic dreams." Mayer, an expert in respiratory medicine and sleep disorders, has taken part in several mountaineering expeditions to the Alps, the Andes, and the Himalayas. As director of the Sleep Disorders Investigation Centre and Clinic of Montreal University Hospital, he is conducting research into dreams and hypoxia. At altitude, he explains, it is common for sleep cycles to be irregular and disturbed, something that in Ingrid's case was compounded by illness.

Such disturbances made her and Lou more prone to having hypnagogic dreams, which are often reported as hallucinations, varying from poorly formed shapes to vivid images of people and animals. They happen mostly at the onset of sleep or during periods of relaxed wakefulness. Similar dreams, known as hypnopompic states, occur at sleep offset. Both can be experienced in successive sleep cycles.

But this doesn't explain why the couple *both* sensed the same Tibetan woman. Lou Whittaker has his own theory about the visitation.

"There is such old history on Kanchenjunga. I think she was a strong spirit that had enough influence to break through our reserves and make us feel that she was there."

LIKE LOU AND Ingrid Whittaker, many mountaineers have sensed unexplainable presences in the high mountains. In 1983, the Australian mountaineer Greg Child was high on Broad Peak in Pakistan when his climbing partner, Pete Thexton, became seriously ill. For hours, through darkness and a storm, Child struggled to get Thexton down the mountain. Throughout the ordeal he had the sense of a presence behind him, gently guiding him in the right direction. "I kept turning around, puzzled to find only darkness behind me," he writes in his book *Thin Air*. "But there was definitely someone, or something, there."

Five years later, the British climber Stephen Venables became the first person to ascend Everest by its Kangshung Face. He was forced to spend a night just below the summit, where he was kept company by an old man. As he began his descent, in an exhausted state, the man encouraged him to keep going. Together they crawled down to the South Summit, where they were joined by Eric Shipton, the long-dead explorer, who helped to warm Venables's hands.

According to a close friend of Steve Swenson, from Seattle, during a night he spent close to the summit of Everest in the 1990s, Swenson saw several "disembodied heads." He was nagged to stay awake until sunrise by the heads of a Japanese woman and a Punjabi man, who then encouraged him to hurry as he broke camp. Finally, a third head gave him directions as he climbed down the mountain.

During an expedition on Kanchenjunga in 1978, Joe Tasker climbed alone to a snow cave on the mountain, where he sat waiting for the arrival of "an indistinct group of people I imagined were also on the climb with us." His climbing partners, Doug Scott and Peter Boardman, admitted to the same sensations. After reaching the summit, when they were heading back to the cave, Boardman was at the back of the group, convinced that there were others following him.

"It was not a thought that needed verification," writes Joe in his book *Savage Arena*. "He was simply aware of the presence of someone behind him, just as firmly as he knew we three were in front of him."

On Everest, in 1975, Doug Scott sensed a presence that spoke to him and guided him while he was climbing difficult sections. Nick Estcourt, who would dream his death on K2 three years later, had a more dramatic experience. Early one morning, he was moving up the fixed ropes between Camps 4 and 5. When he was about 200 feet above Camp 4, he got a feeling that he was being followed. Turning around, he saw another climber. He assumed it was one of the team, trying to catch up. He stopped and waited. The climber was moving extremely slowly. Estcourt shouted down to him, but got no reply. Eventually he decided to press on. Several times he turned around. The figure was still there.

"It was definitely a human figure with arms and legs," he recounted to Chris Bonington, the team leader, who wrote about the incident in his book *Everest the Hard Way.* "At one stage I can remember seeing him behind a slight undulation in the slope, from the waist upward, as you would expect, with the lower part of his body hidden in the slight dip."

After a time, Estcourt turned around to find the slope below him empty. He could see all the way back to Camp 4—it was impossible that the person could have retreated without him knowing. And if he had fallen, he would have seen traces of that as well. When finally he returned to the rest of the team, he quizzed them as to who had been on the rope behind. No one, they told him.

At the Laboratory of Cognitive Neuroscience in Lausanne, Switzerland, scientists have been studying the link between mystical experiences and cognitive neuroscience. They point out that the fundamental revelations to the founders of the three monotheistic religions—Moses, Jesus, and Mohammed—occurred on mountains, and included such components as feeling a presence, seeing a figure, hearing voices, and seeing lights. These similarities of experience suggest to the scientists that exposure to altitude might affect functions relying on brain areas such as the temporoparietal junction and the prefrontal cortex. Prolonged stays at high altitude, especially when linked to social deprivation, can lead to prefrontal lobe dysfunctions, which are commonly found during ecstatic experiences. Also, the physical and emotional stresses of climbing at altitude release endorphins, which are known to lower the threshold for temporal lobe epilepsy, which in turn might evoke such experiences.

In their book *High Altitude Medicine and Physiology*, British doctors Michael Ward and Jim Milledge reported that tests conducted on climbers during Himalayan expeditions indicate that above 18,000 feet thought function and perception become increasingly impaired, and above 28,000 feet,

hallucinations are common. Dr. Charles Houston, a legendary American mountaineer and the co-discoverer of high-
altitude pulmonary edema, told me such hallucinations could
be caused by miniature temporal lobe seizures, triggered by
fatigue, low blood sugar, personal crisis, or anxiety. They
could also be the result of hypoxia, in which there is a diminished supply of oxygen to the brain. By scanning the brains
of hospitalized patients suffering from hypoxia due to other
causes, scientists have shown neural irregularities, including fluid pockets and swelling of the brain, or edema. When
the brain is hypoxic, control of the cortical function is weakened, which impairs the climber's judgment, but also creates
a type of euphoria that makes difficult tasks seem easier. This
euphoria is similar to the state of enhanced ability and senses
brought about by the flood of endorphins, dopamine, sero-
tonin, noradrenaline, and adrenaline during high stress.

Greg Child has a simpler theory. "Going to blow-your-
mind high altitude creates a world inside of ourselves. When
you're down here you're not so tuned into the same things as
when you're up high or in some extreme circumstances, wondering if you're going to make it through the next few hours."

British mountaineer Adrian Burgess, in our interview, put
it even more succinctly: "The higher you go, the more weird
things get."

MOUNTAIN GHOSTS have appeared at lower altitudes. One
winter in the late 1960s, Dougal Haston, a Scottish climber,
was staying with a friend in an alpine hut in Argentière, near
Chamonix, France. They were its only occupants. At around
2:00 A.M. Haston was woken by the sound of someone walking heavily across the floor of the room above them, then
clumping down the wooden stairs. The latch to their room rattled. The footsteps went back up the stairs again. Then, silence.

Haston believed in ghosts, but didn't want his companion to think he was crazy, so he said nothing. In the morning, however, his friend asked him if he had heard strange sounds in the night. They decided to search the place but found no trace of anyone having been there.

Bad weather forced them to spend another night in the hut. At 2:00 A.M., the footsteps returned. The door latch rattled. This time, the men were ready. They sprang up and yanked open the door, but there was no sign of anyone in the hallway. Despite being brave mountaineers, neither could face going upstairs. They left the hut early the next day. Just before heading out, Haston checked through the visitors' book, in which climbers recorded the routes they had completed on surrounding mountains. He was shocked to find a note about the hut guardian being killed in an avalanche. It was a fate that would befall Haston himself, a few years later.

Adrian Burgess stayed in the same hut in 1972. He didn't know about the ghost, and only learned about it a few years later. The hut was about to be demolished, and there was a lengthy discussion about whether its replacement should be built on the same site or relocated because of the resident spirit.

Burgess is skeptical about the idea of ghosts and spirits on mountains. "In some places I climb," he told me, "if the ghosts of dead friends were coming to visit me there would be so many of them it would be pretty crowded. I mean, if it was true, the entire alpine hut system would be crawling with howlers. Anyway, thankfully none of them have ever tapped on the tent door. I'd be scared shitless."

MANY CLIMBERS are reticent about admitting to paranormal experiences, for fear their peers will think them crazy. Not so the Mexican climber Carlos Carsolio, who in 1996, at the age of thirty-three, became the fourth and then-youngest person to climb all fourteen of the world's highest peaks. We had a long conversation about his experiences. He never used supplementary oxygen on his climbs and he's had many hallucinations, including the "third man" syndrome, which he says is a normal phenomenon up high. What he calls his "moments of extended reality" are quite another matter. They are, in his words, "a step more."

One of Carsolio's most profound experiences was in 1988, after his solo ascent of Makalu, the world's fifth-highest mountain. By the time he began his descent, night had fallen, and the wind was very strong. He was extremely weak, struggling with the beginning of pulmonary edema and beginning to freeze. His headlamp faded, the windblown snow covered his tracks, and he was soon lost. He had been in this kind of situation before; he knew what he must do to survive.

"I stopped fighting the cold," he recalled. "I became one with it. Then I became part of the mountain and I didn't get frozen. I used my energy in a positive way."

He started to talk to the mountain and the different entities it was revealing to him. "Some of the seracs were female, some of the rocks were male. They were guiding me, telling me where to go. But some of the presences were evil and wanted me to die. The two sides were fighting over this. I was talking with them. With the friendly ones in a friendly way, with the bad ones in a fighting way."

These conversations went on for hours as Carsolio struggled down through the storm, searching blindly for a narrow snow bridge that he knew was the only safe route through a section of dangerous crevasses. Suddenly he felt a strong presence. He recognized it as a climber he'd known who had died on Makalu—later, he would discover that the man had perished in the very area in which he sensed the presence of his spirit. Eventually, he came across the snow bridge, and from there reached his high camp. This would have been impossible, he believes, without the help of his climbing friend's spirit and the friendly entities.

"I cannot understand how else I found the bridge, in such a huge place with the wind and the dark night and no lamp and frozen glasses and my exhaustion. It was like finding a needle in a haystack."

He collapsed inside the tent, still wearing his crampons. Two hours later, when the sun woke him, he could barely breathe and was coughing up blood.

He had a tape recorder in the tent. He managed to record a brief message, saying goodbye to his family and friends. As he signed off, however, he decided he didn't want to die in a tent on the side of a mountain. He would prefer to die fighting. He started crawling and sliding down the mountain. After several hours, a Polish team passed him on their way up the mountain. He called to them, but they thought he was so close to death that they simply carried on without offering help. By now, his team at base camp could see him through binoculars. They watched his torturous progress—descending a few feet then lying down for half an hour. Finally some Spanish climbers came by. They gave him oxygen, water, and food, and stayed with him until he felt strong enough to carry on alone to the safety of base camp.

Carsolio counts such harrowing experiences among the most memorable and treasured of his life.

"It's not about the adrenaline," he insists. "These extended moments are different. They take me to another dimension. They are why I wanted to climb alone and to do such hard routes, so that I could reach them."

FOUR YEARS LATER, Carsolio went to Kanchenjunga with a team that included Wanda Rutkiewicz, a legendary Polish mountaineer. They arrived at base camp in mid-March, but by early May they had made little progress on the mountain, and the team was ravaged by frostbite and illness. Only he and Rutkiewicz, twenty years his senior, were fit enough to continue on and attempt the summit. Rutkiewicz set out two days ahead of him, but she was slowed by age and a nagging injury from a previous trip and he soon caught up with her. They spent a night at Camp 4, at 7,900 feet, and left at 3:00 A.M. the following morning. Determined to make the summit in a fast, light push and get back the same day, they took a minimum of food and water and no bivouac gear.

After a few hours of climbing, Rutkiewicz slowed to a crawl. She urged Carsolio to go ahead, insisting she would catch up with him after a rest. He climbed all day, regularly looking back at her figure growing ever-smaller on the slopes below him. It was 5:00 P.M. before he reached the summit. The sun was setting, and already the cold of the night was seeping through to his bones. His food and water had run out. It was essential for him to descend as quickly as possible. Carefully, he picked his way down the icy slopes, conscious that exhaustion, hunger, dehydration, and hypoxia could easily add up to a fatal mistake. After three hours, when he was less than a thousand feet below the summit, he came across a familiar rope and followed it to where Rutkiewicz was huddled in a tiny snow cave. Like him, she had nothing to eat or drink. Worse, she was inadequately dressed in a light down suit designed for lower altitudes. She asked Carsolio for his jacket, but he knew he would freeze without it. He encouraged her to descend with him to their high camp but she insisted she wanted to spend the night in the snow cave. She would wait for the sun to come up and warm her, she said, and then she would go for the summit.

Carsolio was horrified. But he was too much in awe of her to argue. She was one of the world's best Himalayan climbers. She had years of experience behind her, and far more expeditions than he had undertaken. Rutkiewicz was a legend, and he was her acolyte. He sat with her for fifteen minutes until he realized that he was becoming dangerously cold. He stood up. He bid her farewell.

See you later, Wanda.

It was a decision he'd always regret.

"I knew she was in a state of exhaustion and cold but I had not the guts to tell her to go down."

He waited for her all that night and for much of the next day at their high camp. Eventually he could wait no longer.

"As I was climbing down to Camp 2," he recalls, "suddenly I knew, right at that very moment, that Wanda was dying. She said goodbye to me. I was climbing down, the terrain was hard, I was much focused, but suddenly my mind was filled with her presence, her femininity. I felt it very strongly."

A storm forced him to stay at Camp 2 for much of the next day. When finally he set off, he left behind food and water for Wanda, even though he knew there was no hope. Wrung out by grief, physically spent after a week on the mountain, he started to descend a huge, steep wall of ice and rock. On the way up with Wanda, they had fixed this section with ropes, so it should have been straightforward. While moving from one rope to another, however, sorrow overwhelmed him; he lost his focus and forgot to tie a crucial figure-eight knot. Presuming he was secure, he stepped back into thousands of feet of air. The fall was short; his arm caught in a loop of the fixed rope. He was hanging, in shock, when he heard Wanda's voice.

Don't worry. I will take care of you.

"I have no doubt that it was real," he insists. "I was not hallucinating and I'm not crazy. I'm sure it was her. I received it as a message; it was not exactly in words, it was another dimension, a feeling, a presence. I started to cry because I felt guilty about not having told her to come down. I did not take care of her and now she was taking care of me." He tried to gather himself, to start rappelling again, but huge sobs racked his body. "I was crying and crying, and then I felt her presence again. It was very peaceful. It was like a mother hugging her child."

Finally, he reached the glacier, where the rest of his team was waiting.

"I was back in the real world, the normal world," he said. "But this experience—it was very deep. When a climb was not so demanding I never had such experiences. But when it was really extreme, especially when I was on the edge of dying, somehow in that moment, *poof!* The channel was open."

Fitz Cahall

UNSEEN BUT FELT

THE TRAIL disappeared beneath the whiteness. Shielding my hood with an arm, I strained, squinting to pick a path up through broad valley walls. I knew the pass lay beyond in the whiteout, but vertigo swelled behind my eyes and I could see nothing. I looked down at my feet, nestled six inches deep in the previous night's snow. Somewhere beyond us, I knew, Sawtooth Ridge's granite flanks were gathering snow-fall; beyond lay the nearest exit from the Sierra on Yosemite National Park's northern boundary. We were nearing the first of the two 10,000-foot passes we would need to cross; I took comfort in the fact that we had already crossed a dozen much higher.

Behind me, Becca cradled her injured hand close to her heart. In the cold, we'd been forced to remove the splint and sling that we'd used to protect the healing wound. Five days earlier, as we strode across talus, a rock had shifted, sending Becca for a tumble. Her thumb had been pinched between a flat rock and sharp stone blade, severing an artery and chipping the bone. The emergency-room stitches were still fresh. We'd discussed calling it a trip, but neither of us wanted to leave. We'd keep walking even if we couldn't climb.

California's High Sierra should have been bathed in sunshine during the fall months, but two days earlier, a gentle rain had begun to fall and had built into a steady downpour, drenching us to the skin and sending the golden larch leaves fluttering to the ground. That night, the steady drum of rain on our open-floored tent gave way to the whisper of snow. We hastily gathered our camp, set out, and walked directly into a wall of white. We could have turned back; that would have been the conservative call. But there didn't seem to be anything conservative about this storm. We could retreat back to the tree line, crawl into our soaking tent and damp sleeping bags, and hope for blue skies. But our lightweight gear was meant only for summer squalls, and staying put would probably earn us an embarrassing helicopter ride home.

We had history with the Sierra. That same October week six years earlier, we'd been ten miles to the north when an unforecasted storm rolled through, leaving three feet of snow, stranding dozens of hikers, and killing several climbers on Yosemite's El Capitan. It had closed the high country for the remainder of the winter. I had the same feeling about this storm. Both had been preceded by a heat wave, then a day or two of unsettled weather. The day's forecast had called for 60°F and sunny. It was 25 degrees and snowing an inch an hour. Becca and I both knew it was time to head for the exit.

In the flat dawn light, I looked at Becca and uttered a one-word question. "Go?"

"Go," she echoed, without hesitation.

WHY? THAT WAS the question I fielded most often before we left. Our expedition was an ambitious, stubborn, and even borderline-inefficient approach to climbing. We'd have to walk almost the entire length of the High Sierra, 300 miles, from southern Sequoia National Park north through Yosemite. We would carry climbing gear the entire way and climb as much as our rations, our bodies, and the weather would permit. It sounded more like a never-ending approach than a climbing trip. "Why?" was a pretty valid query.

Before Becca and I left in August, I'd given out several answers. I'd been thinking about this trip for a decade after hearing about it over a campfire. I wasn't getting any younger. Then there was the fact that men I admired had done this trip in a similar fashion. First, of course, there was John Muir. Then David Brower, the legendary activist, made a very similar trip in the 1930s. Over the course of two months, he and his cohorts ticked off over fifty summits and concluded their route with a moonlight climb of Matterhorn Peak.

Or maybe I'd say that I wanted to prove that you didn't have to travel to Pakistan or Baffin Island to have a truly profound adventure—that it could be found in our backyard ranges. That it was possible to take a climbing road trip without a car or even a road. That modern adventure is more a reflection of creativity and individuality than it is of setting or environment.

The people closest to me knew better.

I was looking for an escape. I was drinking too much. Sleeping not enough. I'd pushed through writer's block simply because I didn't have time for it. The quiet spectre of depression was tapping at my shoulder. I relied on the theory that an animal in motion is less likely to be caught. Keep moving. Don't rest. Don't think. Just get to the trip. In the clutter, the noise, the constant motion of my life I was struggling to hear the quiet. If you never come out of the mountains you never have to answer a phone.

Secretly, I'd hoped that the trip would provide some quick,

easy answers. They would snap from the sky as quick and complete as a lightning strike. I was waiting for someone or something to save me.

"I CAN'T SEE the trail," I howled back at Becca, just three steps behind me. We had progressed no more than a mile and a half from our camp. I used my trekking pole to break the untouched snow. At least the change in texture helped ease the vertigo.

"I don't think we should go back," she yelled.

A trail isn't necessary for upward progress. I repeated that thought silently three or four times and stepped forward. We would have to create our own path toward our first destination, Burro Pass. I took another step and the talus shifted. My feet skated on the six inches of snow and I fell directly into a stranded-turtle position. I struggled beneath the weight of the sixty-five-pound pack. The trip had whittled fifteen pounds off my six-foot-two-inch, 160-pound frame. With the pack on, I felt top-heavy.

Neither Becca nor I could bring ourselves to say it outright, but our margin for safety was as slim as it had ever been. A mistake, a misstep, a twisted ankle, a blown-out knee, would mean one having to leave the other behind to fetch help. The steep talus slopes offered no flat ground for our tent, but the situation was still fine, I reminded myself. Our bodies would stay warm as long as we kept moving. We would pause only to eat and drink. We'd navigated in whiteouts before. We'd done enough skiing in the densely forested Cascades that orienting with a compass wasn't hard. We simply had to keep heading uphill, hit the ridge, and find the pass. Without the trail, travel over the jumble of rocks would be excruciatingly slow, but we'd just have to be patient.

Just beneath those rational thoughts, the other side of reality gnawed. It was October. It was the Sierra. It was snowing so hard it was difficult to open our eyes. Our gear was too light. We were seventeen miles from the nearest road, wet from head to foot. I wasn't sure if we were making the right decision. Only hindsight would tell, but my instinct was to keep walking. Keep moving.

Right about then, the lightning started and the storm swallowed us. Our footprints led back into the swirling white. I reminded myself to appreciate the rawness of the moment. This was obviously a day we would never forget.

FOR THE FIRST week of the trip, phantom cellphones ringing in my pocket haunted me as I dreamed incessantly about work. I chased away thoughts that I was shirking responsibility for my business and my life. Instead, I fished. I even caught fish. I imagined my mind being like a dry fly about to be swallowed whole.

We put up new routes. Climbed old, forgotten ones. We followed in the footsteps of Muir into the "walls of the celestial city." I read books. We remembered that approaches aren't something to be reviled or rushed, but an integral part of the wonderful process of alpine rock climbing. There were strings of days when we saw no one else. We lounged naked on granite slabs next to deep, crystal-clear pools. Becca and I began to think as one, completing daily tasks in wordless unison. Answering questions the other was about to ask. Eventually, the phantom cellphone stopped ringing. The worries about shirked responsibilities faded.

"This is the most beautiful place I've ever seen," I repeated endlessly. "You just said that," Becca would say, with an amused but loving smile.

When cramps and diarrhea racked Becca's body, I pulled weight from her bag and nursed her as best I could. And when stress-induced shingles bled the enthusiasm and strength from me, Becca quietly took over, fluttering through camp to handle the evening's chores and organize gear for the next day's climb. These small acts of caring grew to fill the great empty spaces of the Sierra.

The questions of life in the flatlands remained. Should we leave the city and move back to the Sierra, even if it meant struggling with work again? Would that make my bad days better? Could we afford to start a family one day? Should I let go of my work completely, take a job writing press releases, and leave at five P.M. every night? Were my creative passions killing me, or was I plenty capable of doing that on my own? After forty-two days in the wilderness, no answers had come and I'd stopped asking. There would be no neat solutions.

What was obvious was that I was happy out here. That my mind and body loved the rhythm of the rising and falling sun. That sleeping ten hours didn't make me a lazy slob. That humans weren't necessarily designed to know what day of the week it was. That our community's habit of labelling grueling climbs, chattering teeth, and lightning storms as "suffering" was nothing more than a flair for the dramatic. Suffering, my ass, I realized. Out here ideas drink from inspiration like tree roots soaking up spring melt. This is thriving.

But I couldn't stay out here forever.

I WINCED with each lightning strike on the ridge just above us. I took another tentative step upward. Then another. I'd lost the trail completely.

"At this rate we are going to spend the night out here," I said. My thoughts had turned to spoken words.

"Not here. Not tonight," Becca answered steadily.

I took another step forward. The blanket of snow hid what was a mess of jagged talus. I slipped again. A few minutes later, Becca ripped the stitches in her hand. Our progress slowed. We needed a path. We needed a trail.

I waited for the smallest gap in the clouds, hoping to orient off the Matterhorn, the same mountain Jack Kerouac had summitted with poet Gary Snyder on a cold October day and made famous in *The Dharma Bums*. I hoped they had better visibility. No break came. I moved forward simply because there was no other clear direction. I stabbed with my ski pole.

Then, like a gift, the tracks appeared. Right in front of me were the unmistakable hoof prints of a deer. They ended four feet ahead, as if the animal had been plucked from the storm. From the tracks' position it should have been standing right in front of me.

I stopped.

"Follow the tracks," I muttered to myself. "Trust this animal's instincts. It will lead you."

I took another step forward, looked right and then left for the shadowy form of a buck. I think I even looked up toward the sky. Nothing.

I motioned Becca on to investigate. I stepped two feet to the left to make room for her and right onto the relatively uniform ground of the trail we'd lost earlier.

"I've got the trail," I said, surprised. "What do you think?"

Wordlessly we both answered the question. *Go.*

Each step became more decisive. When the trail became obscured or switchbacked, the buck's tracks appeared. We were moving quickly again, steady, with sure footing beneath us. Forty-five minutes later we paused briefly atop the pass to appreciate the force of the wind. Squeezed by mountain walls, it accelerated through the pinch and wiped away any signs of the deer's trail. The cloud ceiling lifted to offer a momentary view of the path into and out of the next valley. We were leaving Yosemite. We reminded one another to pause, to take notice of the snowflakes' unique patterns before they melted on our jackets. Cold, wet, and physically exhausted, we were speeding toward our lives in the flatlands. Even days like this can be gifts. Then the shivering started, so we walked.

The day moved forward in the sharp resolution that comes with heightened concentration. I will never forget the booming concussion of the string of lightning strikes as we crossed the second pass. Or nervous amusement of watching Becca covered in rime and snow and clinging to tree branches in the third-class cliff systems we'd accidentally wandered into. Over the course of that day, we drew upon every tool we'd gleaned from our decade of adventure together. But whenever it got really bad—when we'd again begin to doubt our blindly staked path and pull out the compass and topo map to begin whiteout navigation—the buck's tracks would appear. His presence unseen, but felt.

It would be tempting to imbue these moments with deep meaning, but the more I replay that day, the more I realize that to interpret them as anything other than facts would be to deny their beauty. There was a blizzard. We were dangerously exposed to lightning and cold. We lost the trail and slowed when we desperately needed to move quickly. Deer tracks appeared. We followed them because that seemed like the best option.

Eventually, the flawless granite turret of the Incredible Hulk emerged through the snow and clouds. Three miles beyond we could see Little Slide Canyon, snowline, and the flat valley below. We lurched downward through 3,000 feet of talus. Knees wavered with exhaustion. Blood trickled from scraped ankle bones. We fell repeatedly. In the gathering dusk, we waded thigh-deep through flooded, stinking beaver ponds and then we collapsed onto a rain-soaked trail lined with sage and hugged each other.

Three miles of flat, wide trail remained. Becca took the lead and, for the final time, tapped into the unseen, shared reservoir of energy from which we'd been drinking liberally on this trip. Too tired to ask questions or even formulate a sentence, I followed in her slipstream. An hour later, we staggered into a massive campground and wandered, lost, among the darkened forms of hundreds of slumbering RVs. We had returned to a day-to-day wilderness that no map or compass could lead me through.

Jan Redford

END OF THE ROPE

I STAND AT the base of El Capitan, my hands flat on the warm rock, straining my neck to stare up three thousand feet of granite. A thin red line of nylon climbing rope lies against the blank face and disappears up out of sight.

Jake throws his backpack on the ground and starts to dig out the gear.

"How high are we going?" I ask in my most laid-back voice.

"About eight, nine hundred feet. Don't worry. We'll be up and down in a couple of hours."

"I'm not worried. Just wondering."

Reaching into my shorts pocket, I pull out my tin of Copenhagen. I take a pinch of the tar-black tobacco, tuck it into my lower lip, tamp it down with the tip of my tongue, and spit out a few floaters. The nicotine buzz spreads through my body, calming my nerves, heating and numbing my mouth.

Jake stops sorting gear. "You're not going to spit that down on me, are you?"

"Why, am I going first?" Even though I've never ascended ropes, somehow following feels safer, even though dead is dead if you fall from 900 feet.

"Yeah, I'll come up behind—clean the anchors and drop the extra ropes."

We're not here to rock climb, just retrieve ropes, but at least I'll get to hang off the most famous hunk of rock in the North American climbing world. Jake and his partner Mike spent the last three days on Horse Chute, then they used the bolts on this blank wall to rappel back down, leaving the ropes behind. They were planning to ascend the ropes and finish the climb after re-stocking their food and water, but Mike copped out. Now the ropes have to come down.

I spit a long, dark stream of tobacco juice into the rocks.

"That's a disgusting habit." Jake sounds irritated, not his usual self.

I learned to chew snuff two years ago in Wyoming on a three-and-a-half-month outdoor leadership course where I also learned to rock climb—my big dream come true. At first I chewed to gross everyone out and to prove girls can do anything guys can do, but now I'm addicted, in spite of my terror of mouth cancer and the fact that Copenhagen smells like pig shit and gets stuck in my teeth.

Jake hands me a tangled pile of nylon slings and two yellow ascenders.

"Here's your jumars. We'd better get going. We've got less than three hours of daylight left."

He steps back, his arms crossed over his chest like a teacher. Except I've never seen a teacher with forearms the size of my calves. Rock climbing half the year and ice climbing the other half has turned him into a scruffy, red bearded, dark-eyed Popeye.

After I scoop out my tobacco and take a swig of water, I attach my jumars to the rope and clip an etrier—a six-foot ladder made from webbing—into each.

"Okay, I'm ready."

Jake studies me through narrowed eyes. "I thought you said you'd used jumars before."

"I have. I jugged up a tree once to hang the food."

Jake shakes his head. "Shit." He grabs two pieces of nylon webbing that are curled up at my feet. "You forgot your daisy chains."

Daisy chains? He slips the webbing through my harness in a girth hitch and attaches one to each of the jumars hanging from the rope. "That's your lifeline."

Looking down at the mess of gear hanging from my harness, I can see that the daisy chains are the only thing securing me to the rope. If I let go of the jumars, I'd fall to the ground. This is starting to look more complicated than rock climbing.

"Your harness is doubled back?" He grabs my harness and jerks it roughly.

"Yeah, yeah." I pull away.

After climbing in Alberta for almost two years, I know how to put on a harness. But when Jake turns his back, I check my buckle, just in case. Right here in Yosemite, a woman leaned off a ledge to rappel and fell to her death because she hadn't done her harness up properly. One stupid, split-second mistake.

I slide the top jumar as high up the rope as I can reach, slip my sneaker into one of the loops of the etrier, and step up. But the rope swings me around and my body slams into the rock.

"It'll take a bit to get the stretch out of the rope. Here, I'll hold it for you."

"I can do it!"

Jake throws up his hands defensively and steps back to watch.

Fumbling with my etriers, it occurs to me he's talking to me like I'm an idiot, the way I overhear boyfriends talking to their girlfriends at the bases of climbs. But I came to Yosemite to *really* climb, not to follow some hot-shit climber around.

When I climb with women, we alternate leads. When I climb with guys, it's too easy to give up the sharp end of the rope. The best thing I could do is swear off men altogether. Become a lesbian. But given my track record, it doesn't look like there's much chance of that happening.

Finally, I'm off the ground. When my weight is on one jumar, I can reach down and slide the other one up the rope. I transfer my weight back and forth like that, slogging upward, as if I'm on some defective step machine at the gym. Not that I spend much time at the gym. My idea of training is ski touring, climbing, or hiking, then drinking beer and doing finger pull-ups on door jams when I have a male audience.

"You're doing good, Jan!"

About eighty feet up, halfway to the first anchor, I have to stop and flex my fingers, stiff from their death grip on the jumars. This gets the scabs on the backs of my hands bleeding again. For the past few days, we've been crack climbing, and my jamming technique is less than perfect. I notice Jake doesn't have one scrape.

By the time I get to the first anchor—two bolts drilled into the rock—my feet and hands are numb. I shouldn't be getting pumped so quickly. Not after working ten-hour days on a trail crew in Alberta all spring and summer, and rock climbing or hiking in the Rockies every day off. But going up these ropes seems to use a whole different set of muscles.

I secure myself to the anchor, unclip my jumars and transfer them to the next rope above me.

"I'm off!" I yell down to Jake, to let him know he can start his ascent.

While I rest against the wall, I watch Robbie at the base, starting a climb with a couple of students. He's on the Yosemite climbing rescue team with Jake. They get a free campsite and showers, and a small pittance for each idiot they rescue off a climb. Business is brisk.

I check my jumars twice before I unclip from the anchor to put my fate back into these pumpkin-coloured pieces of metal. Slide, step, reach, slide, step, reach. My technique is getting smoother, and after a few minutes, I start to enjoy the motion.

"Can you speed it up a bit, Jan? It's getting late."

Jake is already near the top of the first rope. As I try to go faster I lose my rhythm. Sweat trickles down my sides even though the sun is gone and I'm only wearing a tank top and shorts. We decided to go light, since we wouldn't be on the rock long. Not long enough to need food, or warm clothes. Jake has a water bottle clipped to his harness, but we've left the packs at the base.

Jake and I met last spring, on my first trip to Yosemite Valley. He lives here in Yosemite half the year, Alaska the other half. Right now we're slumming at Camp 4, the climbers' campground. There are no showers, no hot water, and the toilets overflow daily, but it's only a dollar a night per person. Jake is camped with the rescue team; I'm at Site 27 with the friends I came down with from Alberta, co-workers at a kids' outdoor camp near Calgary. I'm sharing Niccy's tent, but she's heading back north, so I'll be homeless soon, and Doc is heading back to North Carolina, leaving me without transportation. Jake invited me to share his tent and I declined.

Jake is twenty-five, four years older than me, and has never really had a girlfriend. It shows. He still thinks you get the girl by being agreeable. I told him I wasn't looking for a boyfriend, that it would interfere with my climbing. I considered telling him I already have someone back home, but that would have been stretching it, since I'm between boyfriends. Sort of. Randy was never really my boyfriend, since he already has a girlfriend, though she *is* living back East. And that little thing with Scottie the night before I left for California can hardly be considered "a relationship," since I fell asleep in the middle of it.

Jake is waiting at the bottom of the rope, so I transfer to the next rope as fast as I can and keep going.

"Rope!" He warns anyone at the base as he drops the first rope, then glides effortlessly up the second toward me.

Jake's among the top climbers in the Valley. I wish I *could* be drawn to him romantically. We can talk for hours, the way I talk to girlfriends—comparing our screwed-up childhoods, talking about what we want to do if we ever "grow up"—and he's always giving me things, like a gear sling that's too small for him or his favourite wool earflap hat. But I must have read too many Harlequin romances in high school, because I have an image fixed in my brain of a hairy-chested guy who'll scoop me into his arms and rip off my bodice or my harness or whatever, without stopping to ask my permission.

Someone like Max, for instance—the mountain guide from Alaska. He's the latest, totally unexpected, complication to my love life. He doesn't ask.

At the top of the third rope, I unclip and transfer to the fourth. I let myself look down. How long would it take for my body to reach the ground? Five, ten seconds? A wave of dizziness forces my focus back to the rock in front of me. When I took my first lead fall in the spring, here in the Valley, it was only fifteen feet, but I felt like I was never going to stop. It felt like a rite of passage. Like losing your virginity.

"Rope!" The next rope slithers all the way down the face to the ground.

As I slide my jumars rhythmically up the rope, my thoughts stray again to Max—his big dome tent and thick foamy, how he tossed me around like a weightless rag doll. I have to stop to let a shudder travel through my body.

I didn't even like him when I first met him. He's loud and obnoxious and hyper—too much like me. And we look funny together, my five-foot-one-and-a-half to his six-foot-four. But that body... He's lean and dark, with hands the size of dinner plates, a thick mop of black hair, and a bushy moustache under the biggest nose I've ever seen that isn't plastic. He's so... swarthy. So Harlequin. He told me he'd had his eye on me since that humiliating day when I was on my way to a climb with Niccy. I was walking backward, waving at him, and I fell over a log. He said when I popped up laughing, he knew he had to have me. I gave him my usual line—*I'm not looking for a boyfriend*—the same line I gave Jake, but he just laughed and said, "Bullshit."

After a couple of days of fending him off, I gave in one evening while Jake was up on this climb. So my resolution to focus on my climbing and forgo men has lasted approximately two weeks. Something that is becoming a bit of a pattern in my life—if you can even have a pattern at twenty-one.

The fourth rope goes more quickly, but the whole step/slide/reach routine is getting monotonous. In spite of the cooling air, I'm sweaty and hot and my mouth is drier than dust. I shouldn't have had that last chew.

"Rope!" Jake drops another.

"Jake, I need water!"

I expect him to say, "Just wait there, I'll bring it up," in his accommodating fashion, but instead he bellows back, "Just hold on till we get to the top!"

There's something different about Jake today, something in the tone of his voice. He's no longer fawning. His new impatience is almost attractive.

I start to jug up the next rope.

At the next anchor, I'm surprised to find that there's no rope above me. Between my rhythmic jumaring and pornographic fantasies of Max, maybe I've lost count. I clip in and yell, "I'm off!" then hang from the bolts to take the weight off my feet. When I look down I see boulders turned to pebbles, and massive ponderosa pine to shrubs, and my bowel constricts.

When he's halfway up the last rope, Jake yells, "Why'd you stop?"

"I'm at the end."

"You can't be. There are six ropes."

I look back up at the blank rock.

"There's no more rope! I'm at the top of the last one."

"Maybe you can't see it. The last one's black."

"Hey Jake, I'm not blond. I think if there was a rope above me I'd see it."

He ascends the last bit quickly, till he's hanging beside me. He looks up, his face streaming with sweat. "What the fuck?" I watch his colour drain away beneath his tatty red beard.

"Where's the rope?" His voice is hoarse with panic. I've never seen him unravel like this. He sags against the rock. "Jesus fucking Christ!"

"Jake, did you drop our last rope?"

"Jake?"

Jake pounds the rock with his fists till I'm sure he'll draw blood. He pounds and curses and there's nowhere for me to go. We're hanging off the same bolts. But I've been through similar episodes with the men in my family—my dad and brother, one fuelled by Scotch and the other by rum and coke—so I know what to do. I stare off into the valley and let myself detach until I barely register the rage spewing beside me. Tufts of smoke rise from barbeques by the Winnebagos. My stomach growls.

As I wait for Jake to calm down enough to figure out how to save us, the reality of the situation starts to sink in. I'm hanging, clipped by a locking carabiner and one-inch-thick nylon webbing to two bolts, 700 feet up a vertical wall of granite, with no way down. The bolts are drilled 150 feet apart, the length of a climbing rope, which means that with two ropes we could descend. With one rope, we're screwed.

Eventually, Jake pushes a flop of wet hair off his face and looks around. "Mike must have taken the last rope down when he came up for his haul bag. Un-fucking-believable."

The sound of laughter comes wafting up from the base.

"Robbie's still down there with his students!" I lean out from the rock and scream, "Robbie!" I can't see him, but I know he's there.

Jake puts his head in his hands and groans, "This is fucking embarrassing."

"Embarrassing? Are you serious? How else are we going to get down?"

Jake hesitates, then his voice pummels my eardrum. "Robbie!"

Eventually Robbie moves into our view and looks up. Waves both arms above his head.

After Jake is forced to broadcast our predicament to the whole valley, Robbie disappears back with his students. I wait for him to run down the hill through the trees and out to the road, but he doesn't reappear.

"Why isn't he going down?"

"He'll finish up with his clients first."

"You've got to be kidding." I put my forehead on the cooling rock. "So now what?"

"Just let me think."

Refusing to look down, I stare at the wall and think of Max, how safe and protected I felt under his huge body. I wonder if he'll notice when I don't come back, but I've only done two climbs with the guy and one night in the sack. He's as much my boyfriend as Randy or Scottie. A familiar longing jabs at me. Sometimes I crave someone who would notice whether I was dead or alive at the end of the day. Someone who could keep track of me, tether me to the ground so I'd stop floating off on any little breeze that blew my way.

I close my eyes and kiss the rock. *Please keep us safe.*

"The guys can't get to us in the middle of this wall." Jake sounds calmer. "We have to get to that crack system. It's the only way down." He points to a crack in a left-facing corner. It looks very far away to me.

"Maybe we should just wait for a rescue." I have an urge to curl into a ball and hang from the bolts, like a pupa.

"No, we have to get as close to the ground as possible. I'll have to pendulum."

Jake sets up the rope and lowers himself fifty feet. He runs across the rock away from the crack as far and high as he can go, lets gravity swing him back, and sprints toward the crack, straining for it, but it's too far away. He plunges in a long arc below me, runs back to the top of the pendulum, higher than before, then races again across the rock. Again he misses. This goes on and on, until finally he scrabbles at the edge of the crack and his fingertips—conditioned from vertical miles of climbing—clamp down like vise grips. They hold his 180 pounds.

By the time Jake lowers me over to him it's getting dark. He grabs my harness and pulls me toward him to clip me in. I let him. I don't give a shit anymore how tough he thinks I am. I just want to get down alive. Once I settle my feet on the small ledge, the blood rushes back into my legs.

We're both clipped into a single rusted piton poking out from the crack, and a carabiner that Jake has wedged in as a backup. We have no equipment with us to use as anchors to rappel from, so we have to rely on any gear previous parties have left behind.

"How old do you think that thing is?" I ask, rubbing the goosebumps off my bare arms.

"I don't know. Old. Probably put in on the first ascent in the seventies. It's all I could find."

"So now what?"

"I'll keep going down, see if I can find some bolts. You'll have to unclip in case the anchor doesn't hold."

Jake watches me closely to see if I understand. I do, but I wish I didn't. If the anchor fails while Jake descends and we are both clipped to it, his weight will pull me down and we'll both die. If I unclip, just Jake will die, and I'll be clinging to a two-foot ledge in the dark, 600 feet up without an anchor.

"That's fucked."

"I know. Don't move till I tell you to. If it holds my weight, it'll probably hold yours. I'm really sorry. I don't know how I let this happen."

After I unclip, Jake slowly lowers himself onto the rope. Neither of us takes our eyes off the piton. Fear eats at the inside of my belly, nauseates me. I don't want him to die.

"Maybe we should wait!"

"We'll be okay. Just don't move." He forces a smile as he lowers himself below an overhang and out of sight.

On the valley floor, headlights move toward the village, like a procession of fireflies. My legs cramp. I'm thirsty and hungry and can only take tiny little breaths because I'm too scared to move.

You're not as tough as you think you are. That's what Max said to me when I pulled out my tin of tobacco. Maybe he's right.

"Jake!" No answer.

I wrap my arms around myself but can't stop shivering. The rope is still tight from his weight, so he hasn't found an anchor yet. I pinch the piton lightly with my fingers for the false sense of security it gives me. One slip of my feet and I'm gone.

If I had just paid attention while I was jumaring, I could have said something. Before he dropped that last rope. As usual, I just bumbled along with my brain on pause. Even when I go first, I follow.

I call down again.

"Jake!"

The rope goes slack. He's found another anchor.

"Rap down slowly!" His voice is faint.

With the rope through my rappel device, I lower my weight onto the piton. Jake weighs about seventy pounds more than me, so I should be okay, unless his weight shifted the pin and now it's ready to pop. I start to descend into the black night, cringing as the rope runs through my rappel device in quick jerks, putting more strain on the anchor. My jumars and etriers dangle from my harness, clanging against the rock, the only sound except for my breathing—short, quick sips of air.

"Be careful. I barely made it to the anchor." Jake appears just below me and off to the right, still several feet away. Relieved to see him, I descend faster.

"Watch your brake hand! You're going to run out of rope! STOP! NOW!"

As the words rip from his mouth, I feel the tape that marks the ends of the rope and I instinctively squeeze before the last bit of nylon can slip through my rappel device. Three inches. That's all that stands between me and the paper bags of shit at the base that climbers jettison during their multi-day climbs. If Jake hadn't shouted at that moment, I would have rappelled right off the end of the rope.

I hang, over 500 feet up the wall, paralyzed. I don't weigh enough for the rope to stretch those extra few feet to the anchor.

"Jake. What do I do?" To keep from crying, I clench my teeth.

"Just don't move. Don't let go. I'll get to you." I can hear him unclip from the anchor but don't dare move my head. By the time he rigs up a sling and hauls me over to him, I'm shaking like an epileptic.

"It's okay. We have a good anchor now." He clips me into two bolts and I slide my back down the wall to sit on the ledge. My feet dangle into nothingness. Jake sits and puts his arm around me but I can't calm my body. Can't stop the tears.

"I'm so sorry. We'll get down. I promise." He passes me the water and I gulp it down. Terror has sucked up the last of my saliva. "The guys should be here soon, but I think we can get down another pitch."

"I don't think I can move."

"It's okay. We'll take our time."

We watch the headlights creep along far below on the road. I hear the rumble of a car in dire need of a new muffler, just like my own car, Baby Boat, and out of the blue, homesickness explodes in my chest. I want to go home. I want a home to go home to but I can't even narrow "home" down to an address. Home is Canada. Home is my car. The most stable thing in my life right now is a rusted-out Dart that won't start unless I shove a stick in the carburetor to open the choke.

Jake eventually breaks the silence. "Can I ask you something?" His voice is strained.

"What's the matter?"

"I just want to know something." He pauses. "Why Max?"

His dark eyes shine and his mouth twists under his beard. Shame courses through me, like I've been caught screwing around. But Jake's not my boyfriend.

I clear my throat. My mouth is so dry. "I don't know. It just happened."

It just happened. Like everything else in my life. Like hanging off El Cap, without a rope, waiting to be rescued.

Jake removes his arm from around my shoulders. A shiver courses through me as I lose his body heat. "I thought you didn't want a boyfriend."

"I didn't think I did."

"Max is thirty-eight. He's almost old enough to be your father."

"I know."

"He just separated from his wife."

"I know, I know."

Max doesn't seem seventeen years older than me. He's young for his age. Playful. Just the other day he said, "I bet I can bench-press you," and got me to put on my harness so he'd have something to grab on to, then lay on his back and hoisted me into the air like I was a barbell. Jake would have no trouble doing the same thing—I've watched him do endless pull-ups—but the thought wouldn't even occur to him.

"I don't get it," Jake says.

What am I supposed to tell him? *You never bench-press me?*

While I search for the right words, I wonder how he found out, but anyone could have told him. Max does have a nice tent, but a millimetre of ripstop nylon doesn't offer much privacy.

"They're here," Jake announces in a low monotone, as though the zombies have found our hiding spot.

I lean out and look over the edge. The blackness below is punctuated by a procession of headlamps bobbing through the trees. I want to dance on the ledge and yodel, partly because I know that I've survived the night, and partly because I won't have to continue our conversation.

"Thank God. I could use a beer."

"Don't get too excited. It'll take them a couple of hours to climb high enough to shoot us another rope. Hopefully they brought the rope gun with them." Jake stands up. "I'll head down and find another anchor."

Suddenly a blast of white light pins us to the rock, like wild animals caught in headlights. When my eyes adjust, I see two huge spotlights tilted up toward us from the ground; half a dozen bodies flutter around them like moths.

"Hey Jake! What the fuck you doing up there?" someone hollers.

"Jake, you moron! Is this whatcha gotta do to get a date with a chick?"

Jake turns his back to the taunts and sets up to rappel.

I yell down, "You assholes sure took your time! We're freezing our nuts off up here!"

Jake leans out from the rock and starts to descend.

AT TWO in the morning, we walk through a quiet Camp 4. Neither of us speaks. Most of the tents are dark, but the occasional fire still crackles in a campsite, with climbers huddled around in pile jackets and down vests. There's no sign of life in the sagging two-man tent I share with Niccy, nor in Max's big yellow dome beside it. Jake and I say goodnight and he turns to leave, pauses, then comes back and gives me a hug.

"Sorry 'bout the fuck-up."

"Hey, don't worry about it." I punch his arm. "At least now I can say I've been rescued off El Cap."

I wait until he fades into the night, then kneel in front of Max's tent and unzip the door.

Freddie Wilkinson

A SHORT CLIMB
WITH UELI STECK

or
How I discovered the Swiss
Machine was really human after all

THE HIMALAYAS at dawn.

A golden beam of light strikes the summit of Mount Everest. It steadily spreads to the lesser summits of the Khumbu Himal, illuminating one vertical, icy arena after another, seeping down toward the still-darkened valley below. The beam from my partner's headlamp has faded and a glow soon lights Makalu's shark-fin pyramid to the east. We pause to don crampons.

"It does not matter how slow we go," Ueli Steck tells me in clipped English. "Only that we never stop moving."

I'm about to follow perhaps the greatest living solo climber of our age up a mountain wall 800 metres high—roughly two and-a-half times the height of the Empire State Building. Naturally, we will begin by climbing as high as is possible without a rope. If either of us falls, it's understood that he'll die.

Above, the north face of Cholatse points like an arrowhead straight toward the heavens. A faint crease runs down the centre of the face: our line. It's spattered white, the etchings of a thousand spindrift avalanches from a hundred storms. At two-thirds height, this natural pathway is split by an overhanging rock buttress and breaks into two systems: twin ramps rising away from each other to reach the two ridges that bound the northeast face. Both of these variations have been climbed before.

Our plan—or rather, Ueli's plan—is the *direttissima*: to finish straight up the rock buttress in between.

After a few minutes of hiking, the terrain gradually steepens. Instead of carrying our ice axes like walking canes, we begin to plunge the picks directly into the slope in front of us. A streak of névé, seventy degrees steep and marble-smooth, leads over the first cliff band, a 100-foot-high escarpment of shattered rock. Ueli scampers up this section, but as I begin to follow him, some hard-wired mental breaker flips within my frontal lobe. My body surges with energy, yet I move with an inconsistent glitch.

At the top of the first pitch, Ueli casually leans off the tethers connecting his harness to his ice tools to snap a photo of me climbing. I slurp in a deep breath and try to reboot. We move higher, meandering up a fifty- to sixty-degree sheet of alpine ice peppered with small rocks. I find myself following the path of least resistance; Ueli chooses a different line a few feet to my right. We share the occasional word of excitement, but mostly we climb. We keep moving.

Each swing of my tools thuds into the névé like a dart hitting a bull's eye. I'm an experienced climber and I can objectively evaluate every placement I make: each one is "bomber"—completely solid. Even if my other hand and both my feet were to cut simultaneously, I know it will hold. Or so the climber in me says. But the other part of me—the part who is a son, brother, and husband, who loves life dearly and doesn't want it to end—knows that my existence rests on a centimetre or two of steel.

Between my feet I can see the beautiful curve of the mountain wall, sweeping over the lower rock band and down the long, arching snowfield across our tracks to end in a crumpled pinch of talus above an emerald-blue glacial lake.

It wouldn't be a clean fall, but I wouldn't stop, either.

THE WORLD first heard of Ueli Steck in 2002 in the inaugural issue of the magazine *Alpinist*. Ueli, with Canadian Sean Easton, had pulled off an incredible ascent of the east face of Mount Dickey, in the Ruth Gorge of Alaska. In only three days, the pair merged big-wall climbing with cutting-edge mixed techniques—the equivalent of ascending a face half-again as big as El Capitan with ice tools and crampons. Because the ascent was so startling, and occurred on a relatively low-altitude peak lacking big-name stature, it garnered little mainstream attention. Only the true alpine crazies recognized "Blood from the Stone" for what it was: a groundbreaking achievement that heralded the arrival of a new talent.

In the following years, Ueli steadily racked up one of the most impressive and diverse lists of climbing accomplishments in the history of the sport. He soloed 5.13. He redpointed 5.14 on rock, M12 on mixed terrain, and competed in the Ice Climbing World Cup. In the greater ranges, he made several bold attempts to climb the south face of Annapurna, one of the most formidable walls in the great Himalayas, and orchestrated a series of brilliant raids on numerous 6,000-metre peaks scattered around Nepal. Simultaneously, he came within a whisker of making the first "on sight" free ascent of El Capitan in Yosemite Valley.

And all along the way, there was the Eiger. For Steck, who grew up in the country north of Interlaken, the nearby mountain has been home turf since he was a kid. He first climbed its classic North Face—perhaps the most storied alpine route in the world—at the age of eighteen. In 2001, he put up a line of his own on the wall, calling it "The Young Spider." Five years later, in 2006, he returned and soloed the same line in winter. The next year, he turned his attention back to the original route on the Face. The first time he climbed it alone, in 2004, he carried a rope to self-belay on tricky sections and was pleased to make an uneventful ascent in ten hours. Steck kept training and kept getting better. In 2007, he broke the North Face speed record, shaving nearly an hour off the existing record of 4:40 held by Italian Christoph Hainz, bringing it down to 3:54.

Steck was fast becoming a climbing star in the Alps but he was still relatively unknown in the United States. This all changed the next year, in 2008, when he returned again to the Eiger. He was in the best shape of his life. As he later explained, "The [2007] record meant nothing to me—I knew that was not my real best. I had just been faster than the others."

On February 13 of that year, he started the timer on his watch—and began sprinting up the opening snowfields of the North Face. Two hours, 47 minutes, and 33 seconds later, he was on the Eiger's summit, having taken more than an hour off his own record. All within less than a calendar year, he then went on to solo both the north face of the Grandes Jorasses (via the Colton-MacIntyre Route, in 2:21) and the north face of the Matterhorn (via the Schmid Route, in 1:56)— thereby claiming the speed records on the three most iconic faces in Western Europe.

Steck's achievements might still have been lost among the larger outdoor audience were it not for a film about his exploits released in 2010 by the adventure film company

Sender Films. Over the previous decade, Sender's creative partners, Nick Rosen and Peter Mortimer, had established their street cred by capturing the global elite of the climbing world in action. Although similar alpine feats had often been reported "after the deed" in words and photographs, never before had the intense, intensely personal experience of free-soloing up a big mountain face been captured so vividly.

"I grew up in the youth program of the Swiss Alpine Club," Steck deadpans at the start of the movie. "Swiss mountaineers, they're really traditional... if there's one thing, especially: you can't run on crampons," he continues—as the video cuts to several clips of him literally jogging up and down mountainsides, legs pumping more in the manner of a distance runner's measured stride than a technical alpinist's jerky movements.

Later in the film, viewers see Steck's front points skate across the blank slab of the Hinterstoisser Traverse and the pick of one tool pop off a thin limestone edge before settling on a more secure placement. A helicopter-mounted camera, shooting from otherwise impossible angles, illuminates with heart-pumping clarity the insane exposure of the Eiger's nearly 6,000 feet of relief.

It would be hard to conjure an image that better embodies the general public's perception of risk than the final shot of Ueli racing toward the summit ridge. For an audience of the uninitiated, there can only be two explanations for this sort of behaviour: either Ueli Steck is crazy or he is Superman. And throughout the movie, Ueli appears quite sane.

As a finishing touch, Mortimer and Rosen titled their film *The Swiss Machine*. The moniker would stick, and I played a small role in its inception. The two filmmakers, who are friends of mine, had asked me to provide a supporting interview about Steck's ascents. At the time, I knew him only in passing, though as a climber myself I felt qualified to put the immense psychological and physical demands of his solo ascents in perspective.

"Does he sleep?" I asked, rhetorically.

At the end of that interview, Rosen asked if I'd be willing to call Steck "the Swiss Machine" on camera. I thought it an apt description, and I went along with the gag.

By an odd quirk of fate, I ended up climbing with the Machine only six months later.

Sender Films planned to continue documenting Ueli's adventures in the Himalayas the following spring, as he did a series of warm-up climbs with Italian alpinist Simone Moro before attempting a trilogy of 8,000-metre summits. Less than a month before departure, Moro had to drop out. Steck suggested we team up instead.

I had three weeks to train.

IN PERSON, Steck has straw-stock-blond hair and a gap-toothed grin. He is thin but gangly, both taller and longer-limbed than he may first appear, and he walks with a peculiar, pigeon-toed gait. Among strangers and new acquaintances, he smiles often and says little. He seems shy.

We rendezvoused in the Khumbu Valley in early March of 2011. Steck's expedition strategy this time around derived from one of his mentors, the great Swiss alpinist Erhard Loretan. In 1990, Loretan, with fellow national Jean Troillet and Polish legend Wojciech Kurtyka, climbed back-to-back new routes on both Cho Oyu (the sixth-highest mountain in the world) and Shishapangma (the fourteenth-highest). Steck's goal was to knock off both summits and then move on to Everest, a trifecta that had never before been accomplished in a single season.

Once you've acclimatized for one 8,000-metre peak, you might as well do more: so his thinking went. Although Steck would be approaching the three big peaks from Tibet, he had come to the Khumbu Valley first for a month of acclimatization before moving on to the windswept Tibetan plateau.

"There are no shortcuts to climbing above 8,000 metres," Steck told me, one hand karate-chopping the air in a quick motion to accentuate the point. Steck often speaks in short declaratives and employs illustrative gestures. The more time you put in at moderate altitude, he explained—say, 4,000 or 5,000 metres—the stronger you will be. The Khumbu, with its pleasant Sherpa villages replete with German bakeries, juniper-scented guest houses, and intermittent Wi-Fi signals, made for a far more convivial environment to recover in between training climbs.

On a rest day in Namche, I watched as Ueli, clad in trail-running gear and white wrap-around shades, left our hostel for a casual training run. He clattered down an alley past a few yaks and then took a left turn up the town's endless, terraced flights of stone stairs, past a gang of western hikers labouring with oversized packs. The trail up the Khumbu Valley is probably the most popular trekking route in the Himalayas, a major physical endeavour in its own right for legions of mountain enthusiasts the world over. When people saw Steck coming up the path, easily jogging past them as they gasped for breath, whole cattle trains of tourists stopped to stare.

Steck enjoys the Khumbu for more than just its training environment. It reminds him of his own heritage—his home, the Jungfrau region of Switzerland, where he cut his teeth as a young alpinist and still pushes the limits. "You can do everything in my valley," he says. "We have year-around sport-climbing; we have the Eiger." The Jungfrau's tightly bundled network of trains, roads, huts, and lifts provides seamless access to all manner of mountain terrain.

Although we held permits for two 6,000-metre peaks, our expedition had no base camp per se. We would stay in tea lodges along the main Everest trekking route, beginning each ascent by striking out directly in the early morning from a comfortable bed—a style not dissimilar to how one might embark upon a climb in the Alps.

Steck also made an unexpected pronouncement.

"If you do not stop this kind of solo climbing," he told me, referring to his speed climbs in the Alps, "It will kill you. No question." His hand chopped in another definitive gesture as he spoke. Ueli had resolved to step away from high-end soloing. His partner on all three 8,000-metre climbs would be Don Bowie, a Canadian-American with two 8,000-metre summits already to his credit, including K2.

Of course, "solo climbing" doesn't kill anyone; soloists kill themselves. This, I realized as we prepared for our ascent, was the deeper conundrum Ueli faced: here he was, an elite-level athlete in the prime of his career—someone who had already achieved so much, such a highly specialized statement of physical excellence in the uncompromising face of death—gradually realizing that he could only reach his ultimate potential by sacrificing his life to the sport.

In short, Ueli Steck needed a vacation. He had come to the Himalayas that spring seeking new horizons. He sought to push his cardiovascular limits on the highest peaks on Earth; but he was not seeking the same level of mortal danger he'd faced on his speed ascents in the Alps.

There was one problem.

Alpine climbing is not black and white. It's balancing one set of risks against another, a continuum of weighing a set of rewards against the likelihood of drawbacks should one fail. Whether tied into a rope or untethered, climbing alone or in the company of another, the danger in the situation hinges on the character of the participants rather than on the style of climbing they choose.

I STOP a thousand feet up Cholatse. We have been cruising, moving up casual grade II mixed terrain. Now, above us, a vertical passage looms. The frozen flow narrows to a single channel only a body-length wide; the colour of its surface changes subtly, from a de-saturated blue to an opaque white. I know I have reached my limit.

In fact, Ueli and I had discussed this precise set of circumstances—specifically, that we might reach a point in our climb where I'd feel unequipped to continue without a belay, yet might be sucked into following him into the void beyond.

"We will use the rope when you want, Freddie," he had assured me.

I look at the pitch now facing me. It takes me less than two seconds to assure Ueli I am ready for the rope. His shoulders give a barely perceptible shrug. The rope comes out.

There is no need to discuss who will lead, either. "You can film, I will lead," Ueli had told me before the climb.

Ueli ties in and proceeds to sprint up the pitch. At the steep bit, where the angle tilts a few degrees and the colour changes imperceptibly, he pauses to grunt—and continues on, with nary a piece of protection between us. Sixty metres above me, Ueli runs out of rope and builds a belay.

The opaque white isn't Styrofoam ice. It's mashed potatoes—"snice," compacted snow of nebulous consistency. You might find placements to bear a portion of your weight, but if your feet were to cut, your tools would not hold. I don't second-guess my decision one bit.

"That was more tricky than I was expecting." Ueli shrugs again at the top of the pitch.

He continues to lead; I continue to film.

A rope, like any tool, is only as effective as the user makes it. Steck seldom places more than two or three pieces of protection, which means that a fall would probably leave him badly maimed: a broken ankle at the least and perhaps much worse. This is par for the course in high-stakes alpine climbing. Even if one were inclined to take the time to stop and place more gear, the terrain itself affords scant opportunities. Legions of alpinists have sketched their way up similar passages; Steck himself had previously climbed this face, solo, in 2004. What struck me was how he moved without hesitation or doubt. He was unquestionably in the zone.

We gain height quickly, following a zigzag path across runnels of ice as a cloudy sky slowly wraps around us. We are more than halfway up the face when the first flakes begin to fall.

IT IS TEMPTING to attribute much of Ueli Steck's temperament to his Swiss-German background—something he himself will allude to in good-natured fashion.

"You know, I am Swiss, so I like to wake up in bed, drink an espresso, go climbing, and return home on time for dinner," he often jokes. His website states that he "emphasizes himself through his great self control."

Yet even by the standards of his own culture, Steck is an intensely focused individual—the kind of person who naturally unwinds alone rather than socializing with other people. The more I got to know him, the more I realized he was not really shy but an unapologetic introvert, somebody quite comfortable in his own skin. One-on-one or with close friends, or when discussing matters of mutual interest, he is open, engaged, and friendly. Yet he has little tolerance for idle chitchat, the kind of superficial human interaction we Americans excel at.

"I'm not into a lot of 'blah-blah-blah,'" he explains, one hand pantomiming a sock-puppet mouth opening, closing, and opening again. "I like to be alone, sometimes."

Steck credits his family with his work ethic. The youngest of three boys, he compelled himself to keep up with his older siblings. "We grew up in this small Swiss town, and ice hockey was just the sport to do..." he reminisces. "My father was strict, but to play ice hockey, he was always fully behind us, my parents always supported us." When Steck's athletic imagination turned toward climbing, his dad had only one piece of advice. "He said, 'I don't care what you do, but I'm happy when you do something, and not just hang around... but I'll tell you something: if you do a sport, you should try to do it as good as you can.'"

Steck did his mandatory service in the Swiss army, where a bit of a rebellious streak surfaced—he occasionally smuggled fresh bread and pastries to his unit when the opportunity presented itself. After finishing his time, he found work as a carpenter and climbed as often as possible. The noted Canadian climber Will Gadd remembers meeting him on a summer trip he made to the Canadian Rockies around 2002 and cheerfully recalls one near-miss Steck experienced while descending from a climb in the Bugaboos. "Ueli dropped his headlamp about fifty feet down into a bergschrund; unfortunately, Ueli was attached to his headlamp," he told an audience at the 2009 Banff Mountain Film and Book Festival, "and he broke a few ribs. Stephen Holeczi, Josh Briggs, and one other climber ended up rescuing him, which they often point out."

Soon after, Gadd and his wife Kim Csizmazia stayed with Ueli in Switzerland while competing in the 2001 World Ice Climbing Competition. "Ueli's climbing results at that time were not impressive," recounted Gadd, "but I have never seen anyone try so hard while training and climbing. He was already beating himself from normal metal into the iron of a superhero."

Hard work, tempered with the occasional unexpected brush with death: these two themes pop up again and again in Steck's athletic career.

In 2005, while making the first free-solo of Excalibur, a 5.10d rock climb in Switzerland, he arrived safely on the summit—only to find that the harness and rope he had stashed for the mandatory rappel descent had been ravaged by mice. Steck cobbled together enough uncompromised sections of rope to get off the mountain pillar alive. "We Swiss like to plan for everything, and this was not something I had planned for," he told journalist Martin Gutmann at the time.

In 2007, he launched up the south face of Annapurna, hoping to solo the massive alpine face, one of Himalayan alpinism's most fearsome challenges. Less than a thousand feet into the climb, an errant stone fell from the mountain above and struck him in the head. Steck came to at the base of the face, helmet smashed and body bruised but otherwise fine, having fallen an estimated 200 metres.

"It was important for me to understand whether I was pushing it too hard, or whether it had just come down to bad luck," Steck later told journalist Tim Neville. "I decided in the end it was just bad luck."

It was also in 2007 that Ueli redoubled his training. Indeed, there would be no room for unconsolidated snow, unexpected squalls, or bad luck in general on his next round of ascents. Speed alpinism, as he has freely acknowledged, is more a daring athletic performance—mountain as racecourse—than an act of throwing oneself at the unknown wilderness. "I have always considered myself an athlete rather than an adventurer," he wrote on his blog.

In preparation for his Eiger speed rematch, for example, Ueli was coached by Simon Trachsel of the Swiss Olympic Medical Center through a year of intensive, periodized training. As his physical condition began to peak the following winter, he ruthlessly dropped weight from his frame to reach an optimal 141 pounds. Steck and Trachsel calculated he had a two-week window in which to make an attempt before his body would inevitably weaken.

Favourable conditions prevailed that season on the Eiger, but Steck knows all too well that this kind of luck will one day run out; hard work can only protect you for so long. Pierre Béghin, one of the greatest French alpinists of his day, was killed on the south face of Annapurna in 1992. Béghin's young partner, Jean-Christophe Lafaille, survived to become a leading soloist himself, only to be lost and killed while attempting to solo Makalu in 2005. Tomaž Humar, a leading Slovenian soloist, died in 2009.

"When I look at Tomaž Humar, you know, he had his Dhaulagiri," Steck says, referring to the Slovenian's most notable achievement. "And after... he tried to keep up with that."

AFTER TEN or more pitches of ascent, a 100-metre step of vertical climbing leads to the upper wall. The ice has sublimated away from the rock underneath: it's hollow and vibrates like a steel drum with each swing of the axe. Ueli runs out of rope, but he's in the midst of a long run-out, far from easy ground. The terrain affords no opportunities for reliable protection. I have no choice but to remove the anchor and begin climbing myself to generate slack for him to continue. We simul-climb for a hundred feet before he drills in a reliable ice screw and puts me on belay.

We've arrived at a fork in the road: the overhanging buttress looms directly overhead. Easier lines of escape ramp off to either side. The wispy contrails of a spindrift avalanche appear from the clouds above us. It's already mid-afternoon, and we are both thinking the same thing.

"Straight, to the right, there are good pinnacles," Ueli says, pointing at a corniced-topped fluting poking out of the murk above.

Our home for the night is a narrow ice ledge the size and shape of a sectional sofa. We hack into the slope with our tools in a vain attempt to make it flat. There's enough room for us both to lie down, but we don't trust the arrangement enough to untie from the rope. Two inches of snow has collected on my bag by the time the sun sets and the mountain plunges into darkness.

The snow has stopped when we wake the next morning, but soon after sunrise, clouds return to the face. We made it through the bivvy in relative comfort, but another night wouldn't be much fun. Rappelling what we've already climbed wouldn't be a good idea, either: there aren't enough reliable cracks in the rock, nor is there enough solid water-ice from which to craft reliable anchors. Over instant coffee and granola bars we discuss the situation and our goal of climbing the *direttissima* shifts to making it up and over the mountain by the path of least resistance.

Ueli leads on, up a steep rib of unconsolidated snow and mixed steps. There's barely any protection, but Ueli continues to fire. I belay and watch as he swims up a long patch of seventy-degree rotten snow, moving back and forth from one foot to the other like a prize fighter finding his rhythm. I've only experienced that kind of confidence on a handful of days myself, though I've seen it often in other partners. But normally, people get tired—you go all guns blazing to lead a few pitches of terrain, and then you bonk and let your partner take over. What's striking about Ueli isn't that he climbs at a notably higher standard than many of his peers, but that he is capable of maintaining such high performance for so long.

What's truly impressive about Ueli, I realize, is that he's always *on*.

We reach Cholatse's 6,440-metre summit after six hours of climbing, and immediately we begin tromping toward our descent route, the southwest face, as fast as crampons will allow.

This is familiar ground for me, too, having climbed Cholatse from this side a decade earlier. We scramble down a few hundred metres of steep penitentes, across a rock tower, and down a steep, snowy couloir. By late afternoon, we're on a glacier, winding through a small icefall toward the Gokyo Valley below.

"There's one more ice wall we will need crampons for," Ueli says, shouldering his pack after a quick water break. From somewhere deep in my memory bank, a recollection sparks.

"No, Ueli," I say. "If we cross the glacier here, there's a climber trail on the other side of the moraine."

Ueli looks at me and then continues in the same direction as before, but I'm certain I'm right. "We came this way in 2001," I say. "Trust me, Ueli."

Finally, the Swiss Machine is willing to let me lead.

THE WORST climbing accident of Ueli's life occurred in August, 2010. Strangely, it occurred on the Wetterhorn, a peak in his home region of the Jungfrau, rather than on a far-flung Himalayan giant; and the accident befell not him, but his partner that day: thirty-year-old Nicole Steck, his wife, a passionate climber in her own right. As the couple hiked up a casual approach trail toward the mountain, the path passed next to a waterfall. For a few metres, the footing was damp. He watched as Nicole slipped off and fell thirty metres.

The accident momentarily made headlines and Twitter feeds across Switzerland, media attention that was appalling to Ueli's sense of privacy. Although Nicole has since made a full recovery, it's obvious to those who know him that the experience, more than any other of his near-misses, has left Steck a changed man.

"Fuck, I'm thirty-five, and maybe, you know, I had already the high point of my career, it's possible I cannot top it," he confessed to me near the end of our trip. "You have to accept that, and go the way of it, or otherwise you get really strange and weird."

At the same time, he recognizes that on his best solos, he never thought he could fall. "You're not expecting you could die up there. You just think: no problem, I do it. I just go for it, and I do it. It's not like I might not make it back, and I don't care."

The temptation to "just go for it" will likely remain within Ueli's character for the rest of his life. Indeed, he occasionally sounds like a recovering addict when he talks about his sport. "It's my character, my whole life ... I was so committed; you shouldn't be so committed your whole life, otherwise it's a dead end.

"I've been working for two years to get away from this solo climbing. Because it's dangerous, if you do it too long, if you do it too much, you're gonna die, for sure. You can look to the history, and all these climbers die at some point.

"I had this situation last fall, conditions were so great on the Eiger. It would be easier, I make the decision Monday, go take the car Tuesday morning, and I'm back for lunch, no big calling up friends ... I really had to say 'no, you're not going alone.' So, I start to try to find a friend, and it came up I had an old friend, a mountain guide. I ended up phoning him up and we went and it was so much fun.

"But I had to make the step—picking up the phone."

POSTSCRIPT: *Ueli and I parted ways in Kathmandu. He rendezvoused with Don Bowie and crossed by jeep into Tibet, and I flew to Alaska. Arriving at Shishapangma base camp first, he and Bowie proceeded directly to an advance camp at the foot of the south face. After his time in the Khumbu, Steck felt acclimatized and ready. Bowie, who had not spent any time acclimatizing beforehand, knew he would need several weeks to prepare. With his partner's blessing, Steck launched up the face alone.*

He was on the summit ten and a half hours later. "I promised my wife not to do any solos anymore. But this is not really a solo," he wrote on his blog. "In this area a roped party would not really belay. You would lose too much time and it is not really necessary. I thought I could do it, and I could already see the exit."

The team moved on to Cho Oyu, where Steck and Bowie together made a relaxed, multi-day ascent via its normal route. While he was on the mountain, Erhard Loretan, Steck's old mentor, who had climbed both Shishapangma and Cho Oyu in a single expedition, was killed climbing in France. It was Loretan's fifty-second birthday.

Finally focusing on Everest, Steck and Bowie made a high bivouac on May 20 and set out for the summit at nine P.M. Bowie turned back at 8,000 metres when his feet began to freeze. Steck continued on, weaving through groups of commercial clients trudging along using supplemental oxygen. Above the third step, he paused. A passing climbing Sherpa told him he was less than an hour from the summit. But there was no sensation left in his toes.

"For a moment I have thought to ask a sherpa if I could breathe ten minutes of oxygen, then I would have had again warm feets," Steck wrote. "But then I would have stood on another peak." Steck resisted the urge to just go for it, turned around, and returned home to Switzerland. He had come within a whisker of pulling off the trifecta.

Don Gillmor

THE DESCENT OF MAN

I STOOD UNDER a cloudless sky near the peak of Mont Fort, staring at the glaciers of the Grand Combin, shining like starched sheets. Mont Fort, at Verbier, Switzerland, is one of the steepest ski runs in Europe. Most of the people who rode up on the tram went back down on it. My friend Ken and I had come to Europe to ski and escape ourselves. We were in our fifties, a shadowy decade. Looking down at the canton of Valais, I felt a combination of exhilaration and fear and simple awe. The world laid out, endless in its possibilities. The price, though, was a treacherous descent. It was late in the season and the moguls were large, rutted from spring thaws, and shiny with ice. A few skiers picked their way down carefully, making long, hesitant traverses across the hill.

We stood in that familiar lacuna, waiting for the right moment to go down, a moment when the path was clear, when courage was high. After several minutes, Ken launched himself. On the second turn, he crossed his skis and fell.

He slid quickly on the ice. Both skis blew off, then both poles. He hurtled down the steep hill headfirst, picking up speed, his helmeted head bouncing off the moguls. It occurred to me that he might not stop until the bottom, more than 300 metres below. There was a crevasse near the bottom, off to the side. It was marked with colourful racing poles to warn skiers away.

Beside me, near the tramline, were the remnants of a speed course that had been set up a month earlier. Speed skiing means simply getting into a tuck and going as fast as possible. The skis are 240 centimetres long, and specific aerodynamic helmets and clothing have been developed for this rarified sport. There are only about thirty courses in the world.

Speed skiing requires a very steep start and a long run out. The fastest anyone has ever gone on a pair of skis is 251.4 kilometres an hour, achieved by an Italian, Simone Origone. What is remarkable is that he reached that velocity in fifteen seconds, roughly as fast as the 690 horsepower Lamborghini Aventador—which gets to 250 km/h in 14.4 seconds. It was Origone who set the course record at Verbier with a speed of 219 km/h.

When I was young, speed was a visceral affirmation, an extension of my natural optimism (that I wouldn't crash, that I would live forever), and part of my inchoate search for limits and meaning. But speed had become something else in middle age. I still sought it; as a way to prolong youth, perhaps. Yet skiing had become a balance between hope and fear—the hope that it would preserve me, that it would amplify my existence, and the fear that it might do the opposite.

Ken had managed to get himself turned around so that his feet were pointing downhill. People stopped to watch him, a Gore-Tex missile heading toward the crevasse. His boots sent up sprays of snow as he rocketed down. The late morning sun was brilliant. Had we waited another hour or so, the hill would have softened up.

Ken skied, he had told me, to take himself out of his own head, a head that was filled with screenplays, resentment, political rants, women, and, more than anything, himself. A head that struggled to contain an expansive ego that now flowed over the moguls 100 metres below.

The act of skiing is instinctive and ultimately solitary and at a certain age it provides welcome relief from our thoughts, our mortgages and disappointments. We were both aware that there wouldn't be many more years of skiing like this. We could ski into old age, but it would be something else again.

Switzerland was having a nervous year. More than half of Verbier was closed, a brown ring around the bottom of the resort. While it was late April, this was still unusual. Swiss glaciers, like glaciers everywhere, were in retreat; they lost eighteen percent of their surface between 1985 and 2000. Seventy percent of them could be gone in the next three decades. The glaciers feed the Swiss river system, and half of the country's power is hydroelectric. Low river levels will affect energy, transportation, and the many ingenious farms scattered through the valleys and crawling up the mountainside.

Swiss ski resorts have already felt the effects of glacial retreat. In 2005, Andermatt wrapped the disappearing Gurschen glacier in a protective foil made of polyester and polypropylene, designed to keep the sun off and the cold in. Mont Fort followed suit.

Standing at the top of Mont Fort in the perfect spring sun, the snow receding below me, Ken slowing down, I wondered if the sport would die before I did. Perhaps we would all go together.

Two hundred and fifty metres below me, Ken finally came to a stop. He lay motionless for more than a minute, then one arm rose and weakly waved, indicating he was alive, at least. His head wasn't occupied with the messy details of his life now. He was mentally gauging the pain, tracking its source and intensity. Was anything broken? Had the helmet saved him from concussion? He had a bad back that was now much worse. He had knee issues, a sore wrist, a lifelong case of existential angst, and he travelled with a cache of celebrity-grade painkillers that would come in handy.

I started down, stopping to pick up his skis and poles, moving carefully on the ice, muscles straining, my head empty of conscious thought, reduced to a purely physical being, focused on survival.

I LEARNED to ski on a small hill perched inconveniently on the endless Canadian prairie. Mount Agassiz had a modest vertical of about 150 metres. It featured one T-bar and a rope tow that, in memory, ran off the flywheel of a tractor and was operated by a grumpy farmer who cursed us when we fell off or slid backward on the ice. The hill was a three-hour drive from Winnipeg and rarely seemed to be warmer than -20°F; we had to stop every half hour to warm up in the modest chalet. From the summit you could see conifers and low scrub and hardscrabble farmland that had been cultivated a century earlier by hopeful immigrants. My Scottish great-grandfather had tried to farm to the east, but finally gave up on that impossible land and moved to the city to become a minister in a particularly pessimistic branch of Calvinism (called, paradoxically, the Free Presbyterians).

Mount Agassiz took its name from Jean Louis Rodolphe Agassiz, a nineteenth-century Swiss geologist who was the first to suggest that the Earth had experienced an ice age. He argued that this ice age had replaced the biblical deluge; that it wiped out all (sinful) life, which then began anew. Agassiz kept his faith and resisted Darwin's evolutionary theory for his entire life. But the mountain named after him was formed during the Pleistocene epoch, when glaciers ploughed through Manitoba, leaving a few upturned hills that were gradual on the side where the ice was advancing and dropped off sharply where the ice had pulled down huge slabs of rock as it went by. Geologically, this glacial till plain was an unlikely spot for a ski resort.

When we were seventeen, a group of us drove 1,500 kilometres across the frozen plain to ski at Lake Louise in the Rocky Mountains. Going up the Olympic chairlift, staring back at the immense scale of the valley and the Slate Range that stretched beyond it, I saw not just the possibilities of the sport, but the possibilities of life. Chief among them was the concept of freedom. In part it was the post-adolescent freedom of being on the road, of being in another place, unsupervised. But the summit of Lake Louise invited a larger sense of freedom, a phenomenological escape that changed my sense of the physical world. And there was the simple joy of that speed, the harmless physics of the prairie given way to something else.

Our Banff trip was a collage of hard skiing and wasted nights. Our lack of success with the few girls we met was epic. We turned to adolescent stunts, locking one of our number out of the hotel room, naked. We drank beer in crowded taverns and wished we were dancing with girls and stayed until closing time, hoping for a miracle, and woke up at 7 A.M. and ate pancakes and caught the first lift up.

None of us returned to Mount Agassiz. It was irretrievably diminished by then, a fondly remembered childhood relic. The following year I moved to Calgary and started skiing seriously, getting out fifty days or more each year. But after six years, even the yawning scale of the Banff area became too familiar. It began to feel as finite as Mount Agassiz had.

In 1978, after graduating from university, I went to France to ski. In the Grenoble train station I met a man my age wearing a ski jacket who told me that Val d'Isère was the place to go; that's where he was heading. He looked like Robert

Redford and introduced himself as Bob. He had seen the Redford film *Downhill Racer* several times and had adopted the star's mannerisms. Occasionally he'd act a scene from the movie without crediting it.

At the time, *Downhill Racer* was a touchstone for a certain kind of skier. Redford's character, David Chappellet, was a perfect late-sixties anti-hero, handsome and aloof and a bit of a shit. The movie trailer had a voiceover that asked the quasi-existential question, "How far must a man go to get from where he's at?" *Downhill Racer* was a gritty, European-looking film, and I wanted to be like Redford, though not as badly as my new friend Bob did.

I spent the whole season in Val d'Isère, living in the basement of a massive eighteenth-century stone house with Bob and a handful of expatriates. The scale of the resort was immense; we could ski to other villages, to Italy.

Going up a large tram one day, a man who turned out to be from Brooklyn recognized me as North American and said, "Want to take a walk on the wild side?" In an urban setting, this could mean a number of different, largely uncomfortable things. But here it meant he knew the secret location of some incredible powder-filled bowl. So I followed. We climbed and traversed for three hours from where the lift let us off, into Italy, sweating heavily and panting in the thin air.

We finally arrived at a massive, very steep, untouched bowl. We hurtled down, floating in the bottomless powder. The run took less than two minutes, but that speed and the ethereal sensation of moving through the light powder made it feel longer, a suspension of not just gravity, but time. A thrill. The sensation of weightlessness made me feel I had transcended my physical self.

The freedom, the possibilities of life that I'd first felt at Lake Louise were all magnified in Val d'Isère. Just over the mountain was the world conjured by my literary imagination: Paris and Spain and doomed love affairs with tragic Europeans.

In spring my peripatetic Calgary girlfriend flew over and the tenor of my expatriate life changed. We skied and argued, then left for Italy. We ended up in Greece, admitting finally that our relationship, which had been pretty much defined by break-ups, wasn't working. She decided to fly home and I stayed in Athens. After she got in the taxi to the airport, I walked to the harbour and sat on the hard sand of a vast, empty industrial beach. On the horizon, a figure approached in the heat shimmer, a woman carrying something. It turned out to be a wooden box, filled with cigarettes, which she carried with the aid of a neck strap, the kind that cigarette girls in 1930s nightclubs used to have. She stood over me. "Cigarette?" she said in a heavy accent. She was perhaps forty, and her legs, which were at my eye level, had small bruises on them. I bought a package of Marlboros and sat on the deserted beach smoking, pondering the end of my relationship with my girlfriend, and what proved to be the effective end of my relationship with skiing for the next decade.

BACK IN CANADA, I moved east, where skiing withered amid the dwarfish hills of Ontario. I was trying to be a writer, and my world became almost exclusively urban. On those few occasions that I did get out skiing, I was reminded of Mount Agassiz and its limitations and the whole experience depressed me. Years went by without getting out on a hill.

In my thirties, I inched back to the sport, going to Quebec a few times. But by my forties, something else had changed. One March I drove to Jay Peak, Vermont, where a large thermometer at the top of the hill informed me it was 61°F. The snow was heavy and wet, and it was like skiing through peanut butter. A storm of tropical force that had been lurking on the other side of the mountain suddenly released a hard rain. Those of us who wanted to persevere were issued green garbage bags with armholes.

By fifty, both winter and myself were getting unreliable. I couldn't count on snow, and I couldn't count on my ability to negotiate some of the runs that had once thrilled me. Skiing claims to be our oldest sport (a 5,000-year-old ski was found in Sweden) and now it is showing its age. The sport and I appear to be going through some of the same issues: doubt, deterioration, financial worries, environmental dread. As I lose strength and stamina the glaciers retreat in solidarity, the snow dries up, the resorts dwindle. The number of U.S. ski resorts dropped from 727 in 1985 to 485 in 2008. Mount Agassiz closed in 2000, though I didn't hear about it for another decade.

As the esteemed glaciologist Lonnie Thompson has warned us, glaciers are disappearing at an accelerating rate. Kilimanjaro—that Hemingwayesque symbol of mortality and loss—could vanish entirely within a decade. Ninety-nine percent of the glaciers in the Alps are in retreat. "As a result of our inaction," Thompson wrote in his 2010 article in the journal *Climate Change: The Evidence and Our Options*, "we have three options: mitigation, adaptation, and suffering." Not coincidentally, these are the three options that late middle age offers.

LOUIS AGASSIZ was the first glaciologist, before the word was coined, his reputation made with the publication in 1840 of his two-volume *Études sur les glaciers*. He described the landscape transformed by glacial activity as if it were a woman's body, with a breathless and detailed *pensée* on the striations and valleys, the rounding and hollows, the cruel results of time and friction. Agassiz wasn't a brilliant scientist; he mostly synthesized what was already out there, including the work of colleagues who were uncredited. He was an adept promoter, a quality that flowered after he moved from Switzerland to the U.S. and embraced marketing as a faith. Although his fame didn't last, he became one of the best-known scientists in the world.

The mid-nineteenth century was the golden age of glaciers, and Agassiz's work spurred a taste for both exploration and research. Glaciers were mysterious, holding ancient secrets, and the Industrial Revolution had yet to begin its carbon-spewing assault in earnest. And they'd seized the imagination of English Romantic poets, who saw in them a spiritual grandeur, an expression of the sublime.

Agassiz's reputation climbed quickly and brightly but then quietly subsided in middle age. He refused to embrace Charles Darwin's evolutionary theories, and held to the increasingly discredited idea that species remained identical throughout history. Agassiz also adhered to Catastrophism, a school of thought advocated by his former teacher, the French paleontologist Georges Cuvier. Catastrophism stipulated that the earth's timeline was short, and defined by violent events that produced severe climate change and resulted in extinctions. Cuvier was careful never to link his theory to religion—none of his papers refers to Noah and the Flood. But Agassiz made the link, viewing glaciation as the event that did the Flood's—God's—work, equal parts geology and miracle. Scientifically, he was left behind.

Before the end of the century, Agassiz's ideas were replaced by the prosaically named theories of Uniformitarianism and Gradualism, which posited that geologic change occurs slowly over long periods of time.

But Agassiz may have the last laugh, now that Catastrophism has come back under another name—climate change. At the time he published his seminal study of glaciers, the Colum-bia Icefield that is located at the northern border of Banff National Park was roughly twice the size it is now. In geologic terms, 187 years is a blink. But the glacier has retreated 1.5 kilometres since then.

The implications are profound, and not just for tourists and hikers. The Columbia Icefield is actually a collection of thirty glaciers, and the meltwater from them feeds three oceans, the Pacific, the Atlantic, and the Arctic. It is the hydroponic apex of North America, the kingpin of continental glaciers. It is no exaggeration to call its retreat a catastrophe.

Glaciers don't melt at arithmetic rates. As they become smaller and their bulk provides less defense against the warm-ing climate, and as more detritus is exposed and its darker hue attracts more sun, they melt at something that is closer to a geometric rate. Like certain people, one day they are suddenly old. You saw them only a year ago. And now, in the glare of the supermarket, there they are, the face subtly collapsing, a blur-riness, a weight in the eyes that hadn't been there before. Or perhaps it had always been there, but you just hadn't noticed it.

THE YEAR I turned fifty, a scattered group of old friends reconnected via email and decided to return to Banff to ski. We came from Winnipeg, from Vancouver, San Francisco, Hong Kong. I flew out from Toronto. I hadn't seen some of them in thirty years. We caught up, reminisced. We recalled making fake IDs by photocopying a paper version of a class-mate's birth certificate and using Wite-Out to eliminate his name. We made multiple copies of the blank version, typed in various whimsical aliases, soaked the paper in tea to age it, put them in a dryer, then ironed creases into them. With these small masterpieces we were able to get into the Voyageur

Tavern and see a 300-pound stripper named U.C. Moore wrap her giant panties around a friend's head, scaring all of us.

There were missing friends too. A suicide, and the usual complement of tragedy, medical issues, alcoholism, divorce, and debt.

I was long married, the father of two, in reasonable shape. I had a touch of plantar fasciitis, a small arthritic spur on my hip, and an ongoing bout of existential nausea. "Something has happened to me," Jean Paul Sartre wrote in *Nausea*; "It came as an illness does, not like an ordinary certainty, not like anything obvious. It installed itself cunningly, little by little; I felt a little strange, a little awkward... I was able to persuade myself that there was nothing wrong with me, that it was a false alarm. And now it has started blossoming."

This confronting of existence alights at some point, a quiet argument that we carry within us. Where is this all headed? The answer too obvious to state out loud.

Skiing was a perfect, if temporary distraction. The act of negotiating a steep hill requires concentration. And unlike many other sports, it doesn't force you into the unpalatable head of your opponent. It is pure experience.

Both Sunshine and Lake Louise had expanded dramatically since I'd last visited, twenty years earlier. The forty-five-minute wait at the Olympic chairlift was gone; the high-speed lifts eliminated line-ups. The frequent breakdowns that had left us swaying in bitter crosswinds for nervous lengths of time were also mercifully gone. We were still good skiers, among the better skiers on the hill, but that was because everyone under the age of forty was on a snowboard. We were part of an evolutionary slow fade.

At lunch the next day, my friend Martin checked his phone constantly for news of pending interest-rate hikes. His nickname was Captain Leverage, I was told, due to his heroic relationship with debt. He had stayed in Winnipeg and when his father died he'd taken over the family manufacturing business. I remembered his taciturn father washing his Cadillac in the driveway, his beautiful mother pouring vodka over Tang crystals in the kitchen.

Neale was the only one on a snowboard, though it wasn't a nod to hipness or progress. He'd had a leg injury that made skiing painful, but somehow allowed for boarding. He had aged very little, and was married to his high school sweetheart, the woman he'd been dating when I left Winnipeg thirty-three years earlier. His life seemed miraculously intact, though this was an illusion. There had been two previous marriages, three kids, and two divorces.

I spent time with Paul, my closest adolescent friend, who was now a successful developer in Vancouver. In the mornings, as he drove the rented SUV up to the mountain, he would phone his father, who was in a nursing home with Alzheimer's, talking to him in cheerful, repetitive tones.

Paul and I recalled a summer night out at the lake when he was behind the wheel of his mother's Thunderbird, an otherwise responsible boy, heading for law school, racing wildly on the Number One highway in the dead of night. Trying to pass a white Grand Prix on a blind hill, that reckless teenage faith. The memory still brought an unsettling frisson of mortality.

All of our worlds held secrets now. Certainly that had been true of an absent friend who had killed himself by driving a jet boat into a bridge support on the Red River. He had managed to keep his world contained until that last desperate act. This anarchy lies in many of us, I suspect; not necessarily suicidal ideation, but the anarchy of a mind overburdened by disappointment and doubt, or simply time. The hill had been a testing ground for us when we were young, a release of pent-up energies. It was more relief now, the visceral experience of skiing displacing other thoughts and worries. Another kind of freedom.

IN 2004, the European Project for Ice Coring in Antarctica drilled to a depth of 3,270 metres, providing a geologic record that goes back 800,000 years. The methane and CO_2 that are trapped in bubbles in the ice provide a record of carbon emissions that stretches back to the mid-Pleistocene epoch. During glacial periods, CO_2 concentrations varied between 180-190 parts per million by volume (ppmv). During warmer phases, that figure rose to roughly 280. After the Industrial Revolution, CO_2 concentrations showed a spike. Then, from 1975 to 2005, emissions increased seventy percent. The current concentration of CO_2 is 391 ppmv, the highest in eight hundred millennia. If this trend continues, the sport of skiing may erode at a rate that is faster than the glaciers.

Switzerland noted a 3.7 percent decline in skier visits in 2012. At Whistler, the 2001 figure of 2.3 million skiers dropped to 1.7 in 2009. The 2011/2012 season in the U.S. started with the weakest snowfall in twenty years, which prompted a 15.7 percent decline in skiers from the previous year.

Snow conditions are increasingly unpredictable, though partly mitigated by sophisticated snow-making machines. But the unreliability of snow means that there are fewer advance bookings, as skiers wait to see where the snow is. And this creates problems for resort owners. The recent economic downturn has taken a toll as well; uncertainty, in all its forms, particularly plagues the ski industry, which needs both snow and prosperity to survive.

There is a point in middle age when you feel that there is still time to right the ship, that whatever you have neglected— health, teeth (a particularly sore and expensive point), partners, finances, children—can be dealt with by a concerted push. If we just cut out carbs, buy flowers, start putting money aside *today*; if we sit down and have that conversation about drugs with our teenagers, all will be well. Climatically, this is the moment that many people feel we are at: if we install solar panels, buy a Prius, rein in our consumption. But there are scientists who feel we have passed that point; regardless of our best efforts, we've already done too much damage, and it will all come crashing down.

THE WORLD'S glaciers are disappearing, but they contain only about four percent of global ice cover. It is the polar ice sheets that pose the biggest risk. In 2006, the legendary Northwest Passage—impetus for three centuries of exploration—was free of ice for the first time in recorded history. In 2007, an apocalyptic year for ice, satellite photographs showed that twenty-four percent of arctic ice had disappeared in the previous twelve months.

This left 4.17 million square kilometres of polar ice, a record low that only held until 2012, when a new low of 3.32 million square kilometres was announced. In the 1980s, the sea ice covered an area roughly the size of the U.S.; now it is half that.

As the polar ice melts, water seeps to the bottom of the ice sheet where it acts as a lubricant, helping large pieces to slide into the sea. In 2010 an ice island four times the size of Manhattan broke off Petermann Glacier in Greenland, where temperatures are currently rising at 2°C per decade.

If all the polar and glacial ice melted, the seas would rise by sixty-four metres, according to Lonnie Thompson. The oceans would actually go higher than that due to thermal expansion: as the water heats, it takes up more space. Hundreds of millions of people in coastal cities would be vulnerable. Perhaps we can avoid, or at least forestall, some version of this disaster. But the political record is one of obfuscation, weaselling, and environmental summits that yield hopeful mantras and little action.

The Gradualism of the nineteenth century may be behind us. Climate can change on a dime, more or less. The Catastrophic lurks. Exhibit A for this theory is Ötzi, the Tyrolean ice man, whose frozen body was discovered in the Eastern Alps north of Bolzano, Italy, in 1991 after it was exposed by a melting glacier. His body had been in the ice for 5,200 years. He'd been shot in the back with an arrow, and had managed to escape his enemies, only to bleed to death. Within days of his death, there was a "climate event" that was large enough to cover and preserve him for fifty-two centuries. Otherwise, he would have begun decaying or would have been eaten by scavengers. Evidence suggests that the climate event wasn't local. The isotopes in the water molecules that compose the remaining ice on Mount Kilimanjaro also show a decrease from the same time period, indicating colder temperatures. A very sudden and prolonged cold snap seems to have begun in the Middle East, 5,200 years ago.

Ötzi was forty-five, relatively old in the Copper Age. It is thought that he might have been a shepherd. Because his corpse was the best-preserved example of primitive man, it has become one of the most minutely studied in history. His lungs were blackened by campfires. He showed degeneration of knee and ankle joints, and had tattoos that may have been related to pain relief treatments. He was lactose intolerant, and may have been suffering from Lyme disease. The arrowhead that killed him was still lodged in his back. Perhaps he was a skier. Whatever else he was, Ötzi was a middle-aged man with health issues, trying to survive in a hostile environment.

As Ötzi sat on the mountain, bleeding out, what was he thinking? Perhaps he was thinking about his beautiful mate and their golden children, or maybe he was thinking about the cruelty of this world, the difficulties of finding food, of avoiding enemies and predators. Or he was looking at the stars trying to divine man's purpose. Maybe all he thought about was the pain of that arrow in his back, the coldness in his limbs. *Whatever* he was thinking, while he was thinking it, everything changed. The earth suddenly got much colder. It snowed for days, temperatures plummeted, and he was buried along with his dreams of love and survival.

We dream of those things still. As we age, perhaps more so. We descend, becoming increasingly conscious of the speed, of the blur in our periphery, those events just out of reach.

Masa Takei

═══════════

HUNTING AND KILLING

When some of my friends have asked me anxiously about their boys, whether they should let them hunt, I have answered yes—remembering that it was one of the best parts of my education—make them hunters. — HENRY DAVID THOREAU

TWO OCTOBERS AGO, a friend and I loaded his truck and headed out from Vancouver into the Cariboo-Chilcotin. We passed beyond the wet coastal mountain ranges of British Columbia into semi-arid lodgepole pine country. It was my second season hunting, and we had yet to get a deer. Plenty of signs, enough droppings for me to fashion a life-sized buck, some sightings—but still no success.

The first morning out we awoke in the pre-dawn dark to find sleet encrusting our tent. We set a rendezvous time and my partner headed into the half-light to stake out a clearing he'd picked the evening before. I went in search of a clearing of my own. I found a copse of trees with a good view of fifty yards of game trail. But, as I grew cold and impatient, I began to stalk the strip of forest between the road and the clear-cut, where I found fresh tracks.

Now, approaching midday, the sun was finally warming the landscape. My partner had called me on the radio. He'd quit early and was waiting for me back at the truck. I was only a stand of trees from the road when I spotted the buck's eyes peering at me from above a freshly fallen tree, his small antlers jutting up.

My focus narrowed. My breathing quickened and the deer joggled in the field of my scope. The first shot, through thick branches, missed completely. My second, after he'd bounded away and stopped broadside to look back, hit home. A solid shot through the engine room.

The deer, a spike buck muley, lay in the yellow grass facing me, his eyes clouded over as if with cataracts, an entry wound the size of a dime in his chest. All I remember, standing over him, was a feeling of sadness and shame, as if I'd done something wrong. My rifle hung heavy in my hands. I keyed the mike on my radio and told my hunting partner where to find me. I felt as if I were turning myself in.

MY PATH TO hunting started—as many things do—with lunch. I was a thirty-seven-year-old MBA who had taken a left turn from management consulting into freelance writing. Either way, I rarely got my hands dirty. My friend Ignacio—"Nazzy"— and I were eating Chinese food in a grudgingly gentrifying part of Vancouver. It was 2008, the depths of the Great Recession, when both an economic and environmental apocalypse seemed nigh. Just how nigh was reflected by our conversation, which had drifted to contingency plans for the imminent SHTF—"Shit Hits The Fan," in survivalist-speak—situation.

"I'd head to Patagonia," said Nazzy, between bites of General Tao's chicken, "and live off the land." He was from Peru, but he would bypass home and keep going to where animals far outnumbered people.

"You know how to hunt?" I said, eyebrows raised in skepticism.

He nodded with an air of gravitas. Nazzy and I had met in business school almost a decade ago, and though I'd come to realize that he possesses many skills, from ice climbing to tango dancing, he'd never mentioned hunting. Besides, he was just too doe-eyed, compact, and cuddly-looking to be a hunter. Or so I thought.

As it turned out, he'd grown up hunting with his father, a diplomat. Together they'd taken a wide range of fauna on three continents. His father also hunted with a posse of companions known as Los Magnificos, whose exploits had become legendary. But now, in their twilight years, they were known more for their doddering misadventures, careening their trucks off the road and blasting away with their guns but rarely hitting anything. They were nicknamed after a popular TV show, *Los Magnificos*: what we in North America would call *The A-Team*.

By the time coffee came around, Nazzy and I had decided that we'd hunt together. Los Magnificos, Vancouver Chapter. At the time, DIY food collection and locavorism were on the rise, and we found ourselves gripped by the ideal of self-reliance, by the urge to connect with something primal. I'd always eaten meat, and for meat to end up on my plate, something needed to have died. Just because I didn't do the killing myself made me no less complicit. I could see what author David Adams Richards meant in his memoir *Facing the Hunter*: "...those who eat meat should be morally obligated to kill at least once in their lives that which they eat."

So Nazzy and I plunged into the acronym-rich bureaucracy involved in becoming a ticketed hunter in British Columbia. First was the PAL (Possession and Acquisition Licence), needed to purchase and pack a gun. We spent the weekend in a community centre with biologists, biathletes, and armoured-car guards. (In that class, evenly split between men and women, only one other person gave hunting as his reason for being there.) We handled decommissioned firearms and didn't fire a single shot. Instead we answered multiple-choice questions.

Next came the CORE (Conservation Outdoor Recreation Education). We needed that for a B.C. Resident Hunter Number Card, with which we could buy our hunting licenses and species tags. The CORE was another weekend course, another multiple-choice exam, this time in a Masonic hall. Finally, we were legally entitled to hunt. But all this didn't make me a hunter any more than my CPR certification made me a doctor. I still didn't have the slightest clue where to start.

WHEN IN DOUBT, buy some gear. The item of equipment that figures most prominently, of course, being The Gun.

Ideally, we would each have a rifle handed down to us from our fathers. It would be an old Remington Wingmaster, the deep gun-blue burnished to a dull silver in spots from the repeated touch of hands, patches worn like familiar trails through the forest. Instead, the gun that my father passed along to me, when I was six, was a plastic, belt-fed toy machine gun, complete with bipod and scope. I'd accumulated an array of other toy guns, ranging from gunnish-looking pieces of driftwood to an exact replica of a Smith & Wesson .44 Magnum revolver that I'd built from a plastic model kit. I'd outgrown these toys, but nevertheless I'd spent a significant amount of time with "guns" in my hands—without learning a thing about gun safety, gun care, or the responsibility involved.

The Los Magnificos Vancouver Chapter—JP, another friend from business school, had joined Nazzy and me—convened early one morning to gear up at a local gun store. It was the store's annual sale and, as we rounded the corner, we saw a lineup that went down the block and disappeared around the far corner. There was an air of festivity as people enjoyed complimentary coffee and donuts while they waited for the doors to open. We took our place in line.

I'd done some research (Remington, founded in 1816, is one of the oldest continuously operating manufacturers of anything in America). But we relied on Nazzy for his superior knowledge. This first season, we three would share one rifle until Nazzy could bring his own back from Peru.

Inside the store, the atmosphere shifted. There's something proudly utilitarian about a gun shop, with fluorescent light shining down on unadorned shelves. Behind the long counters, the walls were lined with gun rack upon gun rack, and they were emptying at an alarming rate.

I noticed a group of prosperous-looking men being served at one counter, behind which were the "black rifles"—civilian versions of weapons used by the military and law enforcement, designed for use against two-legged animals, the kind that might shoot back. These were the kinds of weapons at the heart of the gun ownership debate in America. I shied away from this area and the cases containing the handguns too. I didn't want to be grouped with these people: gun nuts. As far as I was concerned, hunting legitimized my boyhood fascination with guns. I was shopping for a tool, not a toy, and definitely not a weapon.

Strictly speaking, to be able to take down any game animal in North America all you need are three firearms: a .22 rifle for small game, a large-calibre rifle for big game, and a shotgun for birds. Anything more is gratuitous. But for some, guns are like tattoos. Once you've acquired one, you're in danger of accumulating many others.

We waded up to the counter, and JP and I stood aside.

"We're looking for an all-weather thirty-ought-six," Nazzy said. (As he'd explained to us beforehand, given the wet conditions we'd be hunting in, we'd want a rust-resistant finish and a stock that wouldn't swell with the moisture. The .30-06 was a versatile calibre.)

"We're sold out."

"Okay, how about a three-oh-eight?"

The salesman unlocked a sleek rifle with a black synthetic stock and matte stainless barrel from the rack and brought it back to us.

"Ruger. A good brand."

Nazzy removed the bolt—the sliding mechanism that extracts the bullet from the magazine and pushes it into the chamber—and looked up through the barrel at the lights above us. It was a brand-new gun, so inspecting the bore was not strictly necessary, but we were suitably impressed. He passed the rifle to me. It was heavy. I tried to think of something perceptive to say. Fully retracted, the bolt seemed loose and rattly.

"The bolt seems loose and rattly," I said.

"It's a Mauser-style controlled round feed, based on the Mauser 98k. One of the most reliable rifle actions ever developed," said Nazzy. "It's meant to be like that."

"Oh," I said.

I passed the rifle to JP, who pointed it at the salesman, who patiently redirected the muzzle to one side with a forefinger.

"We'll take it," said Nazzy.

THE NEXT TIME Los Magnificos VC met, several weeks later, it was to go to the range and "sight in" the scope. When you screw a scope onto a rifle, the crosshairs aren't going to line up exactly with the bullet's point of impact. The object, in making minute adjustments to the crosshairs, is to get the perfectly straight line of sight through the scope and the slightly arcing trajectory of a bullet to meet exactly—at say, 100 yards.

When shooting at a deer or other large game, you're not aiming for general centre of mass. You are shooting to hit the vital organs, to deliver death as quickly as possible. Given the anatomy of a deer-sized creature, this is typically a dinner-plate-sized target, centred about six inches behind the shoulder. Broadside, this will mean a heart or double-lung shot. A head shot is riskier. The brain is less than the size of a fist and, being an extremity, the head will move more erratically.

The worst possible case, worse than a clean miss, is to leave a wounded animal loose in the wild to die a painful, protracted death. Bullet placement is everything.

At a rifle range out in the suburbs, we were assigned a shooting lane next to a couple of disenchanted youth with baseball hats askew. They were shooting Glocks and a sniper-style rifle with a muzzle brake, a device at the end of the barrel that redirects the exhaust gases. When they shot the gun, the sonic blast caused our organs to jiggle in our rib cages.

On the other side of us, a tall, pale fellow in reflective eye shields had a European-made AR-15, the kind of thing you see U.S. soldiers carrying in Iraq. He took dozens of offhand shots from a standing position. We were a long way from any combat zone, so perhaps he was training for the apocalypse.

Between getting pinged in the head with hot, spent brass from the left and being deafened through our earplugs on the right, we spent a couple of hours sighting in our scope. This would be the only target practice I would get before attempting to shoot a live animal.

GEAR ASIDE, I was still up against the biggest hurdle a newbie hunter faces: the business of how to hunt. It is, one could say, a natural act. But even a baby tiger needs to be taught how to catch its prey. And urbanite humans, whose kibble comes neatly packaged, have lost the skills involved in hunting for our food.

My father hadn't hunted and neither had his. An intergenerational passing of hunting knowledge is ideal, but if that link is broken you have to get it where you can. Before that first successful hunt, I spent time with a people for whom hunting was a necessity and a source of pride: the Inuit of Northern Labrador. I was on a writing assignment to explore Canada's newest national park, the Torngat Mountains. We stayed in a base camp encircled by a 10,000-volt fence to keep the predatory polar bears at bay. The Inuit, the only people allowed to carry firearms in the park, acted as our guides. They also supplied the camp by hunting for fresh meat.

This remote park sees fewer visitors each year than Everest. It's a harsh land, where kilometre-high mountains, containing some of the oldest rock on the planet, curve straight up from the North Atlantic's frigid waters. Turquoise icebergs float in surreal contrast to the green scrub that clings like tattered velvet to granitic islands. Tivi Etok, a local Inuit artist in his eighties, recalled that when he was growing up, "To be a candidate for marriage a man had to be a competent hunter: a provider." Among the most important milestones in his life, he said, were "my first fish," "my first rifle," and "my first seal." One of our guides talked about shooting, at age eight, his first ptarmigan—which, following tradition, he gave to his grandmother. Historically, the good hunters were among the most respected members of their society.

I joined them on their hunts for caribou and seal. One day the hunting party landed on the shore of an inlet to gut a seal one of the hunters had shot (while standing on the rocking deck of a small boat, using a beat-up .22 with no scope). Once the entrails were exposed, everyone dove in with their knives, slicing off pieces of the liver to eat raw. Then they took scoops of the brain. They bagged the meat, the fat, the hide, and the intestines to take back to camp. I was honoured with the gift of one of the eyes to eat, which I did, squeezing the viscous liquid into my mouth. While I can't describe the precise flavour, I remember the feeling of freshness, the vitality of eating it straight like that. It was like shucking a fresh ear of corn, still radiating the sun's energy.

But what I learned in Labrador was that successful hunting is a long sequence of decisions and actions, based on knowledge of the habits of animals and the local terrain. The act of shooting the animal is both nothing (it represents a blip of time in the overall venture) and everything (the exact point when you've taken a life).

Which is why, the first season Nazzy and I hunted, we got skunked. It wasn't until late in our second that I got that first spike buck and learned, firsthand, what it means to take another mammal's life.

It would take me a full two days before I stopped feeling terrible. On the drive home, Nazzy parsed my emotions for me, separating the feeling of sadness from the shame. The shame, I felt, was pure socialization, a holdover from my childhood when I had watched Man, the Hunter, kill Bambi's parents. In any culture in which hunting plays a natural part, this emotion would have been as inexplicable as if I'd felt shame over buying my first car. But my sadness went deeper, and was harder to articulate.

But before I had the luxury of analyzing these unexpected feelings, we still needed to field dress and butcher the animal. Being apartment dwellers with nowhere to hang the carcass, we had to butcher it into manageable sections right there. The two of us dragged the deer to the roadside by its front legs. I didn't like how the head dragged along the ground, the tongue lolling out. It felt disrespectful. But I had to get it into my head that though the animal was still warm, Elvis had left the building. From the truck Nazzy retrieved a book, *Dressing & Cooking Wild Game: From Field to Table*. While he read out step-by-step instructions, I cut.

The first incision was tougher than expected. I was scared of perforating the stomach. The knifepoint just did not seem to want to pierce the thick hide. I started and stopped several times, relocating the notch of the sternum again and again. When I finally pierced the skin, the blade sunk in several inches and, just as I had feared, I perforated the stomach. The entrails bulged outward. The knife separated the abdominal wall with a faint tearing sound as the dull knife split the hide. Material the colour of fresh-cut grass spilled out into the body cavity and the pungent smell of G.I. juices wafted up.

Still taking directions from Nazzy, I slit right down to the anus. Then, turning around, I planted the blade's edge up under the sternum, gripped the handle with both hands, and rested an elbow on each knee. Leaning back, I leveraged the knife up through the bone, which separated with a shudder. I kept going until I'd sawed up through the neck, a few inches shy of the jaw. I reached up into the neck and severed the trachea as high as I could. It had the feel of plastic, flexible air-duct tubing encased in a gluey membrane. I carved around the anus.

All that was left was to slice around the diaphragm, then cut and pull apart the connective tissue that held the organs in the body cavity. That struggle finished, we tipped out the guts and were left with meat, bones, and fur.

The sloppiness of the initial gutting done, we searched for a tree from which to suspend the carcass using some cord and a couple of climbing carabiners.

We made cuts down the insides of the legs and around the knees, attempting to keep the hair out of the meat. We sawed off the head and lower legs, then peeled the cape back. By this time, it didn't feel like it was a living creature that we were stripping down; rather, just a massive piece of bone-in meat. Then we got into the major cuts: the backstraps, the shoulders, the roasts. As we worked, we heard the sound of a truck approaching and Nazzy hurriedly hid the book. Four hunters drove up and leaned out the window to chat. They hadn't had any luck, they said. We made some remark about our deer being small, to which one of them responded, "Well, it's meat, eh."

After four and a half hours, we were finished. I cut the spike horns off and said my last thank you to the animal. We left the hooves, spine, ribcage, head, and cape in the brush beside the road for the birds and scavengers.

The year after that, I moved up to Haida Gwaii to build an off-grid cabin and learn to live off the land. There, hunting is more than a seasonal activity. The Sitka black-tailed deer are an introduced species that, lacking any natural predators, have proliferated exponentially from the first eight animals brought over from the mainland in 1878. Now estimated at over 200,000, they've ravaged the landscape, but have compensated for this by being exceptionally tender and tasty. The hunting season was once year-round, but now it runs from June to March, nine months long compared to two or three elsewhere. The bag limit is fifteen deer a year, compared with one or two in other regions. Because of this, I've been able to pack about a decade of hunting into one year. Hunting has become an integral part of my life.

One evening hunt, alone, reminded me of the subtle things I had come to love about hunting. The light was fading as I left my cabin and biked to a clearing I'd scouted. I would lose shooting light within the next half hour but I resisted the urge to move too fast. This would be about the journey rather than any destination.

I put a gumbooted foot down and broke a small twig. With the next step, a minute later, I snagged the toe of my boot under a long blade of grass and snapped that, too.

In my bones, I felt that I would see a deer here. I could even smell something "deery"—the fresh breath of biomass coupled with the pong of wet fur. Even at the rate I was moving, about as fast as a baby could crawl, my perspective on the world surrounding me changed. I examined sight lines and dug deeper with my eyes into the dark brush, areas that might hold a deer. I kept all my motions, the back-and-forth sweep of my head, slow and smooth.

My index finger was on the trigger guard of my rifle and my thumb rested on the sharp point of the safety. I was taking in the natural environment, savouring it in a way that rarely happens when I'm in the woods. When I hike, I'm mostly thinking about how far I have to go, or chatting with companions.

Here, I was aware of the wind, its direction, where my left foot was and where my right foot was about to go. The sound my hair made as it brushed against the collar of my rain jacket. I took in the game trails and tracks criss-crossing in all directions, the distant chatter of a squirrel, even the incessant thump of waves on the nearby shore. A stand of trees changed form and mood with every step I took.

Fifteen minutes later, I stepped into full view of a clearing to my left. My heart bumped as I saw the unmistakable form of a deer taking unhurried steps toward a hillock at the clearing's edge. My thumb pushed the safety halfway forward but I didn't even get a chance to shoulder my rifle. With several flicks of its tail the deer stepped, head down, out of my view.

In full stalking mode, I crouched so that my pack wouldn't catch on a tree branch that drooped over the path. I was still in slow motion but moving with a purpose, straining to listen for branches breaking. I wanted to intercept the deer before it slipped into the forest.

I came to the end of the road, a pond to my left. A large, sedge-covered hill separated the last clearing from this one. I could wait for the deer to crest the rise, or I could make my way toward it. The light was dissipating fast and soon it would be too low to make a shot.

I pushed through some alder saplings toward the water, treading carefully toward the hill. Then an unexpected movement caught my eye. On the far edge of the pond another doe had emerged from the forest and was ambling along the shore, its reflection moving in the water. I froze. When I moved forward, gravel crunched beneath my feet. The doe paused and looked around, cupped ears swivelling, scanning, then continued on its way.

I knew that if I dropped the deer at the far end of the pond it would be that much harder to drag back to the road, but the deer might disappear into the thick brush at any time. I needed to trust that it would continue along the water's edge. Instead of trying to get closer, I spun the magnification dial on my scope to full strength and knelt as I raised the rifle to my shoulder. I was always surprised by how much brighter the scope made the landscape.

The deer seemed unaware of me despite my bright orange jacket. I centred the crosshairs behind the shoulder and followed the deer. It moved behind a bush and I panicked, thinking I'd missed my chance at a clean shot. I put my head up and saw that it would soon emerge from the other side if it continued on its course.

I picked out a tree and chose that as my marker; when the deer reached the tree, I would take my shot. I waited, both eyes open, as I peered through the scope, keeping the deer in context with the background, all the while aiming at the shoulder.

When the doe reached the tree, I let out a low whistle. It stopped dead in its tracks, on high alert. I pulled the trigger and the gun jumped. Everything exploded. As the air settled, I could see the deer sprint up the far bank and disappear into the treeline.

If the animal was wounded, it was best that it not think it was being pursued, since it would run deeper into the forest. I waited a few moments, stooping to pick up the empty casing.

I found the deer laid out at the bottom of a slope just within the edge of the dense forest. I gently touched its eye to make sure there was no life. I slung my rifle over my shoulder, then grabbed hold of the deer's front legs and dragged it back up the hummock and down into the clearing.

Using the climbing rope I'd brought for just this purpose, I made a loop around the deer's neck and pulled it along so that it slid with the grain of its fur. By the time I got back to my mountain bike, I was sweating.

I pulled out a game bag and dragged the deer off the road and into the forest. Drawing my hunting knife, I field dressed it by headlamp. But first, I stopped and gave the deer thanks, something I'd forgotten to do in my initial haste. I placed a hand on the warm body and lowered my head, eyes closed, fervently willing that my gratitude be conveyed.

Twenty minutes later, I cut the liver and heart from the gut pile and put them into the canvas game bag to cool. I would eat them when I got back to my cabin.

Now, the problem of getting the deer home. Using the rope looped around its neck, I lashed its head to the handlebars and draped it lengthwise along the bike with the seat up in its body cavity, legs hanging on either side of the frame. It looked like it was levitating. For a fraction of a second, I considered riding the bike by sitting on the deer's back, but I decided that would be offensive to the dignity of the deer— and probably dangerous. It would have been apt revenge for the deer to stick a hoof into the front wheel and send me over the bars.

It was only a couple of kilometres to get back, so I decided to walk along the dirt road, pushing the deer beside me. The full experience began to sink in. At the path leading to my cabin, I stopped for a while with my companion on the bike beside me to appreciate the bright clusters of stars above.

The outing encompassed much of what I enjoy about hunting. But "enjoy" is not quite the right word. I find it satisfying, engaging, rewarding. First, there are the places we go in search of game. Places that we otherwise would have no reason to visit: estuaries, forested slopes, fog-bound marshes studded with Tim Burtonesque trees. Even the clear-cuts, piled with slash or scrubby young second-growth, have something to offer, if only the distinctive water-drop call of a raven. A saw-whet owl may glide past as the moon comes up, or the first frog of the season will chirrup out in the bog. Every trip has yielded some sort of reward, even if it's simply the time spent outdoors, being out for a sunrise or a sunset.

The other thing I appreciate about hunting is the time I spend with friends in a shared purpose. I feel especially lucky to have introduced a handful of people to their first hunting experiences.

Then, of course, there's the meat, the ultimate in organic, the reward for hard work. It's as different from store-bought meat as a bleached-out tomato bought in a supermarket is to the rich globe pulled off a vine in your backyard. It's a special feeling to feed yourself and others with what you've hunted and gathered. It's a direct connection to the life forces that sustain us. And to share something so vital with someone is as primal a gift as one can give.

I'm proud of my new skills as a hunter. However, my initial reaction after dropping an animal is still sadness. I still don't enjoy the killing.

A hunter I went out with recently will no longer take the shot. Now in his fifties, he's fine with the stalking, the field dressing and butchering, but the act of taking life is too much for him. As a veteran hunter and retired military search-and-rescue technician, he's perhaps seen too much death already. He said it wasn't so much a rational choice, but something he felt in his gut. Which, from my experience so far, is where hunting resides: not in the head, but in the gut.

Ian Brown

WHAT THE MOUNTAINS MEAN TO US

Did you have too much to drink last night? Are you talking too much? Are you knowledgeable about anything? Is your life a failure? Are you getting a sunburn? What about your lips? Are you going to get lip cancer? —from a notebook kept by the author on a recent ski mountaineering trip to the Selkirk Mountains, listing everything he was afraid of.

Skiing in the backcountry of the Rocky Mountains: it makes me nervous even to type the sentence. I am at best a very amateur mountaineer, but a persevering one. I have travelled, on foot or on skis, on some trip or another, in the Rockies or the Purcells or the Selkirks or the Monashees or some nearby mountains, every year for the last thirty years, hauling my city body out to play in the high country. And whereas I think those visits have transformed the way I see the world, to the point where I believe we *need* the mountains, as human beings and as citizens, I don't qualify as anything more than a tourist mountaineer.

This is especially true in places like Banff and Canmore in Alberta, and in Golden, B.C.—the staging towns for most of our trips. Out here, every other resident is an extreme skier, or a daredevil kayaker, or a radical mountain climber-slash-environmentalist-slash-producer, or a writer referencing post-Nabokovian conceptions of nature.

On the other hand, it was timid mountain tourists like me who helped make Canada's mountains famous 120 years ago. They came out by train and hired guides to haul them up to the top of as-yet-unnamed mountains. Ever since, we tourists have always been considered a necessary nuisance. We pay the bills but we drive the locals crazy.

I spent an evening not too long ago with one of my own heroes, Chic Scott, the longtime explorer and chronicler of the Rockies, who lives in Banff. The man is a national cultural hero, and you can still walk into the Cake Company, his favourite café in town, and have a coffee with him, a fact that to this day gives me a bit of a thrill. You couldn't have done that with Mordecai Richler: he would have eaten you alive. But mountain society tends to be more democratic, because it revolves around the physical: if you go outside, and hike, or ski, or bike, or climb, or curl, or in any way attempt to use your body, you are welcomed into the society of the outdoorsperson, those who seek grace through physical effort. You don't even have to be very good at it, because sooner or later the mountains humble everyone.

Chic and I were talking about the mountains, and life, and work, and the great challenge of trying to combine all three, which is something we often talk about. (The overall problem is that it's hard to find work in the mountains that will make you enough money to let you stay in the mountains.) Then Chic said something interesting: "I'm a mountaineer who's done a little writing. You, on the other hand, are a writer who has done a little mountaineering." And while I think he was being modest, I could tell which side of that divide he was happy to be on. I wished I could say the same.

I was talking to Chic because I wanted to meet an old skiing pal of his, Donny Gardner. Together, these two men discovered or opened up most of the glaciers and big winter ski traverses in the Rockies. Roughly forty years ago, Donny Gardner put on a pair of skis, and with little more than a credit card and a safety blanket in his pack, he decided to ski, on his own, from Calgary to the Pacific Ocean. Which he did, sleeping in a lot of tree wells along the way. It took him twenty-nine days. That's pretty fast—it's about 700 kilometres from Calgary to the Pacific Ocean by ski. But then, Donny Gardner has always been a winter man. He once travelled the fifteen kilometres between Canmore and the town of Banff along the unwelcoming ridge of Mount Rundle—a long way up (4,970 metres) and a long way across—in the winter. The base of his first pair of cross-country skis consisted of a coat of green paint: he figured that might make them slide more.

I heard the story of Don Gardner's trek when I first visited the Rocky Mountains, and I've never been able to forget it. There's something about taking a walk in the woods in the winter—and Don Gardner's ski to the Pacific is still pretty much the ultimate as far as that sort of thing goes—that speaks to all of us. No sooner do I start to think about what skis he was wearing than I start to think about ski wax (which I gather he sometimes disdained), which in turn gets me thinking about the wax wagon, which is essentially a semi-trailer manned by *professional ski waxers* that the Canadian Olympic cross-country team hauls around with them in Europe…which in turn gets me thinking about my own relationship to gear, and how it both reassures and intimidates me—because it's one thing to have good gear, but is it the right gear? And why do I want such precise, act-specific gear? I need my climbing skins and my knife and my Schoeller hoodie; I do not need the titanium pulley and a second, backup thermos. But I take them all anyway, *just in case*: the motto of the mountaineer.

What am I afraid of? A lot, as it turns out. *Do you ski with enough verve? Why are you so nervous? Should you do the dishes tonight?* This is another reason why even lowly altitude tourists like me long for and need the mountains. They help us figure out who we are.

The attraction is partly physical, of course, because the mountains are just so damn big. They're a place from which to see the natural world in a clear and startlingly delicate form, because being in a dangerous place makes you realize what you cherish, and the things you cherish then seem that much. more vulnerable. But we need mountains emotionally, as well. Travelling on foot in the mountains is itself a form of meditation. You repeat the same movement over and over again, like a physical mantra, whether you are walking or skiing or biking or hiking. And by the time you get to the top of the hill, your mind has freed itself to step back and watch its own progress.

In the mountains, you end up having the time to think, and then you think about what you're thinking about. Mountains are both physical and metaphysical. They free our minds by engaging our bodies in a neurochemically liberating way. A walk in the woods in the mountain wilderness may have been the earliest form of Prozac.

We live—as someone tells us every day—in an increasingly crowded and technologically inter-wired world, where distinct regional cultures are melting into a global monoculture, driven by digital technology that forces us to be more and more conventional and "other-directed." The mountains, by contrast—especially these raw-boned, undomesticated Canadian mountains—are one of the rare places left on earth that encourage us to be introspective, and alone. You can't be too social, because you have to concentrate on your next step, and your remoteness forces the demands of the so-called "real" world to fade away. Where else does that happen these days? People come to the mountains to have fun, but they also come because here there's a chance they'll be left alone.

But mostly we need the mountains because, despite their size and their ferocity, they force privacy upon us, and therefore feel more personal. Travelling through high country feels intimate: the mountain has a relationship with you and you alone, an arrangement that is perforce intense, even jealous. After hearing stories about people like Donny Gardner, I started coming back to the mountains regularly—every year, for thirty years, to undertake ski mountaineering trips with the same group of friends. We still spend a week or two every winter, visiting places like the Tonquin Valley and the northern Selkirks and the Columbia Icefield. We have a thing for glaciers, for getting as high and clean as we can.

For this reason I can now reveal a few of the secrets shared by our group of slightly overweight amateur mountaineers.

For instance, we never travel with women (although one or two have been our guides). We get a lot of grief about this from our wives, who refer to our outings as "the penis trips." But in a meditational sense, we want to clear our minds of distractions, even welcome ones: travelling in the mountains in the winter, even at our fairly safe and relatively undemanding level, gives you lots of other things you have to pay attention to, such as not falling down a crevasse, say, or remembering to bring an extra pair of gloves and the stove, in case you get into trouble.

You might ask why a group of men pushing sixty insist upon returning to such dangers annually. I would like to say that I know the answer. But every year the answer changes—yet another reason the mountains are so instructive, because nothing about them stays the same for long. The question is not, will it rain; the question is, how often, and for how long, and what kind of rain will it be? The kind of rain that makes you want to cry, or the sort that makes you grateful, that seems to operate like a giant facial moisturizer, like the one I passed through when I was hiking with my wife around the mountains that surround Lake O'Hara? As we walked along a stretch of uncannily well-spaced, hand-placed granite steps, we were singing a song my wife made up, to the tune of *The Addams Family* theme, about the chivalrous Lawrence Grassi, Banff's great trail maker. The opening line was "The man who built these steps... I love him, I love him."

The longer my pals and I do these trips, the harder they get, and the more theories we have as to why we still want to do them. It isn't simply our desire to prove we are still the men we once were... because we aren't. But in the mountains you have ample opportunity to find out what makes you afraid.

Recently, on a trip into the Selkirk Mountains, I started making lists of everything that worried me. *Do you have your climbing skins? Will you need your watch? Do you have water? Enough water? Lunch? Extra hat? Sunglasses? Goggles? Will your asthma act up? Will you collapse? Will you fall? Do you have your heel ascenders set at the right height? Are you fit enough? Is your skiing good enough? Will you keep everyone waiting at the bottom of each pitch? Have you been a good enough model as a parent to set your lovely daughter firmly on her feet for the future if you die in an avalanche? Are you getting a sunburn?* My list ran on for twelve pages.

But here's another secret: you get braver as you get older—or at least, you get more resilient.

The last time my companions and I visited the Clemenceau Icefield, just west of the Rocky Mountain Trench in British Columbia, we were the first visitors to sign the hut's logbook in two years. The two-storey Quonset hut with three door-sized windows, one on each side. was buried to the roofline. One of my pals who was in the mountains with us for the first time in his life at the age of fifty volunteered to find the door and dig it out. After an hour and a half of digging he got it on the fourth try.

The mountains don't care how old you are. In the mountains—and this is another reason we need them—it doesn't matter how much money you make, or how many servants or hedge funds you have: altitude demands that you earn your pleasure, and because you have to earn it, you remember it. In an age of forgettable instant communication when everything appears at our fingertips, this is a valuable gift, at least if you want to remember what actually happened to you in the blink of time that comprises a single human existence. (On the geological timeline of the mountains, which were formed by a continental scrunching 65 million years ago, we humans are mayflies.)

Of course, things can go wrong, as well. I've often told the story (because the stories are proof that we lived, that we did this, that we filled our time well) of how one of my ski companions once broke a binding on a remote icefield. (The guide told him not to move, and, being a Magoo-like character, he moved anyway, and then he disappeared over the edge of a cornice. We found him fifteen feet below us. I still remember the small, awed way he said "oh" when he landed. The broken binding issue was serious, though.)

We fixed it that night using a strip of an empty white gas can to make a new binding plate, the work done in a circle of Coleman light on a table in the centre of the hut, the rest of us peering down from our bunks, each turn and rivet of crucial importance. (The Ski Repair Channel has potential.) It wasn't just the technical problem of fixing Mackenzie's ski that absorbed us, but the bigger, existential challenge that an accident in the remote mountains creates: his small mishap could have become a huge problem. It didn't, though, thanks to ingenuity, which thankfully shows up a lot in an environment where you have to make do with what you have. In that way the mountains make you both serious and resourceful. People long for that experience.

Above all, mountains are beautiful, especially in winter, when everything is so tightly upholstered in snow, an image you hang on to in your mind back in the city. And there is the sensation of skiing itself, if you're a skier—the silicate powder snow, the grace-kissed runs you never forget. The way we wait for each other at the bottom of each pitch, just in case, just to make sure no one gets left behind. We all do get left behind, eventually, but not up there, not if we can help it.

In the city, we look forward to our trips for months. Then, as soon as the trip starts, we can't wait to get home again, where we can once again appreciate ease and comfort and laziness. You discover after a week in the mountains that laziness has a lot going for it.

But we also never want the trip to be over. "The free mountain and camp life was at an end," Norman Collie lamented when he finally had to head back down from discovering the Columbia Icefield back in the 1880s, which he wrote about with Hugh Stutfield in their classic book *Climbs and Explorations in the Canadian Rockies*. "All our difficulties and struggles would now be with the complex fabric of civilized life, not with the forests, rivers, glaciers, and snow-clad peaks." Life is simpler up there. Everything you do feels necessary, and sufficient. It is a repudiation of the lives we tourist mountaineers live most of the time, measuring our success against the standards of others. I come to the mountains because it makes life in the city less daunting.

Did you take a shit before you set out skiing this morning? Should you have taken another? Did you wash your hands after? Do you smell? Why do you lean so far forward when you ski? And why are you afraid of the steeps—it's just speed. Can you make it to the end of the week? Will your body hold up? Will your spirits? Why didn't you bring more gin? Are you too big, too old, too small? Are you shallow? Does anyone in your life really love you? Will you ever not be lonely? And why are you so worried in such a beautiful place? Why can you not live in the moment?

WE DO try to be civilized on our trips. We spend our days looking out for one another on the slopes, waiting for the stragglers and avoiding slots and avalanches. Then we do it again with courtesies that evening, in the tent or the cabin—holding doors for one another, mixing drinks, waxing someone else's skins as well as our own—to prove that all this is more than self-interest.

Not all our attempts at civilization have been successful. For instance, we have tried on three different occasions to improvise a portable sauna. The first one, a gas stove in a tent, nearly asphyxiated us with carbon monoxide fumes. The second was safer, but produced about as much body warmth as an aspirin in Coke. The third one, also dangerous, worked well enough, but the real danger arose in the two inches of liquid brume that condensed in the bottom of the tent after a couple of skiers had steamed away a day's sweat and effort and filth— a shallow but burning lake into which you could not help but slip. This juice fetched up brilliant red calluses on our behinds, resulting in the worst case I have ever experienced in three decades of outdoor life of what I like to refer to as Baboon Ass. Painful? Imagine your fundament as a rusty and poorly performing ratchet bolt: that begins to describe the sensation.

I imagine Byron Harmon, the first great photographer of the Rockies, felt the same way when he was hired by a mountain tourist named Alan Freeman to photograph Mount Columbia. They required two guides, a string of pack horses, a radio, a typewriter, 8,000 feet of movie film, and a flock of carrier pigeons, just in case. (Mountain tourists tend to over-pack.) Harmon and Freeman took seventy days to travel 800 kilometres to the top of the Saskatchewan Glacier, a pace even slower than ours. On the seventieth day, their last, their food spent, the clouds finally cleared *for the first time,* and Harmon caught his celebrated photograph of Mount Columbia.

I wasn't there, of course, but because of the sauna, and the way the mountains look skeptically down upon any outrageous human ambition, I imagine I know how Harmon felt. The human history of these mountains is so recent that it feels inclusive in that way, and (once again) personal.

Certain landscapes embed themselves in my memory. I remember some of the places we've gone in the mountains the same way I remember favourite paintings, even if it's only a vast rock face with snow blown into every crack and fissure and cranny—a Jackson Pollock painting on the most massive scale imaginable. (That was just below Castleguard Meadows, on the long way up onto the Columbia Icefield, the year I got so scared—we had a new baby—that I turned back.) And I imagine that the mountains remember us, too. I always want to assign consciousness to the mountains at times like that, as if they know what they are displaying for us, and why—as if the uncaring silence of the high winter wilderness is a message, a warning not to become too ambitious or too prideful.

I know this is irrational. Nature has no intent. But something in me—the tourist mountaineer, the environmental romantic, maybe even the Canadian living in a country that is still so wild and spread-out that it never feels like much more than an idea—something in me wants the mountains to be alive, to make sense, and to speak to us. It may just be the effect of all that churchy white space on a suggestible consciousness, or the fact that these western Canadian mountains are rapidly becoming one of the few places left that can still be called an extensive wilderness. Or maybe it's because the mountains make us reach for the best in ourselves, and force us to take a chance, and be less afraid.

BUT THE RAREST and most valuable effect of time spent in the mountains in Canada is that it can still be a private experience. Our lives seem to be lived more and more in public, thanks to the camera phone and the internet and YouTube, and the general transformation of our written stories into visual ones.

But in my experience the mountains are still a private place, a sanctuary for the independently meditating and worrying mind. There is so much pressure these days to think alike. Overwhelmed by information and the incessant pressure to connect, it's harder and harder to know what you really think and feel, as opposed to what you are supposed to feel, what others want you to think and feel. In the hopelessly distracted, spectacle-addicted world we live in, simply being remote and hard-to-reach in the mountains, where the damn cellphone doesn't work a lot of the time, feels like a radical act. A radically human act. Of course, the mountains are a radical place simply by virtue of their uncooperative topography. Every time I see them lifting their heads to the west of Calgary, I begin (after a short jolt of apprehension) to feel independent, to experience the electrical possibility of feeling *new* again. Going high, going into the mountains, going remote rather than accessible, is by definition an anti-establishment act, an act of rebellion against the status quo. *Will I return? What am I trying to prove? Did I put tape on my heels? Should I have a drink of water?*

In the city, where everything feels like it has been done before, many times, where so many high standards have been set, the main impediment to action is all that precedent. How can you work up the nerve to begin anything fresh, when so much accomplishment precedes you? Whereas in the sparsely populated and not easily attained mountains, the trails have not all been broken yet. We can still make our own tracks, instead of following someone else's.

CREDITS

The epigraph to "Ode to Bob" in Helen Mort's poem-sequence "No Map Could Show Them" is from David Mazel's *Mountaineering Women* (College Station: Texas A&M University Press, 1994) and was reproduced with permission of the publisher.

"First Ascent" by Barry Blanchard was previously published in *Alpinist* magazine.

"A World of Ice: Circumnavigating Ellesmere" by Jon Turk was adapted from "Ellesmere: Two Men Alone in a World of Ice," published by *Canoe and Kayak Magazine*, May 2012.

"Norman and the Crow" by Niall Fink was previously published in *Other Voices: Journal of the Literary and Visual Arts*, Volume 22, Issue 1, Fall 2009.

Quotations from the "The Magic Bus" by Niall Fink were taken from the "Supertramp" inscription by Chris McCandless.

"Finding Farley" by Karsten Heuer was previously published in *Canadian Geographic*, July/August 2008.

"Muskwa-Kechika" by Bruce Kirkby was adapted from "Ride through the 'Serengeti of the North,'" previously published in *The Globe and Mail*, September 1, 2012.

"Walking Off the Edge of the World" by Bruce Kirkby was previously published in *Up Here* magazine.

The following sources were used by Bernadette McDonald in "Searching for Humar": Humar, Tomaž, *No Impossible Ways*, Mobitel d.d., 2001; "Modern Gladiator on his Way," *Delo*, August 6, 2005; Duane, Dan,

"Tomaž Humar: Incredible Rescue, Angry Backlash on Pakistan's Nanga Parbat," *National Geographic Adventure Magazine*, November 2005; Wallace, Colin, *Climbing* magazine, January 2001.

"Underway" by Christian Beamish was excerpted from *The Voyage of the Cormorant* (Patagonia Books, 2012) and was reproduced with permission of the publisher.

"Surge" by Erin Soros was excerpted from the novel-in-progress *Hook Tender*. A longer version of "Surge" was aired on the BBC as a finalist for the BBC National Short Story Award, and it has appeared in *The Iowa Review* and *The BBC National Short Story Award 2008* (Short Books).

"Spirit Friends," from *Explorers of the Infinite* by Maria Coffey, copyright © 2008 by Maria Coffey. Used by permission of Jeremy P. Tarcher, an imprint of Penguin Group (USA) LLC.

The following sources were used by Freddie Wilkinson in "A Short Climb with Ueli Steck": Tim Neville, "Speed Freak," *Outside,* March 9, 2012; Martin Gutmann, "Ueli Steck," *Rock and Ice.*

"The Descent of Man" by Don Gillmor was previously published in *Eighteen Bridges*.

Passages of "Hunting and Killing" by Masa Takei previously appeared in "Why I Hunt" in the October 2012 edition of *Western Living.*

Some of the material in "What the Mountains Mean to Us" by Ian Brown, based on a talk given at the Banff Mountain Film and Book Festival in 2012, originally appeared in "The Boys and the Back-Country" in the Winter 2002 issue of *explore Magazine*. That essay was later republished in *Way Out There: The Best of explore* (Greystone Books, 2006). Reprinted with permission.

AUTHOR
BIOGRAPHIES

CHRISTIAN BEAMISH holds a B.A. in Creative Writing from the University of California Santa Cruz and an M.A. in Creative Writing from San Francisco State University. A surfer, surfboard shaper, and writer, Christian is the author of *The Voyage of the Cormorant* (Patagonia Books, July 2012). *Voyage* is the account of his three-month solo surfing expedition down the Pacific coast of Baja California by sail and oar in the eighteen-foot Shetland Isle beach boat he built. Christian lives in Carpinteria, California, with his wife, Natasha, daughter, Josephine, and German Wirehaired Pointer, Rio.

BARRY BLANCHARD: Canadian Mountain Guide and alpinist Barry Blanchard was born in Calgary, March 29, 1959. Twelve years later three boys navigated the Bow River through the western side of the city on a raft of nailed together railway ties, and Barry was at the helm steering the adventure. He found mountain climbing in the books of his high school library, some of which are still in his possession. A six month trip to the French Alps in 1980 set the course of Barry's life: to climb the steepest and most complicated faces of the world's great glaciated peaks. Barry moved to the mountains in 1982 to pursue his Mountain Guiding career (he is an internationally certified—UIAGM—mountain guide) and has included making Hollywood features such as *K-2*, *Cliffhanger*, and *The Vertical Limit* in his professional life. Barry lives in Canmore, Alberta, with his two daughters, Rosemary and Eowyn.

IAN BROWN has been a roving feature writer at *The Globe and Mail* for the past decade. He is the author of three books, including *The Boy in the Moon*, which won the Charles Taylor Prize and the Trillium Book Award, among others, and was selected as one of the *New York Times* 10 Best Books of 2011. He was the host of *Later the Same Day*, *Sunday Morning*, and *Talking Books* on CBC Radio, and of *Human Edge* and *The View From Here* on TVO. He has travelled in the mountains of Alberta and British Columbia nearly every year for the past thriry-five years. He lives in Toronto.

FITZ CAHALL is the founder and host of *The Dirtbag Diaries*, an online radio show dedicated to adventure and the stories that define outdoor culture. He currently works as the creative director at Duct Tape Then Beer, a digital storytelling agency in Seattle, Washington.

MARIA COFFEY is the internationally published author of twelve books, three of which deal with mountaineering themes. *Fragile Edge: Loss on Everest* won two prizes in Italy, including the 2002 ITAS Prize for Mountain Literature, and *Where the Mountain Casts Its Shadow* won the Jon Whyte Award for Mountain Literature at the Banff Mountain Book Festival in 2003 and a National Book Award in 2004. For these titles, along with *Explorers of the Infinite* (2008), Coffey was awarded the 2009 American Alpine Club Literary Award. Originally from the U.K., Coffey lives with her husband, veterinarian and photographer Dag Goering, in British Columbia, Canada. They are the founders of Hidden Places, a boutique adventure travel company, and Elephant Earth, which advocates for elephant welfare and conservation. Maria's website is hiddenplaces.net.

NIALL FINK is a graduate student at the University of Alberta. He works as a wrangler, canoe guide, and hunting guide in the Yukon and Northwest Territories during the summer and lives in Edmonton during the winter. His first book, *I Was Born Under a Spruce Tree,* was written in collaboration with Tr'ondek Hwech'in Elder JJ Van Bibber. To learn more visit niallfink.com.

CHARLOTTE GILL is the author of *Eating Dirt*, a tree-planting memoir nominated for the Hilary Weston Writers' Trust Prize, the Charles Taylor Prize, and two B.C. Book Prizes. It was the 2012 winner of the B.C. National Award for Canadian Non-Fiction. Her previous book *Ladykiller* was a finalist for the Governor General's Literary Award for Fiction and winner of the Ethel Wilson Fiction Prize. Her work has appeared in *Best Canadian Stories, The Journey Prize Stories*, and many magazines. She lives on the Sunshine Coast of British Columbia.

DON GILLMOR is the author of *Mount Pleasant,* a novel set in contemporary Toronto. His first novel, *Kanata,* dealt with 200 years of Canadian history. He is also the author of a two-volume history of Canada, *Canada: A People's History,* and three other books of non-fiction. He has written nine books for children, two of which were nominated for a Governor General's Award. He has worked as a journalist and was a senior editor at *The Walrus* and a contributing editor at both *Saturday Night* and *Toronto Life* magazines. He has won ten

National Magazine Awards and numerous other honours. He lives in Toronto.

NIALL GRIMES was born in Derry, Northern Ireland, and continued growing there for twenty years until he couldn't take it anymore and moved to England. From his late teens, rock climbing has been his passion, and sadly, almost thirty years later, he has found nothing to replace it. He's not much of a reader, but he does enjoy a good joke or a catchy song lyric. In two thousand and something his co-authored book *Jerry Moffatt: Revelations* won the grand prize at the Banff Mountain Book Festival. He cites his time in the Mountain and Wilderness Writing program as one of the ten best things he's ever done.

KARSTEN HEUER has worked as a wildlife biologist and wilderness park ranger for the Canadian National Parks Service for the past eighteen years. During this time he has become a well-known explorer, author, and filmmaker with a penchant for following some of North America's most endangered wildlife on foot and skis. His two bestselling books *Walking the Big Wild* and *Being Caribou* have earned him numerous awards, including a U.S. National Outdoor Book Award, the Sigurd Olson Nature Writing Award, the Banff Mountain Book Festival's Grand Prize, and the Wilburforce Conservation Leadership Award. He lives in Canmore with his wife and son and is the president of the Yellowstone to Yukon Conservation Initiative, a world leader in large-landscape conservation.

KATIE IVES: A graduate of the University of Iowa Writers' Workshop, Katie Ives is the editor-in-chief of *Alpinist Magazine*. Her writing and translations have appeared in various publications, including *Alpinist*, *The American Alpine Journal*,

Mountain Gazette, Urban Climber, She Sends, Circumference, 91st Meridian, Outside Magazine and *Patagonia Field Reports*. In 2004 she won the Mammut/Rock & Ice Writing Contest, in 2005 she attended the Banff Mountain and Wilderness Writing program, and in 2008 she received third place in the UKC/ International Literature Festival Writing Competition. In 2011 she served as a jury member for the Banff Mountain Festival Book Competition.

BRUCE KIRKBY is a writer, photographer, traveller, and adventurer. As a columnist for *The Globe and Mail*, regular contributor to *explore Magazine* and *Canadian Geographic*, and author of two bestselling books, *Sand Dance* and *The Dolphin's Tooth*, Bruce's journeys have taken him across Arabia by camel, down the Blue Nile on raft, and over Iceland by foot.

ANDY KIRKPATRICK: The U.S. magazine *Climbing* once described Andy Kirkpatrick as a climber with a "strange penchant for the long, the cold and the difficult," with a reputation "for seeking out routes where the danger is real, and the return is questionable, pushing himself on some of the hardest walls and faces in the Alps and beyond, sometimes with partners and sometimes alone." The author of two Boardman Tasker award-winning books, *Psychovertical* and *Cold Wars*, Andy has climbed extensively in the Alps and greater ranges.

BERNADETTE MCDONALD is the author of eight books on mountaineering and mountain culture. She was awarded four major prizes for *Freedom Climbers*, including the Boardman Tasker Prize and the Banff Mountain Book Festival Grand Prize. Additional literary awards include Italy's ITAS Prize (2010), India's Kekoo Naoroji Award (2012, 2009, and 2008) and American Alpine Club literary award (2011). She was the founding vice president of Mountain Culture at The Banff Centre and director of the Banff Mountain Festivals for twenty years. Among other distinctions she has received the Alberta Order of Excellence (2010), and the Banff Summit of Excellence Award (2007).

HELEN MORT is from Sheffield, U.K. She has two poetry chapbooks with Tall Lighthouse Press, *The Shape of Every Box* and *A Pint for the Ghost*. Her first collection, *Division Street*, was published by Chatto & Windus in 2013 and was a Poetry Book Society Recommendation. From 2010–2011, she was Poet in Residence at The Wordsworth Trust, Grasmere. She is currently working on *No Map Could Show Them*, a collection of poems about women and mountaineering, which she began writing as part of the Mountain and Wilderness Writing program at The Banff Centre.

JAN REDFORD spent several years climbing, kayaking, and taking on jobs like tree planting until motherhood motivated her to become a French Immersion teacher. Her work has been published in *The Globe and Mail*, the *National Post*, and various anthologies, and has won multiple writing prizes, including first place in *Room*'s 2011 creative non-fiction contest. She is working on a climbing memoir, and will start the MFA program in Creative Writing at UBC in September 2013. She lives in Squamish, B.C., with her husband, not far from her two adult children, surrounded by phenomenal mountain biking trails.

WAYNE SAWCHUK grew up as a logger, trapper, and guide, and is now a conservationist, author, and photographer who fights to protect the country he once logged. He is the recipient of the federal Canadian Environment Award and the Province of British Columbia Minister's Environmental Achievement Award, both given in recognition of his work to establish the 6.4 million hectare Muskwa-Kechika Management Area. He is the author of the coffee-table photo book *Muskwa-Kechika: The Wild Heart of Canada's Northern Rockies.* Each summer Sawchuk leads three-month horseback expeditions into the Northern Rockies, and he is a member of the Explorers Club of New York.

ERIN SOROS has published short fiction and non-fiction in international journals and anthologies. Her stories have been produced for the BBC and CBC as winners of the CBC Literary Award and the Commonwealth Short Story Prize. "Surge" was aired on the BBC as a finalist for the BBC National Short Story Award. *Morning Is Vertical,* a collection of stories with photographs, is forthcoming from Rufus Books. She is at work on her first novel, *Hook Tender,* set in a 1940s logging camp in the coastal mountains of British Columbia and inspired by the oral and archival history of immigrant and indigenous communities.

STEVE SWENSON grew up in Seattle and started climbing in the nearby Cascade Mountains at age fourteen. He graduated from the University of Washington with a degree in Civil Engineering. He has been climbing for forty-five years with over twenty expeditions to South Asia, including ascents of K2 and Everest without supplementary oxygen. He was part of a team that won the 2012 Piolet d'Or award for the first ascent of Saser Kangri II (7,518 metres). Married with two sons aged twenty-two and thirty-two, he recently retired after thirty-five years of project management, design, policy making, finance, and communications consulting related to water and wastewater infrastructure projects.

MASA TAKEI is a freelance writer. Publications he's written for include *Canadian Geographic, explore, Western Living,* and *The Globe and Mail.* He also contributed to *National Geographic*'s guide to Canada's national parks. He writes primarily about outdoor travel and subcultures. For the project he initiated at The Banff Centre, he scripted and hosted a year-long web series for High Fidelity HDTV (now Blue Ant Media). *Masa Off Grid* was also made into an hour-long TV documentary for the cable channel radX. His work has been nominated for National Magazine Awards and a Canadian Screen Award. He now lives in a 320-square-foot, off-grid cabin near a decent surf break on Haida Gwaii.

JON TURK received his Ph.D. in chemistry in 1971 and wrote the first environmental science textbook in North America, but he left academia to engage in extreme expeditions in remote parts of the world. Jon's two-year kayak passage across the North Pacific Rim was named by *Paddler Magazine* as one of the ten greatest sea kayaking expeditions of all time. His circumnavigation of Ellesmere with Erik Boomer was nominated by *National Geographic* as one of the top ten adventures of 2011 and awarded "Expedition of the Year" by *Canoe and Kayak Magazine.* Jon chronicles his journeys and mental and spiritual passages in a trilogy books: *Cold Oceans, In the Wake of the Jomon,* and *The Raven's Gift.*

FREDDIE WILKINSON is a climber from Madison, New Hampshire. He believes that any adventure is only as good as the stories you bring home.

EDITOR
BIOGRAPHIES

MARNI JACKSON is a Toronto journalist, author, and editor whose work has appeared in *Outside, explore, The Globe and Mail, Rolling Stone, The Walrus,* and *Brick,* among other publications. Her writing has won numerous National Magazine Awards and she is the author of three books of non-fiction. From 2006–2009, Marni was Rogers Chair of the Literary Journalism program at The Banff Centre, a month-long residency for professional non-fiction writers.

TONY WHITTOME was for many years editorial director of Hutchinson and of Random House U.K., and he is now consultant editor at Penguin Random House. Apart from fiction, history, politics, and poetry, he has published widely on climbing, travel, outdoor adventure, and environmental issues.